T5-AFW-129

Windows NT™ Security Guide

Stephen A. Sutton

Trusted Systems
Services, Inc.

ADDISON-WESLEY DEVELOPERS PRESS
An Imprint of Addison Wesley Longman, Inc.

Reading, Massachusetts • Harlow, England • Menlo Park, California
Berkeley, California • Don Mills, Ontario • Sydney
Bonn • Amsterdam • Tokyo • Mexico City

Trusted Systems business director and editor: Stephanie C. Bury

Many of the designations used by manufacturers and sellers to distinguish their products are claimed as trademarks. Where those designations appear in this book, and Addison-Wesley was aware of a trademark claim, the designations have been printed in initial capital letters or all capital letters.

The author and publisher have taken care in preparation of this book, but make no expressed or implied warranty of any kind and assume no responsibility for errors or omissions. No liability is assumed for incidental or consequential damages in connection with or arising out of the use of the information or programs contained herein.

Microsoft and MS-DOS are registered trademarks, and Windows, Windows NT, and the Windows NT logo are trademarks of Microsoft Corporation.

Unix® is a registered trademark of AT&T. OS/2 is a registered trademark of IBM, Inc. NT is a registered trademark of Northern Telecom Limited.

Screen snapshots reprinted with permission from Microsoft Corporation.

Find Trusted Systems at:
http://trustedsystem.com

Many thanks to Mr. Joseph Bury for his thorough and keen editorial review.

Library of Congress Cataloging-in-Publication Data
Sutton, Stephen A.
     Windows NT security guide / Stephen A. Sutton.
          p.   cm.
     Includes index.
     ISBN 0-201-41969-6
     Microsoft Windows NT.   2. Operating systems (Computers)
  3. Computer security.   I. Title.
  QA76.76.063S9   1997
  005.8—dc21   96–47632
                                                   CIP

Sponsoring Editor: Mary Treseler
Project Manager: John Fuller
Production Assistant: Melissa Lima
Set in 9.5-point Palatino by Vicki L. Hochstedler

2 3 4 5 6 7 8 9 10-MA-00999897
Second printing, February 1997

Addison-Wesley books are available for bulk purchases by corporations, institutions, and other organizations. For more information please contact the Corporate, Government, and Special Sales Department at (800) 238-9682.

Find A-W Developers Press on the World Wide Web at:
http://www.aw.com/devpress/

Contents

This book thoroughly teaches the security aspects of Microsoft Windows NT. It's a tutorial for those who use the system day to day (its "regular users") as well as those who manage system security (its "administrators"). The line between these two can be a gray one. Indeed one of the strengths of Windows NT is that regular users can gain selected administrative capabilities for which they are trained and trusted. This text supplies that training and is the basis for that trust. If you already know Windows this text is almost a complete tutorial on Windows NT itself, since most of the new features you'll encounter are security features. We divide our presentation into three parts:

Part I: General Use

Targeted for regular, day-to-day users, but an important introduction for administrators.

Part II: Administration

For administrators of all strata. Some sections serve regular users with occasional administrative duties.

Part III: Assessment

Some help for those who must answer the question: Is Windows NT secure enough for me?

You can use this book for self-study or general reference. It has many on-line and "pencil" exercises, complete with answers. It's always better to have NT running as you work your way through the text, but it's fine if you just want to read about its security. While it helps if you're already a Windows user, we introduce the basic Windows elements you need to do our exercises.

Because the book treats the security aspects of Windows NT from a day-to-day, operational point of view, it's a great way for system planners to evaluate its considerable security strengths—with or without NT in house. Finally, this textbook is unlike many others you may have read on Windows NT:

❖ Our mission is to help you *understand* the *ideas* behind NT security. Clicking the buttons in its many window interfaces takes little explanation. Understanding strategies for when to do so and how it all fits together takes much more.

❖ We give you "day-1" examples for setting up your security environment. Use your understanding to build upon them.

❖ Our on-line and pencil exercises are an integral part of your learning experience. Don't neglect them, even if you're a casual reader.

❖ We're not afraid to express an opinion. You may disagree. From such disagreement knowledge is born. And if you occasionally prove us wrong, we've accomplished our goal. You've become an expert!

Happy learning!

I began my journey into Windows NT as a time-worn veteran of high-end secure systems for the Defense community, mostly Secure UNIX systems. I'd spent long years in their planning, architecture, accreditation, marketing and training, and doubted that the successor to MS-DOS could do much to pique my security interest (or confidence). I was indeed surprised. I found Windows NT an impressive security story, not just for its many features, but for its seamless integration of security into the fiber of its networking environment.

The hallmark of effective security is its integration, coexistence, and concession to all the other properties an organization needs to fulfill its daily tasks. Security that is not well integrated fails; security without backward compatibility and flexibility fails; security that is not readily administered fails. It's in avoiding such pitfalls that Windows NT excels. It not only has the security features commonly requested by even highly secure organizations, but incorporates them from the ground up in a modern, scalable, networked operating environment. NT security is indeed the product of a strong and thoughtful commitment from its creators. And the fact that NT is aggressively targeting Internet and intranet security adds considerably to its strength in today's worldwide communications environment.

If you want to make extensive use of NT's security, there are several ideas you must understand and appreciate, but compared to the other aspects of today's complex multivendor, heterogeneous, client-server systems, security is not going to be your major stumbling block. And of course, since you can turn off or ignore many of its security features, you can ease into NT security gradually. (But read the whole book first! Knowing what to ignore and when to ignore it is primary to a phased implementation.)

I'm excited about Windows NT not because its security is "new and revolutionary" (and therefore not proven and difficult to assess), but because it is *evolutionary*. NT incorporates a base of timeless, proven, frequently requested, strong, and effective security features that are readily administered and woven throughout the networking environment. I am impressed with Windows NT security and hope this book leaves you with the same feeling.

—Steve Sutton

President, Trusted Systems Services, Inc.
ssutton@trustedsystems.com

Trusted Systems
Services, Inc.

Trusted Systems was formed in 1986 as a consulting and training company for secure systems. Its founder, Steve Sutton, has been a prominent designer and teacher of secure operating systems and standards for almost two decades. Today, we believe that the success of these systems depends on quality training and education. With a thorough, historic understanding of secure systems, Trusted Systems is committed to simple, illustrative explanations, as we hope our textbooks and courses demonstrate.

Visit our
Web Page!

http://www.TrustedSystems.com

See the mail-in flyer at the back of the text for more information about our consulting and training services.

Trusted Systems Services, Inc.
1107 S. Orchard Street
Urbana, IL 61801-4851
(217) 344-0996 Fax: (217) 344-0901
inform@trustedsystems.com

PART I
General Use

Chapter 1

Introduction

Windows NT is a networking operating environment that will play a large part in the future of collaborative, "client-server" computing. Perhaps no other operating system has been so eagerly awaited or hotly debated. NT is a tour de force of what we expect of modern operating systems. If you've followed its emergence, you can't help but notice a word that appears prominently: "security." It's about time.

The designers of Windows NT have had the rare opportunity to weave security into the fabric of a completely new operating system and they've made good use of it. Security takes no back seat in NT. There's a wealth of security features—many beyond what you might expect. On the other hand, security is neither oppressive nor steals from NT's many other impressive features.

Your favorite applications and working environment are largely unaffected by security. Depending on how your site is set up, the day-to-day user may see little of security. But even in its fullest use, with a little understanding and forethought, everyone can use NT's security features to protect their organization's critical data. Giving you this understanding and forethought, whether you are a regular user or administrator, is the task to which we set ourselves. Our job in the following pages and chapters is to walk you through NT security, one step at a time and always with an eye to understanding how you can take full advantage. In this chapter we begin our journey with a few basics.

In This Chapter We Describe

➡ What we do (and don't) mean by "security" and the NT commitment to it

➡ What in the world "C2" means

➡ The basic differences between "regular users" and the various kinds of "administrators"

➡ The notion of "trust and threats" and why they're so important

➡ Some basic security ideas that set you in the right frame of mind for your day-to-day activities

A special note on what we mean by "NT": You can buy two major versions of Windows NT—one for a workstation client called "Windows NT Workstation," and a second called "Windows NT Server," intended for use on major servers. NT Workstation is largely a subset of NT Server. From our perspective these are just two versions of the same system that we generically call "Windows NT," or simply "NT."

We cover both systems used in the standard enterprise configuration: central NT Servers serving many NT Workstations. Our focus is the security environment that these two versions cooperatively and seamlessly present. We also address security aspects of several of the systems NT closely supports, including NT networks without NT Servers (NT Workstations only), and Microsoft's Windows 95 and Windows for Work Groups (WFW) in the NT security environment. This edition covers Windows NT version 4. However, the nice thing about security features is that they don't tend to change much from release to release. Hence, what you learn today won't likely become outdated for some time. This text applies to NT's faithful implementation on any hardware base.

☞We use the term "workstation" for any computer, not just those running NT Workstation.

Windows NT and Security

Why do you need security? Maybe you don't, but don't be so sure. "Security" protects you from three basic threats to your well-being and general prosperity: where someone sees your electronically stored data who shouldn't see it, modifies your data contrary to your interests, or maliciously destroys your data. If the prospect of any of these brings you any material concern, you need security.

There are few deep secrets to computer features that protect you from these disasters. It's simply a matter of computer system vendors sensing enough market pressure for security that they implement these features. The major problem with security is that it's a "weak-link" phenomenon. It does little good to secure some pieces of a computer system and not others. For this reason it's essential that security be built into the basis of a computer system—from day 1. This is precisely what Windows NT offers.

What Is Windows NT?

In case you don't already know, we'll start with a brief description of Windows NT in general. Windows NT is the appointed, long-haul successor to MS-DOS. While phenomenally successful and beloved by many, MS-DOS is an antiquated operating system that, while still applicable to the desktop (thanks in part to its Windows wrapping and Windows 95 improvements) it has little to offer servers in the ever-more-popular client-server environment. Wouldn't it be great to have a single, modern operating system that:

✓ Runs existing MS-DOS and Windows applications unchanged, handles traditional file systems (like FAT), supports the IEEE POSIX standards, and interoperates with OS/2, LAN Manager, Macintosh, and others

✓ Sports a friendly and powerful desktop metaphor similar to the long-popular Apple Macintosh

✓ Is a full 32-bit implementation that transparently supports preexisting 16-bit applications

✓ Serves the desktop faithfully, bringing true multiprocessing and parallel processing capability on ever-more-powerful desktop workstations, yet "scales" upward through peer server networks like a small office, to full network servers handling hundreds of clients

✓ Has been designed from the beginning as a networking operating system with components that communicate and coordinate without undue and complicated coaxing from administrators

✓ Supports a truly flexible client-server architecture where each workstation on a network can be both a server and client to all others

✓ Allows several users truly to share a single machine, giving each their own working environment invisible to and protected from others

✓ Employs a "kernel" technology that serves true multiprocessing, keeps errant programs from crashing the whole machine, and forms a solid basis for advanced security features

✓ Provides for full, transparent use of multiprocessor computers (ones that have more than one central processing unit [CPU]) and supports forward-looking applications with different portions that are designed to run concurrently (called "threads") on multiprocessor computers

✓ Can be completely administered through Windows interfaces—from anywhere on the net

✓ Has inordinate design attention to performance and extendibility

✓ Ports easily and faithfully to a variety of modern hardware bases, from personal computer (PC) to engineering workstation to departmental server to mainframe

✓ . . . and, more to our point, makes a *dramatic security commitment*

The name of this operating system is Windows NT. It's designed for the long haul and is rapidly taking its place beside the prominent, workhorse, high-end operating systems of the day.

What Is "Security"?

Before we elaborate on NT's commitment to security, we need to define what we mean by "security," for there are many definitions. Someone once defined security as "a warm feeling in your belly." Whether or not it's quite that, it's certainly subjective. While some note that every administrative action and capability affects some vague notion of security, we need to be a little more focused.

By threat we mean intentional and malicious attempts by some person to subvert the work of other people on a computer system, whether it is a stand-alone or distributed system. Usually the penetrators either view, alter, or delete data in a manner not allowed by site policy. Our security is protection against the threat of such a penetrator, whether manifest in their direct on-line activities (like impersonating another user) or by programs and false data they create, which we'll come to know as "malicious software." The penetrator may or may not be a legitimate system user.

We don't include protections against hardware failure in our definition of security, so we don't discuss features like disk striping, mirroring, or many other fine NT features. While we talk a bit about backing up data, it's not our main thrust. Such features are indeed important, but they're not what we call "security."

What about people that aren't malicious, but have the same effect by just plain bumbling? Fortunately the protections against malicious users are effective against those that simply make mistakes, so we don't need to make any real distinction.

Our purpose is not to judge NT's security against any other particular system. Only you can judge how secure your site is, and this text helps you make this assessment. In the end, "security" really is a warm feeling, but one based on a thorough understanding of your security features and how you use them. The following paragraphs describe the common, time-honored security features that help make your environment secure. These are common themes in Windows NT that pervade our discussion.

User Identification (Authentication)

Ultimately, computers serve people. *Individuals* create and distribute information using computers. The first rule of computer security is to identify who the computer system is serving. This is sometimes called **authentication**. The first step and sometimes only visible aspect of authentication is when a computer asks for your name and secret information (called your **password**) before you can use the system. This is called **logging on**. Presumably only you know your password, so if you present the proper password for your name, the computer assumes you are you. From this point on, good computer security systems (like NT) associate and control all your actions on the system with your identity. When you finish your session, you **log off** so the next person to use the computer doesn't work under your identity.

Your identity is defined on the system by your **account**—information about you, including the name by which the system knows you and your password. A good security account also holds any special capabilities you may be granted on the system.

Sometimes computer users need to enter or reference lists of other users. To alleviate tedious bookkeeping, good computer systems have named lists of users called **user groups**. For example, each department in your company may have a group for the people in that department. Systems like NT even let users create and control their own groups.

Access Control

Just knowing who is using the system doesn't keep people from seeing or changing other users' data when they should not. The task of controlling who can see and change data is called **access control**. Access control is particularly important when the items controlled are part of the computer software itself, especially its security software!

While some systems control access by assigning passwords to each controlled item (for example, a computer file, logical drive, or printer), this can be unwieldy. Users need to remember long lists of passwords, although the system can help by remembering their lists for them. But perhaps the biggest drawback is that changing a password (the only way to preclude users from further access) involves redistributing the password. Messy.

For these reasons, systems that authenticate users base their access control on the user name (that is, their account). These systems maintain a tag on an object called an **access control list** (ACL) that determines which users (or user groups) can access that object and how they can access it. ACLs are fundamental to security and we discuss them extensively.

The general metaphor is that when you create a new object on the system (usually a file or directory) you become its **owner,** and as owner you can set the ACL any way you want. This lets you grant or deny access to whomever you like and change that access as often as you deem necessary. For example, you might let some users read but not change a file, others change it, and still others do nothing at all.

Similarly, administrators own and set the ACL on shared system files and directories. They use this to protect the system itself as well as to determine who can run which application programs.

User Capabilities and Administration

There are many tasks necessary to keep a system functional, from setting the time to configuring printers to creating new user accounts. The more sensitive tasks are often called system **administration** and are granted to user accounts designated as **administrators**.

The mark of a good security system is that there are far more than just one kind of administrator. In the best systems, various administrative capabilities can be individually assigned to user accounts. "Full administrators" is the term we use for accounts with all such capabilities, but most administrators have select capabilities. Indeed, the distinction between "regular user" and "administrator" is often inappropriate, because regular users can be given some (usually modest) administrative capabilities.

The goal of administrative subdivision is that users of all classes should be given as much power as they need, understand, and can be trusted to uphold. In Windows NT, membership in special user groups denotes one's administrative capabilities.

Auditing

Despite the best efforts by users and administrators, people (even administrators) can make mistakes or sometimes do things they shouldn't. Security systems record various system activities that bear on security in an **audit trail**. Administrators can check the audit trail either regularly or when they suspect something untoward has occurred. Although auditing is a bit like the proverbial closing the barn door after the horses have bolted, it's nonetheless an important practice of most secure installations.

Malicious Programs

Just because your staff can be trusted doesn't mean the people who wrote the programs your staff uses can. Much-publicized "virus" attacks are but one aspect of seemingly innocent software written by malicious people. Access control goes a long way toward limiting the damage such programs can do.

One of the insidious things a malicious program can do is pretend to be another, legitimate program so as to "trick" you into entering some sensitive information it can then use for its nefarious schemes, like your password. The **Trusted Path** is a traditional security feature that thwarts these programs by giving you a way to know that the program to which you are giving such information is legitimate. It is then your job to divulge only such information through your use of the Trusted Path.

The Network Environment and the Internet

There are two aspects of "network security." The first is simply that security enforcement by individual computers must be coordinated in today's highly interlinked computer environments. Important aspects of this are that critical security information be centralized and that user identity transparently controls their actions on servers across the network. The cornerstone for coordination in Windows NT is called the **domain**.

The second aspect of network security is protecting data in transit between computer systems and securely identifying remote communicants. The only practical way to do this is through various encryption techniques, which are ways of secretly encoding data so networking eavesdroppers can't see or tamper with it. The current interest in the Internet and intranets brings these technologies to the foreground, and no system is leading the way more than Windows NT with its strong, secure base on which such network security can be constructed.

An Introduction to NT Security Features

We now summarize NT's basic security features. You'll find it much like the more general list we just discussed. This is no accident. Windows NT seeks to address almost all the fundamental tenets of modern computer security.

Accounts and Authentication (Logon)

The user account is the basis for security in Windows NT. Before you can use an NT workstation, you must give it the name of your account and its password. This process is called "authentication" or more commonly "logon." You then enter a working session where the parameters in that account determine your capabilities during the session. For example, this account controls your access to network resources, like printers and remote "share" directories, as well as any administrative capabilities you may have. You end your session with a logoff. Implicit in the account strategy is that you only need to identify yourself once to the system—when you log on. You don't give any resource-specific passwords.

Only administrators can create or modify accounts. As we see later, some accounts are valid only for a particular workstation while others are valid at any one or more groups of workstations. When you request resources of another computer on the network, that computer invisibly authenticates you from your session's account and password.

Accounts let several users share a workstation with no interference among them. For example, your entire Windows environment is particular to your account. The changes you make don't affect other users. You can also be given applications and directories for your exclusive use.

Authentication extends into heterogeneous networks like the Internet. Windows NT only serves remote requests from which it has obtained a valid user name and password for one of its own accounts. All its local services on behalf of the remote user are under the auspices of that account.

Passwords and Logon Controls

Accounts are the basis for NT security and a password protects each one. There are many features that let the administrator control the use of passwords and the logon process. For example, your administrator can prompt you to change your password regularly by giving it an expiration date, require your passwords be a minimal length, or prohibit you from reusing one of your recent passwords.

Domains

Windows NT lets administrators subdivide a large network into enclaves of workstations called "domains."

❖ You are typically given a single domain-based account that's recognized at each workstation in the domain. This single account means that administrators don't need to synchronize separate accounts on each workstation in the domain—a security and operational nightmare. Workstations in other domains can recognize your account through "trust relationships" between the domains.

❖ NT makes it more convenient to access the workstations in your domain, since they're the ones you most frequently use.

❖ Domains form the basis by which an entire network is subdivided for administration. An administrator might fully control some domains, but not others.

In short, the domain is a strong security metaphor—a logical way to protect a set of resources in a large, heterogeneous network. If you're familiar with Windows 95, you'll see that a domain looks a lot like a workgroup, but its security properties are beyond compare.

User Groups

A (user) group is a named list of user accounts. Although some groups are maintained only by administrators, most users can create and maintain their own groups. Groups give you the convenience of using a single name in place of a potentially long list of user accounts. More importantly, if you assign a certain capability to a group (like access to your files), new group members automatically gain that capability. There are special groups that bestow administrative capabilities. If your account is a member of one of these, you gain its power.

Access Control Lists

Windows NT attaches an ACL to many resources in the system. An ACL determines which user accounts can access that resource and how they may do so. Your most frequent use of ACLs is for each file and directory on logical drives with the native NT disk format called "NTFS," which is the norm for security. An ACL is a list of users and groups that detail the specific actions each is allowed to perform on that file, like reading, writing, and deleting. When you create a file or directory, you become its "owner" and can set its ACL to afford any protection you like.

The system uses ACLs to protect all of its critical resources, like key security files. (Obviously, only administrators can change these ACLs.) File and directory ACLs have a default mechanism, so you need not agonize over the ACL of each file you create. You need to set only those that are different than your norm. Resources other than files have ACLs, like printers and network share directories, and these ACLs have the same structure and work similarly to those used with files.

ACLs are common in traditional and modern operating environments, whether highly secure or not. We think you'll find the NT implementation among the most powerful and easy to use. ACLs work hand in hand with accounts and authentication, and together these constitute most of Windows NT security.

Trusted Path

The Trusted Path is a traditional, powerful feature that helps protect you against threatening situations, such as when a nefarious programmer develops a malicious program that is designed to steal information (like a password) by masquerading as a legitimate system program. The Trusted Path is a special window, entitled "Windows NT Security," that you call up with a reserved key combination: the Alt, Ctrl, and Delete keys pressed simultaneously. When you press this key combination, NT guarantees that the window that appears is legitimate and trustworthy—not a pretender. You *must* use the Trusted Path for certain security-critical operations, like logging in, unlocking your workstation after you lock it, and changing your password.

Because the system never displays the Trusted Path window unless you enter the key combination, it is your duty never to interact with an apparent Trusted Path window without first entering the key sequence. You should avoid performing a Trusted Path function, like changing your password, by any other means, since those other means are likely malicious pretenders or at least not as secure as the Trusted Path.

Flexible, Role-Based Administration

A common criticism of lesser secure operating environments is that for a user to perform any administration they must be given all administrative powers. Windows NT solves this problem not only with its domain organization, but also by providing several roles that allow related sets of administrative duties to be delegated to lesser administrators under the control of full administrators. These range from Power Users, who act as miniadministrators of their own workstation, to several kinds of Operators on an NT Server. The appropriate accounts are assigned these powers primarily through membership in special administrative groups. These groups, in turn, gain much of their power by holding certain "Rights."

NT administration is flexible across your entire network. If necessary, you can set up the system so that any administrator can manage any workstation from any place on the network. Administrators can also arrange that they have complete control of their own domain(s) with no encroachment from any other domains. You can even limit administrators to specific workstations. Security can be completely administered through window interfaces that appear and act consistently with all other administrative windows.

Security Auditing

In addition to its normal system maintenance events, NT can log a large number of security-relevant events—from logons to administrative actions to access to specific files by certain users or groups. The record for each event contains lots of information about what happened and who caused it. Because this can be a potential drain on system resources, the hallmark of a good auditing system is its ability to save only those events that administrators deem necessary, and in this NT excels. Not only can you specify which "categories" of events are saved, but for file system events (like users reading or writing files) you can specify, per file and directory, which users or groups and which of their actions are to be audited. NT has convenient window interfaces for scanning and managing the audit trail (called the "security log"). If you like, you can even dump them in character format for processing by common applications, like data base programs.

Service-Specific Features

A number of system services, like the Remote Access Service (RAS), have their own special security safeguards, but these never conflict with NT's basic security features.

NT security fully accommodates preexisting applications and, to the extent practical, interfaces its security to other systems with which it interoperates, like Windows 95, Windows for Workgroups, LAN Manager, Apple Macintosh, and Novell Netware.

The final issue we address is whether or not these features will change in future releases. While we can state nothing officially (even to the extent it's known) these bedrock security features are the sort that don't tend to change from release to release. Although you may see them enhanced, the future is unlikely to outdate the security practices you learn today.

The Impact of NT's Security

Finally, we look at the other design goals of Windows NT to see how they interact with its security.

Compatibility

Security need not interfere with compatibility to the many standards NT supports, including MS-DOS, Windows, OS/2, and POSIX. For example, ACLs have been carefully designed to work with programs that don't know about them. In rare cases of unavoidable conflict, the administrator can choose between security and compatibility.

Distributed Processing (Networking)

Windows NT security is designed for the distributed environment, largely through its domain network structure. NT centralizes critical security information on central servers with ample fallback strategies so that server failures do not incapacitate the network. It also accommodates the legitimate need for groups to administer their enclave in a large network in cooperation with administrators of other such enclaves.

Scale

NT security is consistent across its range of implementations—from a stand-alone NT Workstation through small peer networks to large client-server installations based on NT Server—using the same basic features and administrative interfaces. It expands with growth and accommodates sites with wide mixtures of configurations.

Portability to Different Hardware Bases

Including security as an integral part of the operating environment ensures that you don't have "holes" between NT implementations on different hardware platforms.

Reliability and Robustness

NT's access controls can protect files from both skullduggery and accidents. NT's "kernel" design not only prevents programs from adversely affecting other programs and crashing the system, but it is also a key component to its security strength. You can use its Trusted Path to cancel runaway programs readily.

Performance

You'll find that security has negligible overall impact on your day-to-day applications. Considering what you gain, it's a good buy. If you read the various internal descriptions of Windows NT, you will see that its designers thought a great deal about making its security efficient. NT's security auditing is its only potential performance impact. Here your administrator finds many ways to tailor which audit events are recorded so you need not pay even a small performance penalty for events you don't need.

Extendibility

The designers allow for extension of the security features in much the same way as other features. This helps ensure a stream of third-party security products. We mention a few for which to watch in "Third-Party Watch" in the Chapter 13, NT Security Discussion.

Networking Flexibility

Windows NT's broad and flexible networking architecture lets us participate in a wide variety of enterprise networks, including the Internet. It aggressively pursues the latest public standards, including many evolving, secure networking and encryption schemes.

Multiprocessing and Internationalization

Security is fully integrated with these features.

In the end, you need to assess your own security requirements and satisfy yourself that your system and its configuration meets these needs. One of our tasks in the remainder of this book is to help you understand and appreciate the issues that help you make this decision.

Trust, Threats, and the TCB

In this section we introduce some basic security ideas of interest to all users. Chapter 11 expands these topics for administrators. We've introduced NT's security features, but features alone don't make a system secure if the software that enforces those features is prone to tampering by everyday users and programs. A **Trusted Computing Base** (**TCB**) is the key requirement for systems deemed "secure" in today's market. The TCB is the sum total of system software (and hardware) that must work correctly in order for the system's security controls to be fully enforced. The TCB's major responsibility is to ensure that users and their programs only gain access to objects like files and input/output devices according to strictly observed security policies. Further, and most important, the TCB must itself be resistant to attack.

If you're interested in security, you probably read and maybe agonized over "virus" attacks on traditional PC operating systems like MS-DOS or Macintosh. While these systems and, more to the point, applications and additions that run on them, may have certain "security" features, any program can change any part of the operating system or its programs. There is no tamper-resistant TCB. Quite the contrary, there is no protection for any security software, no matter how well intentioned or designed. This is why viruses are so successful against the non-TCB systems. Once an illicit program runs, it can alter the underlying fabric so as to perpetuate its nefarious schemes.

But all this changes with Windows NT because it and most other modern operating systems, including those deemed "highly secure," are designed around a **kernel**.

The key aspect of a kernel-based system is that regular programs cannot change "protected" parts of the system willy-nilly. To the point, they can't attack the TCB itself, which consists of the kernel software and the security enforcement programs and their data files. NT's kernel architecture is important for other reasons. It prevents programs from adversely affecting other programs or single-handedly crashing the machine. While it's quite handy in this regard, it's essential for security.

We talk a lot about **trusted programs**. Any time a program gains the ability to skirt or forego the system's security protections, we had better trust it to use this ability responsibly and according to the system's security principles. We call such a program a "trusted program." Stated differently, we had better configure and use our system in such a way that only trusted programs gain such abilities. Otherwise security is compromised. Trusted programs are part of the TCB.

Common Threats

A security feature is of value only to the extent that it protects against some threat. We don't really need a feature that protects against a threat that is not present on our system. More important, it is of limited value to have one feature that strongly protects against a particular threat when there's another feature that is totally susceptible to it. Whether you are an administrator or a regular user, the most important basis from which to structure your security environment is the following:

Both regular users and administrators should understand the **threats** to your system, then fully apply features that counter those threats. Be continually wary of "weak links"—features or operational situations susceptible to these threats.

Data Snooping and Tampering

Most sites don't want even legitimate system users to see or tamper with other users' data when not appropriate, especially when the system is a widespread network. Within Windows NT, the ACL is a powerful and pervasive counter to these threats. It's your main line of defense.

Password Misuse

Because NT strongly controls who can access system resources, it's important to make sure the person at the workstation is really who they say they are. The key to access controls are based on the account, and the key to protecting use of the account is the password. NT has a host of tried-and-true features to manage passwords. Password misuse is human behavior, and the administrator can customize password use according to users' diligence and trust, and can customize some of the parameters for each account.

Network Penetration

Unless properly protected, uncontrolled computers on most popular networks (whether they are intended to be attached or not) can cause all kinds of security problems. In these situations, malicious programs or users on these computers can not only view all network traffic, they can interject traffic on the network, issuing false administrative commands, or masquerade as a legitimate workstation coaxing other legitimate workstations to send them protected data.

The only real protection to this threat is cryptography. While Windows NT employs a variety of networking protections, like encrypting passwords on the net, it does not encrypt all traffic over NT networks (although some applications do so, like many Web browsers). If your local network has only NT systems (with no others secretly attached), you don't have this threat because untrusted programs on Windows NT cannot directly access the network. However, malicious programs running on traditional non-TCB systems on your network (like MS-DOS or Windows 3.1) can attempt these schemes. And, of course, if your local NT network is attached to the Internet, these threats become a serious concern.

Malicious Software (Untrusted Programs)

We've left the most insidious and intractable threat to discuss last. Most installations run programs not examined and certified as secure. We call these "untrusted programs," because we don't know whether they contain malicious elements and therefore presume they do, or at least one day one of them will! Trusted programs are both expensive and rare, so most sites use untrusted ones out of economic necessity. The good news is that systems like NT (as opposed to MS-DOS) offer specific, strong protection against these programs. Indeed, this is a hallmark of all systems that can be evaluated under formal criteria, like the "Orange Book" that we discuss later. Still, regular users and administrators alike must be wary. The basic threat is simple:

☞Whether you are a regular user or administrator, any program you run gains your current capabilities, and it may be able to use these capabilities without your knowledge.

The first thing untrusted programs can do is expose or modify the data files you've protected with ACLs, either by making openly accessible copies or by changing the ACL. Because regular users cannot subvert the TCB, neither can the malicious programs they use. Administrators are another story. To the extent you have administrative powers, these programs may be able to call up legitimate administrative programs, making changes without your knowledge. Of course, creating such software often requires expert programming and there are cases where you notice the skullduggery.

Accounts that have significant administrative powers should *never* run untrusted programs.

✓ As a regular user you should not use untrusted programs if you're critically relying on your ACLs.

✓ Make the best trust assessment you can of the programs you bring onto the system. Avoid those you deem over the line. It's a good idea for administrators to review all new programs.

✓ Be wary of applications that can attach small programs to documents that run, perhaps unnoticed by you, when you simply "view" the document. (See "Vermin in the Intranet Environment" in Chapter 3, Your Working Environment.)

✓ Protect all program files as if they are a part of the TCB, and, therefore, unchangeable by regular users. This keeps malicious programs from changing legitimate programs into malicious ones—a "virus."

A **Trojan Horse** is a seemingly innocuous program that is secretly malicious. Its innocence tempts you to bring it onto your system and use it, and then it's got your power. A **virus** is another example of a malicious program. It may first arrive on your system as a Trojan Horse, but propagates itself by changing other, previously safe programs turning them into malicious programs also. Trojan Horse programs, viruses, worms, and assorted other vermin are all instances of malicious software and our cautions apply to them all. See "Tips for Security in the Intranet Environment" and "Vermin in the Intranet Environment" in Chapter 3, Your Working Environment.

Some threats are not electronic. For example, the threat of someone reinstalling NT on a workstation requires operational procedures and physical controls. Since these are not a part of NT, we don't address them. Lastly, this list is not necessarily complete for your site. Strive to find your own threats. It's half the battle!

The Right Frame of Mind

Security is a frame of mind. You can learn the features, but if you don't understand their intent and consistently apply them, it is for naught. Here we provide a few guiding principles, mostly for administrators.

Weak Link

Like armies, penetrators seek weakness and attack it. Security is inherently a weak-link phenomenon. If you understand the threats, you can seek to determine your system's vulnerabilities. Be objective. Most weak links hide in your blind spots. Most of all, don't be the weak link yourself!

Security Is a Series of Barriers

Few security features are absolute. The idea is to make it more expensive to steal something than it's worth. The more barriers you raise, the harder a system is to penetrate, even if each individual barrier is not as strong as you might like.

Security Is About Trade-offs

In most environments, regular users and especially administrators must continually trade security against other properties, like compatibility. Focus on threats and countermeasures. Know the security you're giving up. Mindful of the weak-link phenomenon, there's little point enforcing a burdensome security feature when another feature is susceptible to the same threat, even though the first does raise a barrier.

"Security by Obscurity" Is Little Security

Trying to protect your system by hiding information about how its basic features work is sometimes called "security by obscurity." For example, you might think that by keeping secret the detailed information shown in audit records, you can deny penetrators information they could use to skirt auditing.

You've Got to Trust Somebody

While administrative subdivision is strong, it's not absolute. There may be cases where even modest administrators cause damage beyond their apparent scope if they're determined. One of the major uses for separate administrative roles is to keep even highly trusted people from doing things they are not trained to do, and to keep "too many cooks from spoiling the broth." In other words, even thoroughly trusted people should not have special capabilities unless they know how to use them and can be relied on to coordinate with others.

Paranoia Is Self-Defeating

Security is not about paranoia. Perhaps the most exasperating problems come about when an overzealous administrator attempts to impose such unrealistic restrictions that users are forced to circumvent a feature altogether. The classic case is an administrator who imposes fourteen-character random passwords to make them impossible to guess—in which case everybody promptly writes them on the bottom of their mouse pad!

The Importance of Security Plans and Reviews

Full security plans and complete, regular reviews are your constant ally. We suggest some checklists in Chapter 12, Summary and Checklist.

The first rule of survival for all users is to:
Understand the new security features
. . . then . . .
thoughtfully *integrate* them into your environment
in a *balanced* manner according to your site's *threats*
and *review* your situation frequently.

Regular Users, Administrators, and Those in Between

NT allows for administrators with different degrees of security power. These capabilities are assigned to personal accounts, as opposed to common user accounts into which several users may log on (usually a poor practice).

Users with a lot of administrative power are typically given a separate personal account so that they don't carry these capabilities in day-to-day, nonadministrative use of the system. For example, a user, J. Jones, may have a regular user (or Power User) account named "JJones" and an administrative account named "JJones-Admin."

Regular Users

Regular users are the day-to-day users of Windows NT who have no particular security duties. This doesn't mean they can completely ignore security. As a regular user, you have an obligation to choose proper passwords, maintain ACLs on your files and sometimes those of the your coworkers, and a few other duties into which you will settle quickly. Also, your administrator may give you specific capabilities, like the ability to manage printers or shut down your workstation. Use them responsibly.

Power Users

Power Users are regular users with modest administrative control over a particular workstation, usually their personal desktop workstation, like making its files accessible from the network and setting up new accounts that let other people use that single workstation.

Administrators

Generally, full administrators are empowered to manage all the security and other operational aspects of the networking environment, although their power can be inherently restricted to specific domains or workstations.

Operators

Each NT Server's operators group has a part of the full administrator's power related to specific actions, but is always under the control of full administrators. For example Printer Operators fully control printers on particular servers. Operators can't increase their own powers or those of their friends.

☞ The chapter summary directs each of these users to the minimal sections of this text they need to read.

C2 and the NT Security Commitment

The commitment to security in NT is apparent in its wealth of features, but the most visible, popular sign is its commitment to seek a C2 security rating. Chapter 13, NT Security Discussion, discusses this in some detail, but mainly for administrators. While regular users really don't need to know anything about C2 or its evaluation process, a brief description to enhance your appreciation is in order.

The U.S. government (not just the Department of Defense) established a security evaluation process for operating systems in 1983 that remains largely unchanged today. Two cooperating agencies, the National Computer Security Center (NCSC) and the National Institute of Standards and Technology (NIST), formally evaluate specific operating systems for security. The evaluation is done by a team of security analysts from NCSC according to a published criteria entitled the *Trusted Computer System Evaluation Criteria* (TCSEC), more commonly called the "Orange Book" because its cover is, of course, orange. The Orange Book evaluation rates specific operating system software on specific hardware platforms but does not cover widespread networking, which must be done under a separate, newer criteria called the *Trusted Network Interpretation* (TNI), the "Red Book."

The Orange Book evaluation rates a system on a progressive scale of increased security:

(least secure) **C1** ➤ **C2** ➤ **B1** ➤ **B2** ➤ **B3** ➤ **A1** *(most secure)*

In today's market for general-purpose computer systems, the primary focus is between C2 and B1. C2, because anything less is of too little security to be of much value and B1, because it incorporates a special kind of data access control popular in military establishments but currently of little demand elsewhere. While levels above B1 are of interest, they are expensive to produce and likely must wait for a more robust market. Although original U.S. government policies that all systems should be "C2 by '92" are off track, there are clear, market-driven forces for C2 systems both inside and outside the government sector and around the globe.

So what does this mean to you? An evaluation is a point-of-sale stamp of approval for the security buyer. It assures you that a system's security has been judged by an independent authority to meet certain basic criteria. But perhaps more significant is what a C2 evaluation does not mean. As we see later, Windows NT has almost all the features in the Orange Book except military-style access control based on the familiar tags "Secret," "Top Secret," and so forth. Some claim that if it supported this, it could easily be a B2 system and even then with features from higher levels.

The bottom line is that NT has features and strengths beyond a simple C2. It is mostly a weakness of the Orange Book that systems like NT get no credit for these in a C2 evaluation. The good news is that you get considerably more security for your money than you might expect. It serves as witness to an NT design team committed to adding a lot more security than the minimum required to squeak by a C2 evaluation.

Does this mean you are forced into draconian security measures in which you have no interest or need? No. The basic evaluation rule is that a system must be "capable of being used" in a mode that conforms to the criteria. Evaluations make no attempt to force you, the end user, to use a product in a secure manner. It's perfectly acceptable and a great marketing decision for a vendor to let you disable the security features, trading them off against other operational criteria.

NT furnishes a good example of the strategy of letting the customer make these trade-off decisions. A system administrator can disable or just ignore most of the security features in NT. They can maintain a level of security almost invisible to regular users. As a regular user, there are several things you can do to make security unobtrusive. But beware, if you completely ignore security, you may have none. "Capable of being used" means that some parts of the system may not be secure to the extent of other parts. For example, NT's new file system type, NTFS, attaches an ACL to each file and directory. NT also recognizes the traditional FAT file system, which does not have this important security information. Again, the trade-off is the administrator's to make.

About This Book

This text is divided into two major parts: *General Use* and *Administration*, followed by a brief but important *Assessment* of NT security and *Appendices*.

Part I: General Use

Part I is for everybody. If you are a regular user, it's all you need, unless you have been given selected administrative duties or are just curious. The first part of Chapter 12 is also for regular users.

Chapter 2: Accounts and Domains

Authentication is the basis for modern system security. Understanding your account, your system's domain structure, and how they interact are key concepts that start you on your way to using NT's security fully. Chapter 2 is your introduction to the world of workstations, domains, and accounts. You will see how you're authenticated when you first log on and whenever you access a remote resource, how accounts are interwoven into NT's domain structure, and how domains relate to one another through their trust relationships.

Chapter 3: Your Working Environment

NT security comes through many features new to traditional Windows users. In fact, the relatively few differences you see between Windows and NT are the new security features. This chapter presents the security aspects of your day-to-day security working environment: what the Trusted Path is and how to use it, the art of selecting and protecting passwords, and various security restrictions your administrator may place on your account.

Chapter 4: ACLs

ACLs are the very basis for Windows NT security. They alone protect your data and it's important that you learn to use them correctly. Chapter 4 presents a complete treatment of ACLs for files and directories.

Chapter 5: Special Situations

Chapter 5 describes some special security situations some users may encounter, like accessing NT from Windows 95 and Windows for Workgroups. We saved this information for the end of Part I so that it doesn't complicate earlier chapters with scenarios you may never see. We recommend you concentrate on the situations that apply to you.

Part II: Administration

Part II is of interest mainly to users with administrative capabilities. If you are a Power User or Server Operator you need only to understand the topics in Chapter 7, Managing Groups and Accounts. If you're fulfilling one of the other NT Server operator roles, there are no required sections. However, users with even limited administrative capabilities can benefit from a general reading of Part II.

Chapter 6: Planning Domains
The focus of Chapter 6 is broad and fundamental: how to structure your domain environment for security. The discussion includes practical criteria and guidelines for how to divide your network into domains, which involves security and other considerations. Key to this discussion is how to accommodate special situations so you can keep your domain structure simple and logical.

Chapter 7: Managing Groups and Accounts
While the mechanics for managing these are quite simple, for maximum security you need to plan the "balance" among your user security policies carefully, as well as the way you structure your hierarchy of administrators. Chapter 7 gives you many guidelines and examples, including full treatment of the many parameters in the account, strategies for creating general groups, and how you allow which administrators which capabilities in which areas of the network.

Chapter 8: Security Auditing
Chapter 8 is a full presentation of how to structure your auditing policy and how, therefore, to set the parameters of NT's rich security audit system and manage the security log. We walk you through many practical auditing scenarios.

Chapter 9: The Internet and Intranets
No other system is more aggressive at integrating itself into the Internet and intranet environment than Windows NT. Chapter 9 presents the long-term focus of NT, discusses the basic encryption technology of wide area networks, and gives you some specific guidelines for security NT on intranets, including its Internet Information Server (IIS).

Chapter 10: Subsystems and Other Security Features
The basic features we've discussed so far pervade the NT environment. Chapter 10 closes our operational presentation with a few final topics that include the more common of these other uses, like administering printers and integrating Windows 95 into the Windows NT environment.

Chapter 11: The TCB
Security features are to no avail unless the base on which they rest and the software that enforces them is rock solid and impenetrable. While NT affords this stability, it's

up to you to protect and maintain its basic strength. Chapter 11 discusses what constitutes the TCB (the collection of programs and files key to the system's security) and how to protect it. It's an art.

Chapter 12: Summary and Checklist

This important chapter condenses our many recommendations into checklists for both regular users and administrators. It serves as our general summary and pulls together advice presented in different places through the text.

Part III: Assessment

Chapter 13: NT Security Discussion

Chapter 13 presents a general discussion of the merits of Windows NT security as a point of departure for your own assessment of its many security strengths as they apply to your environment.

Appendix A: Secure Installation

Appendix A describes how to configure your system more securely than its standard installation.

Appendix B: Glossary

The glossary is a synopsis of frequently used security terms and their specific use in this book.

Appendix C: Answers

Appendix C holds the answers to our many exercises keyed to the text by numbers in brackets, like "[45]."

Prerequisites

You don't need to know anything about security. It helps if you are familiar with Microsoft Windows in general. We frequently use the Windows NT Explorer and its desktop, and encourage you to explore NT's extensive on-line help system. We don't use many of its built-in applications or control panel utilities.

If you are an administrative reader, it helps if you are already familiar with both security and nonsecurity NT interfaces. However, we start all the security topics "from scratch," so don't worry if you are a novice.

The job at hand is to teach security—and only security. There are many NT nonsecurity topics that you can readily learn elsewhere. The key to security is to *understand* its features, how they interact, and how to integrate them into your environment. It is this understanding that we stress. Toward this end, this text is not a complete user manual that details each aspect of each security interface. This sort of detail is best left to the fine NT manuals and on-line help.

Icons, Conventions, and Typography

Important notes are set aside in boxes with a small icon for each kind of note.

This icon notes an important topic about which regular users and administrators need to communicate. For example, it might notify regular users of some special capability they should ask of their administrator or a special point administrators should make to other users.

This icon indicates a special note, security warning, or other caution.

This icon marks our major "pencil-n-paper" exercises. Some are thought questions where it may be hard to match the answer, the answer may not be unique, or you may be asked to give an educated opinion. Other exercises are more direct. Sometimes we ask short questions within the text. The answers to all questions are in Appendix C, keyed by a number in brackets, like the one that follows this sentence. [45]

This icon marks an on-line exercise, ones you can do at your workstation. It's tempting to plug in the system and start fiddling. Do so if you like, but when your thirst is satisfied, turn it off and "start over again" with us. It's best if you can set up your system like we describe in *Setting up for On-line Exercises* in the appendix *Background and Setup*.

In addition, we use the following small icons:

☞ Important, but not as urgent as the

➥ A list of topics in a section

✓ An item in a checklist

Don't skip the exercises! They are important checkpoints and their answers often introduce peripheral issues not covered in the main text. However, those marked "**OPT**" are optional. (Think of them as extra credit.) Feel free to skip them if you find them too involved.

We use the following typographic conventions in running text:

❖ We use a bold font for terms either defined in the glossary or items of special note, for example: "This is called a **Right**."

❖ We often capitalize common terms that have a special meaning in NT so as not to confuse them with generic use, like the "Rights Policy."

❖ Program names and window titles appear in plain text with an initial capital (e.g. Explorer).

❖ Field names on windows, menu items, and pages on tab windows are italicized, like *Type of Access*. Buttons are bold, like **Cancel**.

❖ We show a program's menu sequence thus: Explorer: Tools→ Find→ Files or Folders...→ {Find Now}, although we may omit the program name when it's obvious from context. The first option after the application ("Tools" in this example) may be a page on a multipage or "tabbed" window. We often refer to windows by the name in their title bar, and place the page, menu, and button sequence you use to call up the window below the window. If a sequence uses a button we indicated the button with the "{}" braces, as in this example:

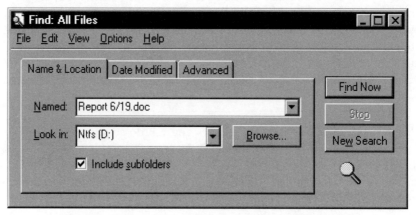

Explorer: Tools→ Find→ Files or Folders...→ {Find Now}

We sometimes refer to an item's **icon menu,** which you call up by selecting an icon or item and clicking the right mouse button (for mice configured as "right-hand" mice). We also refer to an item's **property sheet** that you can usually call up by selecting the *Properties* menu on the item's icon menu.

When you get on-line, call up the preceding window from Windows NT Explorer to see the correlation. Also, select any file or directory on an NTFS-formatted drive. Call up its icon menu and property sheet, select the *Security* page, and select the **Permissions** button. We indicate this window using the window notation:
Icon Menu: Properties→ Security→ {Permissions}

Setting up for On-line Exercises

Setting up for our on-line exercises is a bit of a catch-22 because you need to know a little about administration. You can either have a more experienced administrator help or read enough of your system documentation to get you through this setup.

You can do many of our on-line exercises with a single workstation running NT Workstation or NT Server, but to get the most out of these exercises, set your system as close to the following configuration as you can. You need not use the exact names, but the exercises are clearer if you do. We assume that NT is configured as delivered, except as we note.

✓ You can do almost all exercises with one networked NT Workstation and one NT Server. We call our main domain ACTG and its controller ACTG-SERV, and our workstation in that domain JJONES PC.

✓ Some of our exercises involve a second domain and its controller. We call this domain MANUF with controller MANUF-SERV. MANUF trusts ACTG.

✓ We work mainly in three domain accounts: ACTG\JJones, ACTG\BBrown, and ACTG\CClark. Put these in the Domain Users group. Let these users change their passwords, but don't force them to change it at the next logon. Don't place undue restrictions on these accounts. For example, keep the Accounts Policy liberal. Don't activate the Account Lockout feature.

✓ Put ACTG\JJones in the Power Users group on JJONES PC.

✓ Create a local group on JJONES PC named ProjX that consists of these three users.

✓ Create home directories for these users on JJONES PC, preferably in the standard USERS directory. Set the directory's ACL to give "Full Access" permissions to the respective user and "Read" (**RX**) access to Everyone. Don't forget to define the directory path in the account's "profile."

✓ **Note**: Disable the Guest account on all the workstations including servers.

✓ Create a bland account named LLocal on each workstation but give each a different "Full Name." On NT Server, make it a "local" account.

✓ Create a network share directory named Open on each workstation and give everyone "Full Control."

✓ On NT Server, give the Everyone group the Right to log on locally. (As delivered, NT Server omits this.)

✓ Optionally, set up the "logon banner."

✓ (**OPT**) You need a generic Windows 95 or Windows for Workgroups workstation for our Windows 95 (or WFW) exercises. You can install JJONES PC and Windows 95 (or WFW) on the same computer, because we never use them at the same time. (It's easy enough to first install Windows 95 or WFW and then NT Workstation on the same computer so that you can boot either.)

✓ **(OPT)** A few of our exercises involve an NT Workstation named BETA that's not a domain member. Set up a local JJones account, but with a different password and description than on ACTG. Alternately, you can set up a domain controller in a domain named BETA that does not trust our other domains.

✓ **(OPT)** A few of our exercises involve a third domain named SALES with controller SALES-SERV. Both ACTG and MANUF trust SALES. If you set up SALES, create an account SALES\DDavis like the other accounts you just set up.

Review of Files, Directories, and Trees

It's best if you already know a little something about Windows or MS-DOS when you read this book, but in this section we summarize files and directories to synchronize our terminology. Your data and program files are stored in a set of **logical drives** on your workstation. Each is named by a **drive letter**, like "A:" or "D:" and you can give each a descriptive name, like "Local Files." Drives A: and B: are usually your diskette or floppy drives.

Your working data is organized into files and directories. A **file** can be a letter, a spreadsheet, a drawing, or anything you've created with one of your programs. Each of your programs is kept in a file sometimes called an **executable file** with a name that usually ends with ".EXE".

A **directory** is an organizational tool that holds the names of other files and directories. When you "open" a directory, you see these names. Each drive holds a single directory (called the **root directory** of that drive) that may hold other directories, as well as files, each directory of which may hold other directories (as well as files), and so forth without bound. We sometimes use the word **item** as shorthand for "file and/ or directory." NT shows your directories as little folder icons indicating that a directory is something that holds other things.

☞ If you want to explore with us on-line, you must log on to NT first, although we don't cover logging on until later.

Windows
NT
Explorer

A directory together with all its files and directories, together with all their files and directories, and so forth, is called a directory **tree**. The directory with which we started is called the root directory of that tree. You can conveniently manage your files and directories from the desktop or Windows NT Explorer (see figure).

The left part of this Explorer window shows the components of your desktop with a tree growing from the storage and networking components of your computer. (Trees grow from left to right in this world). The right part shows the contents of the currently selected directory "docs."

Note that the directory Program Files includes a directory Accessories. We say "Program Files is the **parent directory** of Accessories," and "Accessories is a **subdirectory** of Program Files." A subdirectory is a directory in its own right and we only use the term "subdirectory" to distinguish a directory from its parent directory and avoid confusion. Hence we could say: C: is the parent directory of its subdirectory Program Files, and Program Files is the parent directory to its subdirectory Accessories.

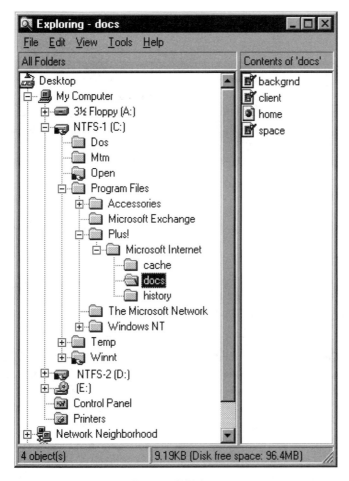

Explorer Window

The left window partition shows directory trees. You can expand or contract trees by double-clicking one of the little folder icons. The right portion of the window lists the file and subdirectories of the folder currently selected in the left window, the one with the "open" folder icon. If you double-click a folder in the right window, it becomes the selected folder in the left window.

Explore trees with Explorer: If you don't already know Explorer, you might want to experiment with it now. In its standard setup, Explorer doesn't do anything drastic like delete files without asking for your confirmation, so don't worry about breaking anything. Feel free to peruse the file trees on all your logical drives.

You can also manage your files just by opening the various icons on your desktop and, successively, their contents. Whether you use this technique or Explorer is a matter of preference.

Special users can make a directory and its tree accessible to other workstations on the network. This is called a **network share directory**. They attach a name of their choice to the share and advertise it on the network. Providing security allows, you can explicitly attach to a network share directory by right-clicking on My Computer and selecting the *Map Network Drive...* option. After you connect, you see the network share directory as if it were a logical drive. For this reason, NT also calls a network share directory a **network drive**. Although the directory and its whole tree is on another workstation, it looks like it's on yours, just like another local hard disk drive letter. You are hard pressed to see any difference. If you're an MS-DOS user, you can use customary path names to access items on the network drive. If you make changes to a network file, like adding an item, the change is actually made on the remote workstation. What you see is not a "copy" of the remote tree, it's the real thing. Use *Disconnect Network Drive...* to end sharing a network drive.

Each of your logical drives (including network drives) has one of three Windows NT disk **formats**. The NTFS format includes an ACL on each file and directory. FAT has none. Floppy disks support only FAT and have no ACLs.

> **Create an Open network share directory**: Create a directory named Open on an NTFS drive, perhaps the one with your WINNT directory. Make it available to the network. Now connect to it yourself ("map it"). If you're doing this with others, connect to their Open directories. Also peruse these directories by expanding the Network Neighborhood both on the desktop and in Explorer.

A remote shared resource like a directory or printer is often referenced by its workstation and advertised share name. For example, you can reference a directory shared as "Open" on a workstation named "ACTG-SERV" as:

```
\\ACTG-SERV\Open
```

When you expand your **Network Neighborhood** either on your desktop or within Explorer, NT automatically accesses share directories as necessary. You don't have to map and disconnect them yourself. However, they have no drive letter. DOS commands must reference them by their full network share path name.

Chapter 2

Accounts and Domains

Authentication is the basis for modern system security. Understanding your account, your system's domain structure, and how they interact are key concepts that start you on your way to using NT's security fully. Your account is the basis for your actions and capabilities on Windows NT. In a full NT environment, your account is bound to a group of workstations called a "domain," and your domain principally determines the other workstations on the network you can access (for example, connect to their network share directories and printers).

In This Chapter We Describe

➡ How and why workstations are grouped into domains

➡ How "browsers" show you the domains and workstations on your network

➡ Logging on to an account, the logon session, and logging off

➡ How domains are related so that users in one domain can gain access to workstations in other domains

Throughout this "general use" portion of this text, our perspective is from NT Workstation (as opposed to NT Server). Regular users almost always work there.

Domains and Workstations

A Windows NT network is a collection of NT computers connected to a network. We generically call each one of these computers a **workstation**, and workstations range from desktop units to large servers that have resources that are shared by many workstations. Typically there could be from a few to hundreds or even thousands of workstations on the network. Each workstation has its own name and each can potentially communicate with any other, although there are a lot of security restrictions and some may not be able to communicate with others at all.

In most client-server environments, NT workstations are grouped into **domains** where each workstation belongs to a single domain. Domains form the components of the master "Microsoft Windows Network." Your usual view of the network is through a **browsing window**. NT uses several similar versions, but the simplest is that of Windows NT Explorer, where you can expand the local network in the left pane to see all the elements in one list. (If you're following along on-line, you need to wait until you log on to open this window and we address this in the next section. At that time we suggest some on-line exercises using this window.)A Typical Browsing Window

The next figure shows a network partitioned into five domains: ACTG (accounting), MANUF (manufacturing), PERS (personnel), RESCH (research), and SALES. (We usually show the capitalized version of names, but some places on your system show otherwise.) Browsing windows list domains, their workstations, and the workstations' shared resources in outline form. Our workstation is named JJONES PC and is a member of the ACTG domain, which we see expanded to show its other workstations. We also see the three network share directories currently advertised by ACTG-SERV.

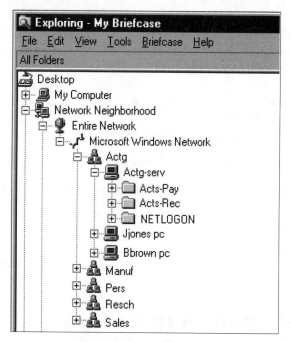

A Typical Browsing Window

Your administrator typically defines domains so that users within a given domain work more frequently with users and workstations in that domain than in other domains. For example, it's common to have a domain for each department in a company like we've shown. The desktop workstations and servers in the accounting department would be put into the ACTG domain. That's why it's convenient that the browsing windows open with your current domain expanded. People who work in the ACTG domain see their own domain's resources by default. Domains don't necessarily restrict the workstations with which yours can communicate, although they might and often do form natural boundaries that you can't cross, often for security reasons. You can expand any of your domain's workstations in the Explorer window by double-clicking it to see the list of network share directories that workstation offers to the rest of the network.

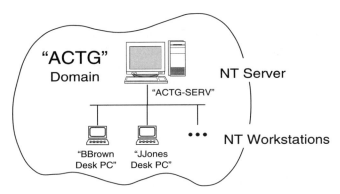

A network partitioned into five domains

In a broader sense, a domain is a natural administrative and security domicile. Typically each domain has its own local administrators that act with a degree of security and operational autonomy from the network as a whole, although there may be a few administrators that can control all domains in a network.

The grouping of workstations into domains is logical, not physical. It's possible for the members of a domain to be widely dispersed and intermixed with other workstations. It's only as common for all the workstations on a "floor of a building" to be in the same domain as it is for all the members of a department (like accounting) to be on the same floor. Only the administrator can define a workstation's domain. There are a few special workstations in a domain:

❖ **Domain Controllers** Each domain has at least one domain controller that serves as the bookkeeper for the domain, a central point of coordination, and security. If there is more than one controller, one is the "primary" and the rest can be held in reserve as backups in case the primary fails. Only the NT version called "NT Server" can be a controller. A domain controller could be someone's active workstation, although they're usually used as major domain servers instead. NT Server has many services not found on NT Workstations.

❖ **Servers** The term "server" is definitely overworked. Generically, a server is any workstation that provides useful services to others on the network. For example, network directory sharing is a service that lets other workstations access part of the server's local hard disk. A "client" is a workstation that avails itself of such a service. The beauty of Windows NT is that any NT Workstation can be both a server and a client to all other NT (and other) Workstations, security allowing.

However, it is common to designate one or perhaps a few of a group of workstations to handle mainline server duties, and it's natural for domain controllers to be servers. (That's why the version is called "NT Server.") Some use the term "server" only for mainline servers running NT Server.

While you never really need to know about domain controller activities, you frequently avail yourself of the services. If there are several domain controller/servers in your domain, your domain administrator usually divides the services among them to balance the load. Domain control and servers both demand the same property of their hosting workstations: nonstop, reliable service. This also encourages them to inhabit the same workstation.

☞ Since our perspective is security, we use the term "server" generically, applying it to any NT Workstation providing services. We never use "server" when we mean "domain controller."

Accounts and the Logon Session

ACTG\jjones

From a security point of view, an **account** is a collection of parameters that govern how Windows NT controls each user that uses the system. Before you can use an NT workstation, you must furnish the name of an account and its **password** in a process called **logging on** (or **logon**). An account is usually for use by one person only and is typically named for that user (for example, "JJones" for someone named J. Jones). One person might have several accounts and presumably only they know the password for each. Only administrators create and manage accounts.

Most accounts are **domain accounts**. A domain account belongs to a particular domain and is valid on all the workstations in that domain. That is, other security controls allowing, you can log on using that account at any workstation in the domain and gain services from all the domain's servers and workstations. A domain account may be allowed in other domains, depending on how the administrators set up the network. In our running example, you can log on using the ACTG\JJones account from workstations in the MANUF domain. (NT often prefixes a domain account with the name of its domain (for example, "ACTG\JJones"), but when the domain is obvious it may show only the account name.)

Logging On and Off

When you approach an NT Workstation, you see a note to press three keys simultaneously: Control ("Ctrl"), Alt, and Delete ("Del"). When you press these keys, you are activating the **Trusted Path**, which in this case starts the logon scenario, as shown in the following figure.

At this point you may see a "logon banner" window with a message from your administrator (the middle window in the figure). Some administrators use this as an "official use only" notice, while others may put some important note about the status of the system. The next window in the sequence asks you for an account name, the

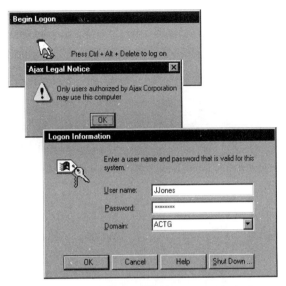

Logon Windows

User name, and its password. The *Domain* field asks for the domain that holds that account, which for now we assume is your workstation's ACTG domain. Notice that the system does not actually show the password you type, but prints asterisks instead.

When you log on NT sets up a familiar Windows working environment and you proceed with your daily tasks. When you're done using the system, you **log off**, forcing another logon. We call the period of time between a logon and logoff a **logon session**. At any point in this session you can log off by pressing the Trusted Path key sequence (the Ctrl, Alt, and Del keys simultaneously) and selecting the **Logoff**... button. (You can also log off from the *Shut Down* option on the task bar's *Start* menu, but the Security window is a better security choice for reasons we cover later.)

Note that this window, called the **Security window**, shows you your account name and logon time. Once you log on, you can't change your session's account identity, although some remote services let you use other workstations under a different account, providing you know its password. Hence, if you want to use another of your accounts locally, you must log off and then log back on.

Some documents (indeed, sometimes this one) may say that "a *user* has access to..." or "*you* have access to...." NT doesn't deal with "users" except through the session's account. Hence, to be precise one should say "an *account* has access to...." In other words, "you" don't "have access to..." unless you know the password of the account that "has access to...." NT doesn't really know you "as a person." (Sounds a bit cold, doesn't it?) It only knows you through the account you present, and takes the account's password as evidence that you are allowed the capabilities within that account, primarily use of the account for various kinds of access both on your current workstation and for services on others.

33

The NT Security Window and Its *Logoff* Option

When you log on, NT gives your account its own personal Windows and MS-DOS environment, separate from any other account. (Note our careful use of the word "account" rather than "you," since if you use more than one account you technically have a separate environment for each, although you can make them look alike.) For example, your Windows environment includes your desktop and task bar layout, color scheme, screen saver, and so forth. Your account usually has a **home directory** on a local drive in which to build your own personal directory trees. When you open many browsing windows your home directory is automatically selected.

Your desktop and MS-DOS environments have little security relevance, so we don't discuss them much. However, there's a great deal of flexibility in how you set them up and manage them. Talk to your administrator for details.

When should you log off? The main security reason for logging out is so that if you leave the workstation, others can't step up and work under your account. However, you can also "lock" your workstation to prevent this, so you log off mainly at the end of the day or when someone else needs to log on.

Introduction: We now begin our on-line exercises. Our view is mostly through the eyes of a regular user named "JJones" on their Windows NT Workstation named JJONES PC in a domain ACTG with domain controller ACTG-SERV. From time to time we'll touch on the other domains we introduced earlier. Unless we say differently, do the on-line exercises from NT Workstation if possible (as opposed to NT Server).

Logging on and off: Practice and explore logging on and off:

❏ Notice whether or not you see a logon banner. Your administrator enables this window and defines its title and message.

❏ Log on using one of the training accounts, like ACTG\JJones. Note that you can select only from the list of domain names in the *Domain* list.

❏ After logging on, use the Trusted Path to log off (Control, Alt, and Delete, simultaneously).

❏ Try a few failed logons with the wrong name or password. Note that NT may remember the name used in the previous logon and present it as the default.

(OPT) Account environments: Explore how each account has its own unique home directory and Windows environment:

Notepad

❏ Log on to one of your training accounts like JJones. Start an application like Notepad and start to open a file. Note that the directory that's expanded by default is your home directory. Use the Desktop Properties window to customize your desktop's background pattern or wallpaper. (Right-click on your desktop background and select the *Properties* menu.) Log off.

❏ Log on to a second training account like BBrown. Note the different home directory and the initial desktop. Log off. Log on to JJones and note the distinct desktop pattern you previously set up. This exercise should convince you that the Windows environment for each account is indeed unique.

Exploring a typical browser: Now that you've logged on, browse the network a bit. Explore a typical browser window and the Network control panel:

Network

❏ Start Explorer and peruse your Network Neighborhood's domains, workstations, and share directories by expanding and contracting the list. You may not be able to expand some workstations because you are not allowed into its domain.

❏ Explore the same territory by expanding your Network Neighborhood icon on your desktop. You should see the same structure as in Explorer. (We generally prefer Explorer because it shows everything in one list, but use the method you prefer.)

❏ Open the Network control panel and note that its *Identification* page shows you the workstation's name and domain.

Secondary Logon

The logon we've just described is called a **primary logon**. Your primary logon is always at the workstation in front of you. You can't do a primary log on "through" one workstation onto another, although you can often get services from that other workstation. Unseen by you, when you request services from another workstation (the remote "server" in this scenario), your workstation (the "client") cooperates with the remote server to log you on to the server by passing the account name and password from your primary logon. Your account must be allowed onto the server for this to succeed and, as we see later, domains have something to do with this. This process is called a **secondary logon**. Note that in this example both primary and secondary logons are to the same account, they're just checked in different places.

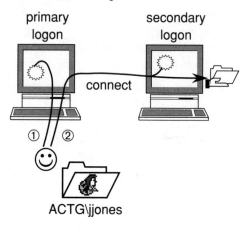

Secondary logons: Network browsers always do a secondary logon when you try to expand a workstation to see its advertised share directories.

❑ Use Explorer to expand all the workstations in your domain. (Note that they are listed directly under the Network Neighborhood for convenience. You can also see them if you expand the entire network down through your current domain.) Secondary logons to workstations in your account's domain usually succeed. They fail only if they don't pass one of the few security controls apart from the domain structure itself.

❑ See if there are workstations in other domains you can't expand. If so, it's probably because they don't allow your account's domain. Hence, the secondary logon fails. More on this in the next section.

Although secondary logon is invisible, and from that perspective commands little of your interest, it is key to how other workstations on the network grant you services. These workstations always ensure that the name and password from your primary logon indicate an account allowed in their domain. If so, they use that account to determine the services you may receive.

Using Accounts across Domains

Each account belongs to a particular domain, hence the convention of prefixing the account name with its domain (for example, ACTG\JJones). Think of this as the full, proper name for an account, even though for simplicity NT often omits domain prefixes from your account's domain. In the broadest case, your account is fully visible and usable on workstations in other domains. This means you can use your account to directly log on or request network services from workstations in other domains. In our example, your day-to-day account and your desktop workstation are in the same domain, ACTG, which is common. But in our example, ACTG\JJones is also allowed onto workstations in the MANUF domain, hence:

❖ From any account in ACTG, you can request services from the workstations in the MANUF domain. For example, you can access network share directories and use printers in the MANUF domain under your ACTG\JJones account. Remember that when you request such services, the server (in MANUF) validates your ACTG\JJones account from its own vantage point, and in our example MANUF allows accounts from ACTG.

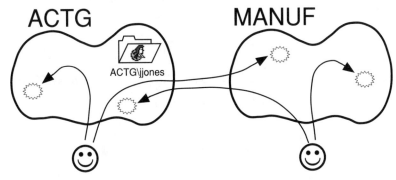

logon: ACTG\jjones   logon: ACTG\jjones

❖ You can also log on using ACTG\JJones at workstations in the MANUF domain. For example, sitting at a workstation in the MANUF domain, you can log on as ACTG\JJones and proceed to read and write documents on that workstation under your ACTG\JJones account.

In short, your ACTG\JJones account is allowed, visible, and fully usable in both domains. However, your administrator can prevent the accounts from certain domains from being used in certain other domains. Continuing our example, your administrators have prevented the accounts from MANUF from being used in the ACTG domain. This means MANUF accounts cannot request services from workstations in ACTG nor directly log on to them. This might well be a security restriction that says resources in ACTG are highly protected and hence not accessible for users in MANUF.

Think of the account's user as being a member of its domain, and think of a domain's users being allowed into some domains but not others. In our example, users from ACTG are allowed into MANUF, but MANUF users are not allowed into ACTG. Again, "allowed into" a domain means you can directly log on to its workstations and remotely access its shared network resources (other permissions allowing). It's a bit like saying MANUF personnel aren't allowed in the accounting offices because there are a lot of sensitive documents laying around. Accountants, however, may freely roam the manufacturing lines.

Further, while SALES users are allowed into the ACTG and MANUF domains, users from ACTG or MANUF are not allowed into SALES. This is because we deem the SALES environment to be the most sensitive and therefore restricted among these three. Only SALES users are allowed there.

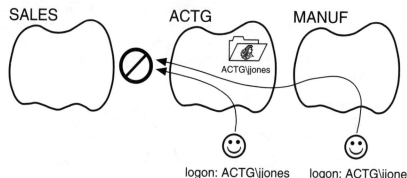

logon: ACTG\jjones   logon: ACTG\jjones

The *Domain* list in the logon window shows which domain users are allowed onto that workstation.

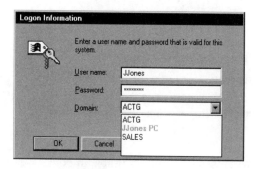

Workstation in ACTG Domain

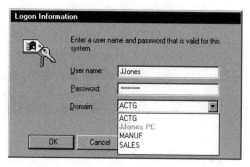

Workstation in MANUF Domain

The left window is from an ACTG workstation; it shows that only ACTG and SALES users are allowed to work there. The right window, from MANUF, shows that ACTG, MANUF, and SALES users all can work there.

On a Windows NT Workstation, the name of your workstation appears in this list but is seldom used in full domain environments. Ignore it for now. (We've artificially grayed it in this figure to deemphasize it.)

NT calls these rules between domains **trust relationships**. We prefer to think in terms of who is allowed where, so if someone says "domain **X** trusts **Y** and **Z**," you could say, "Oh, domain **X** allows user accounts from **Y** and **Z**." Think of this analogy: If your home trusts the home down the street, you allow members of that household into yours. Or consider two countries **A** and **B**. **A** trusts **B**, so it lets citizens from **B** enter **A** and also request information from **A**'s government by mail. **B** does not trust **A**, so **A**'s citizens can neither enter nor request government information from **B**.

Trust is often a one-way street. In our example, while ACTG users are allowed in MANUF (because MANUF "trusts" ACTG), the reverse is not true. For that to happen, ACTG would have to trust MANUF. Administrators define the network's trust relationships and, therefore, who can enter which domains. This is a strong security control, because when you preclude someone from entering the domain, you prevent the skullduggery they might attempt once inside.

You may come across a case where the trust relationships prevent you from connecting to network share directories or logging on at another workstation. See your administrator. NT gives them some clean alternatives.

Network browser windows show you the workstations in all the domains on the network, even ones in which you are not allowed. This is because there are special cases where you can still get services from such workstations using other accounts that are allowed there.

Accessing other domains: In this exercise we show you the perspective of accessing other domains from your home workstation domain. We assume you're sitting at a workstation in the ACTG domain.

❏ Look at the list of domains in your logon window. These are the domains with users who can log on at this workstation. This list is the same for all the workstations in a domain (except, of course, for the entry on an NT Workstation that lists the workstation itself). Log on to ACTG\JJones.

❏ Use Explorer to expand a network share directory on a workstation in the MANUF domain. This succeeds because ACTG users are allowed into the MANUF domain. (You need to make sure a share directory exists and its permissions let you connect. Use our Open share directory if it's set up.)

❏ **(OPT)** Now try to expand a share directory on a workstation in the SALES domain. This fails because users from ACTG are not allowed in SALES. You can't even see the shared resources available on SALES.

Using your account in other domains: In this exercise we show you the perspective of working in your ACTG\JJones account from other workstations.

❏ From a workstation in the MANUF domain, log on to ACTG\JJones. This succeeds, again because ACTG users are allowed in MANUF. Now try to expand a share directory in ACTG. This also succeeds, again because ACTG users are, of course, allowed in the ACTG domain. Had you logged on using a MANUF account, could you expand it like this? [1]

❏ (OPT) Try to log on to a workstation in the SALES domain using ACTG\JJones. Of course this fails because ACTG users are not allowed into SALES. You can't even attempt to use an account in ACTG because it's not in the domain list of the logon window.

Can a user SALES\DDavis log on at a workstation in the ACTG domain (primary logon)? If so, from there could they use a shared resource on a workstation in SALES? Explain. [2]

From the workstation in SALES, you log on to the account SALES\DDavis and then use Explorer to try to expand a workstation in ACTG. Does it succeed? Explain. [3]

(OPT) Exercising Server Manager: From an NT Server and logged on as an administrator, find the administrative tool Server Manager and use it to browse your network's domains (or at least those that recognize your account). Use *Compute→ Select Domain…* to select a domain. Try the items on the *View* menu.

Server
Manager

You may still be a bit confused as to what you can do from where. It's okay. The bottom line is that your account may not be allowed in some domains. If not, you can't log on to those domains' workstations and can't access their network share resources.

A "Master" Domain Example

As an alternative example, your administrators could have configured the domain environment somewhat differently. They could have placed all accounts in a master domain named MASTER that has account administration as its main purpose. People's workstations could still have domains in our example: ACTG, MANUF, and so forth.

In this scenario, your day-to-day work would have been on your ACTG workstation but under the master account MASTER\JJones. This illustrates that your usual account might not be in your day-to-day workstation's domain.

Different Accounts of the Same Name

You could have two accounts of the same name in different domains, like ACTG\JJones and MANUF\JJones. While they may both be for your use only, presumably because only you know their passwords, technically they are separate, independent accounts. In our terminology, you are a different "user" depending on which of these two accounts you're using. However, when you attempt a remote service there are cases where NT "matches" your local account to a remote account of the same name if you know the remote account's password. In this case, these two accounts let you fully use both domains. We talk more about this later.

Summary

You should have a good handle on your account and how it relates to networking domains.

❖ Administrators arrange workstations into domains under the strategy that users within a domain are much more likely to communicate within the domain than with users in other domains. More importantly, domains partition the network for security, letting each domain admit users from some domains and not others.

❖ To use Windows NT you must present a valid account and its password to log on, beginning your logon session. When you're done with your work, you log off. Use the Trusted Path to initiate both.

❖ On NT, your account has a unique Windows environment and usually a home directory for your personal files. These are separate and independent from others who can log on to the same workstation.

❖ Typically, the account under which you log on is a domain account in your workstation's domain that's fully usable within that domain and, typically, some other domains. However, your domain account may not be allowed in other domains. If so, you can't log on to their workstations or access their network share resources.

❖ At a more detailed level, whenever you request the services of another workstation, NT invisibly does a secondary logon. To succeed, your account must be allowed in that workstation's domain and must pass some other controls we talk about later.

❖ We call the rules for which domains allow other domains' accounts "trust relationships," which your administrators define. You really don't need to understand these rules since NT windows seldom show you domains that don't allow your account.

❖ Although domain controllers and servers are an important part of the network, you seldom "see" domain controllers, and see servers only to the extent you need their services.

Quick Check:

✓ Why is the phrase "your session's account can access..." more precise than "you can access..."? [4]

✓ Is your account tied to your workstation in any way? [5]

✓ What names are listed in the logon window's *Domain* list? What do they mean? [6]

✓ Your administrator says, "Domains **A** and **B** trust **C**." Restate this in terms of which users are allowed in which domains. [7]

✓ An administrator gives you, ACTG\JJones, a second account named "JJones" in SALES. Are SALES\JJones and ACTG\JJones the same account? Is this useful? [8]

✓ Considering only the ACTG and SALES domains in our example, from which workstations can SALES\JJones perform a primary logon? Secondary? [9]

✓ What must you constantly keep in mind about the domain trust relationships on your network? [10]

How would an administrator let several people use a single account? Is this good security? [11]

Usually your account is in the same domain as your day-to-day workstation, usually one on your desk. Have you seen any disadvantages when your account is in a domain other than your workstation? For example, might the domain structure prevent you from accessing other workstations in your workstation's domain? [12]

(OPT) From what you've seen by now, suppose you are asked to map out the trust relationships of a network by snooping at its workstations. How do you proceed? [13]

(OPT) Mapping your site: If you're working in a multidomain environment other than your standard example, map out your site's trust relationships as in the preceding exercise. (This may take a bit of leg work.)

(OPT) Printer sharing: Printers can be shared on the network just like directories.
❏ Browse your network's shared printers. Open the Add Printer icon in the Printers directory in My Computer. Connect to a network print server. A browser window appears that works analogous to Explorer, but shows printers rather than share directories.

Chapter 3

Your Working Environment

NT security comes through many features new to traditional Window's users. In fact, the relatively few differences you see between Windows and NT are the new security features. This chapter presents the security aspects of your day-to-day security working environment with the exception of ACLs, which we cover in the next chapter. Don't let the fact that we cover these thoroughly cause you concern. Most of the these new features are simple and intuitive. However, using them correctly and consistently is important to the security of your data.

In This Chapter We Describe

➡ The importance of your Trusted Path and how to use it securely

➡ How to choose secure passwords

➡ The restrictions your administrator may place on your account

The Trusted Path

The Trusted Path is your friend and constant ally. It's critical to security and useful for other things, like stopping runaway programs. Best of all, it's easy to use. First a little motivation about why it's so important.

Stealing Your Password

Suppose NT did not have a Trusted Path. Your screen saver takes over, blanking your screen. You move your mouse and a little window comes up demanding your password, which you happily enter. Your screen is restored to its original splendor. Great security feature, right?

Not quite. Suppose that some innocent-looking program you are currently running blanked the screen, then asked for and received your password, and is on its way to handing it over to the person who wrote this nasty little piece of code in the first place. What you've seen is not your real screen saver at all. Your password has been stolen, and you don't know it, nor could you have reasonably known it. You have been "spoofed." There are certain cases when you want to demand of NT: "Show me a window I can trust—right now—no kidding!" and be sure that the next window you see on the screen is the bonafide, trustworthy window that you requested—one, for example, to which you could safely give your password. This is precisely what the Trusted Path gives you. To activate the Trusted Path, you press three keys simultaneously: Control ("Ctrl"), Alt, and Delete ("Del"). (This is the same sequence you used to log on.) When you do, your windows disappear (they're still there and active, just hidden) and you'll see the Windows NT Security window:

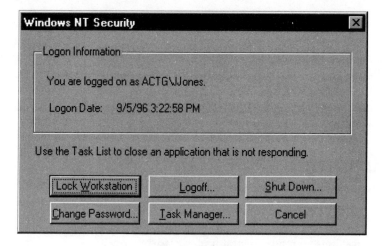

NT Security Window

Windows NT never displays this window unless you press these keys, although it may produce a window that tells you to press them. The Security window even disappears if you don't use it within a few minutes. You've already seen that you must use the Trusted Path to log on and off. We now look at its other options.

Lock Workstation

This feature hides your windows and locks your workstation, but doesn't disturb your applications. Unlock your workstation by entering the Trusted Path, which asks you for your password. Lock your workstation when you'll be away from your workstation and you don't want others to use it. You could alternatively log off, but that cancels your current work. Administrators can unlock your workstation using their own account name and password, but it ends your session by logging you out.

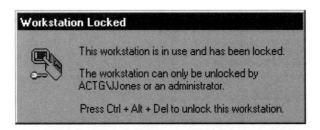

Shut Down . . .

After asking for confirmation, NT logs you off and shuts down the workstation or, at your option, reboots it. Some users may not be able to do this. If you can't and need to, see your administrator. You need a special Right (discussed later). This is the only way to shut down the workstation safely.

☞Don't power down NT without going through this shutdown procedure.

Change Password . . .

This feature lets you change your account's password. Type your old password once and the new one twice. Actually, anyone can change the password of any account of any workstation on the network, providing they know the current password. Type the name of the account in *User name* and the name of a domain or workstation in *Domain* (or choose one from the list). We talk later about when to change your password and how to choose a secure one.

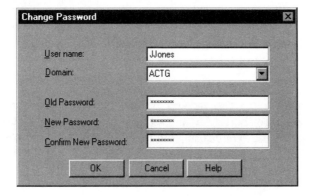

Task Manager...

This option lets you delete active applications (usually when they are running out of control), create new ones, and switch to one of your active windows (usually when you can't find it in the clutter of your screen). Its pages also show you some interesting statistics and the complete list of processes running on your system. While this window is "secure," it's not particularly security relevant.

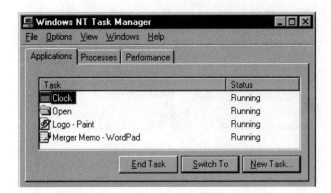

Exercising the Security Window: Explore these scenarios. If you change your password, either remember it or change it back to what it was originally, if you are allowed! Try changing some other account's password. If you can, change the password of a different account on another workstation.

The Trusted Path helps thwart malicious programs. You might thoroughly trust all your programs and be tempted to avoid the Trusted Path where you can. Don't. It's cheap and effective protection. There are only a few cases when you need to enter your password through a window other than one you call up using the Trusted Path.

When you activate a screen saver from the Desktop control panel, you can make it "password protected." After it blanks your screen, you must enter the Trusted Path and your password to restore it. This is an excellent option and we encourage its use. Because it uses the Trusted Path, it avoids the stealing-your-password scenario presented earlier. Legitimate screen savers ask you to unlock them by initiating the Trusted Path. You'll spot any one that does not as illegitimate. Won't you?

Password protect your screen saver: From the Desktop property sheet, select a screen saver, choose a short delay, and set *Password protected*. Exit (**OK**) and wait for the screen to blank. Explore using the Trusted Path to restore it. The procedure is like unlocking your workstation after you use the Trusted Path to lock it.

Why does NT remove the Security window if you don't use it within a few minutes? [14]

An official-looking screen appears and says, "Temporary administrative lock, please wait..." then after a little while prompts you to "...enter your password to continue." Do you do so? (This is hypothetical. NT doesn't do this.) [15] What might a scenario like this have said to enable you to trust it and enter your password? [16]

Observe the following. Always. No exceptions!

✓ Never believe what appears to be the Security window unless you caused it to appear via the Trusted Path keys.

✓ Except for *Task List...*, never do any of the Security window's functions by other means. For example, don't use that little handy-dandy password changing program you got from someone down the hall.

✓ Never enter your password except in a legitimate Trusted Path scenario or in one of the few other cases we describe later.

✓ If you're worried about others using your workstation, use a password-protected screen saver.

✓ Never believe it when a user or your workstation tells you the Trusted Path key sequence has been changed.

Choosing Passwords

Passwords are the subject of much folklore and seem a magnet for unsteady thinking among even well-meaning users and administrators. They are also the underpinning of security on almost all security systems, including Windows NT.

NT's Rules

First, the basic rules:

❑ Each user may or may not be allowed to change their own password. If they can't, presumably the administrator gives them a new one from time to time.

❑ If you can change your password, you must choose one that meets certain tests:

❖ You can use any keyboard character including the blank, which counts as a character. Upper case is distinct from lower. Hence, the passwords "BHTBR" and "bHtBr" are different.

❖ It can be no longer than fourteen characters and may need to contain a minimum number of characters depending on your administrator's policy. The minimal length can be zero, in which case you can choose the "empty" password if you like, although it's obviously not secure.

❖ You may be prevented from choosing a password that is the same as one of your previous passwords, where the number of previous passwords checked is set by your administrator. If so, whenever you change your password, you can't change it again for a certain period of time.

❑ Your password may expire on a particular date. When it expires, NT either forces you to create a new one the next time you log on or you need to get a new one from your administrator. NT warns you when expiration is a few days away.

❑ The administrator can terminate your password at any time. For example, they might do this for a batch of users when they suspect stolen passwords are being used.

❑ If you or someone else tries to log on a certain number of times in a row entering an incorrect password, your account may be locked out and cannot be logged on to. In this case you either must wait for a while before you can log on again or get your administrator to unlock your account, depending on how your administrator has set up the system.

You need not remember these rules in detail. Just change your password when you think you should or when the system suggests. If you can't make the change you'd like, talk to your administrator.

> When NT prevents you from using one of your previous passwords, it also prevents you from changing the new one for a period of time. Why? [17]

When and How to Pick a Proper Password

Why do you need a password? Obviously, to keep other people from using your capabilities on the system, including reading and writing the data to which you have access. But you may work in a small enclave of people who you implicitly trust and who freely share all their data. Who needs passwords?

Well, what about the office visitor with an opportunity to fiddle with your workstation unnoticed? And do you really want some else to be creative with your desktop color scheme or try to be helpful by tidying up your home directory? Most sites need passwords at least for these reasons, although many don't need them to be exceptionally hard to guess. There's a few basic rules for protecting your password:

✓ Don't write down your password.
✓ Don't tell it to anybody.
✓ Choose passwords that are hard for others to guess.
✓ Avoid storing any password (and never store your NT logon password) inside one of your files or in a DOS command (*.BAT) file. For example, you may be tempted to include your passwords in certain *.BAT files you create, for example ones that automatically connect to some networking service. Avoid this.

When should you change your password? Apart from when NT makes you, change your password:

❖ **When it is first given to you by your administrator.** It is a good idea to change your password from one given to you and therefore known by your administrator. It's not that the administrator is untrustworthy, only that they can make mistakes, too.

❖ **If you have an inkling that someone else knows your password.** For example, you may have written it down (despite admonitions to the contrary) and lost the slip of paper or you may see something unusual in your interaction with the system that may lead you to suspect that someone else is working as you.

If your suspicions have any strength, notify your administrator.

❖ **If you have been away for an extended period of time.** If you have not logged on for a while, you may have missed some clues that would have tipped you off that someone else has your password.

❖ **If your account acquires more capabilities.** This applies, for example, when you receive membership in new groups. This prevents anyone who knows your current password from getting these new capabilities.

If someone learns your password and you get a new one, they cannot log on using the old one. However, they may have done many things that last even after you get a new one. For example, they may have subtly changed the ACLs on your files or replaced your well-protected programs with fake versions. The best defense is never to let your password out in the first place.

As for what constitutes a proper password, one that's secure enough, the problem is that hard-to-guess passwords may well be hard to remember. While the password "a%Rrt%$shdGGu*" is certainly hard to guess, you almost surely must write it down. Passwords written down (often on the bottom of a keyboard or, better yet, mouse pad because it's portable) are a large risk. Mostly, it is a trade-off of keeping the password complicated enough to be secure but simple enough so you need not write it down.

Bad Passwords

✓ Your account name

✓ Any part of your real name or the names of your coworkers, family, pets, and so forth

✓ Any word or number from your personal vita, like your phone number, birthday, or automobile license number

✓ Simple passwords like "xxx" or "defgh"

✓ Dictionary words

✓ The same password that you use for some application programs on your system. Such programs probably don't manage their passwords through the Trusted Path, which makes them easy for another program to steal.

✓ The same password you use on another computer system (or domain), unless perhaps the two systems (or domains) are "equally secure." Even if they are, this may not be a good idea. Check with your administrator.

✓ And, of course, a final caution that no self-respecting security book would be caught without: *any of the examples in this book!*

Now that we've told you what not to choose, what's left? There many good schemes but we discuss one that we think is particularly effective. First, choose a phrase that you can easily visualize, perhaps something memorable that happened to you that few others know about, like:

"fell curb hurt ankle ouch"
"chitty bird on tiny limb"
"blue car ate yellow house"

The more uncommon the words and the more incorrect the grammar, the better. Visualize the phrase; carve its image in your mind. (This may sound silly, but it works!) Now condense this phrase to less than fourteen characters by a truncation technique that you never change. Three examples:

1. Use the first (or last) letter of each word. For many sites five or six such characters is a respectable password.
   "blue car ate yellow house"   *shortens to*   "bcayh"

2. Use the first three letters of each word up to fourteen letters:
   "blue car ate yellow house"   *shortens to*   "blucarateyelho"

3. A more complicated technique: reduce each word down to three letters by first crossing out the vowels, starting from the rear of the word, then crossing out the consonants, also starting from the rear:
   "blue car ate yellow house"   *shortens to*   "blucarateyllho"
   "chitty bird on ugly limb"   *shortens to*   "chtbrdonglylmb"

Avoid common words like "big" or "old." Use uncommon words like "olfactory" or "endowment." Stick with the same truncation algorithm so that you can always reconstruct the short password if you remember the long one. It's the long one you're likely to remember.

The strength of the technique you use is really a decision between you and your administrator. Your administrator likely has a better view of what's needed for security and hopefully has some guidelines.

Use the scheme we just discussed to make up several passwords. Choose a little-used account and really change the password to convince yourself that you can remember it without writing it down.

Get some ideas for constructing phrases by doing an exercise with an associate or classmate. Make up eight of these phrases. Exchange lists with your associate and then create variants on each of the eight phrases. You can cycle the lists through several users.

Other Topics

Here we discuss a few final topics to round out your working environment.

Logon and Service Restrictions

Your domain administrator can place several restrictions on your account that prevent you from logging on. NT is quite specific when it tells you why you can't log on.

Account Expired,[1] Locked, or Disabled   Your administrator can prevent an account from being logged on by "disabling" it, or the account can expire. As we discussed earlier, your account can also lock because someone tried unsuccessfully to log on to your account, although in this case it may unlock itself after a period of time.

Logon and Service Hours[1]   The administrator can prevent you from logging on to a particular account during certain periods of the day, and these periods may vary from one day of the week to another. If you're logged in when you pass into a restricted period, you may not be able to gain services from other workstations during the restricted periods. Also, depending on how the administrator has set up the domain, NT Servers may suspend already established services when you pass into restricted periods. However, these periods do not affect activities local to your workstation if you're already logged on. They don't force you to log off.

Logon time periods can be troublesome. Administrators may limit accounts to anything except "normal" working hours. However, your exceptional late-night logons are usually under pressure from the next morning's deadline. Bad time to find an administrator. Know these periods before hand.

Restricted Workstations[1]   Your administrator can prevent you from primary logon at certain workstations. However, you still may be able to gain remote services from these prohibited workstations when you're logged on to another.

---

1. Accounts on NT Server only—not NT Workstation.

Domain Controller Logons[1] Independent of the other restrictions, your account needs special capabilities (a "Right," see below) to do a primary logon to a domain controller or major server. Domain controllers are often critical resources where only administrators can primarily logon.

Rights

Certain actions on a workstation, often actions that are administrative, require your account to have a corresponding **Right**. Each workstation has a list of which accounts are allowed which Rights. That is, your Rights are not inherent in your account, but are instead granted to your account on a workstation-by-workstation basis. Your administrator should give you the ones you need and are trusted to use wisely. A few that you might need include:

❖ Shut down and restart (reboot) a workstation

❖ Log on locally. This is used to allow only administrators to log on to critical workstations, like domain controllers and servers, and can also be a general-access restriction.

❖ Access the workstation remotely. In other words, do a secondary logon from another workstation. For example, you need this Right to connect to a network share directory on the workstation.

❖ Back up and restore files and directories in a mode that overrides ACL controls. With this privilege the Backup program can read and restore any file or directory on the system regardless of its ACL.

There are many other Rights, but none regular users likely need. Your administrator usually gives your account a Right by adding you to some group that has it. You can't see your Rights, nor should you need to. Just run the programs you need and if you have the Rights they require you succeed.

Power Users

There's a local group named Power Users on each NT Workstation. If you're a member of this group, your account has some administrative capabilities on that workstation but on no other workstation, unless of course you're a member of *its* Power Users group. There are two main things you can do as a Power User that regular users can't. First, you can make your own workstation's resources accessible to users on other workstations, like network share directories. You can also create, manage, and share printers. (You need not be a Power User to gain services from other workstations—only to make them available on your own.) Secondly, you can create, modify, and delete local accounts, thereby letting others use your workstation. We haven't talked about local accounts yet, but they are like domain accounts except they allow access only to the workstation on which you define them. They can't be used on any other workstation.

You can also perform some minor housekeeping duties, like set the time, profile the workstation's performance, and change scheduling priority. Power Users are not absolute masters of their workstation and are always under the control of full administrators. They cannot, for example, bestow administrative capabilities on themselves or other users except for creating additional Power Users. Power Users need a modest amount of administrative training.

Tips for Security in the Intranet Environment

An "intranet" is the latest term for a wide area network attached to your local area network (LAN). The most famous intranet is the worldwide Internet. Attaching your small enclave onto a broad network opens a host of security problems. Most of these are quite technical and should be addressed by your administrator. However, there are a few things you can do to protect yourself in this environment. Although also important for the LAN, these tips become particularly important for wide area networks.

Safe Authentication and Protecting Your Password

Many intranet applications require that you enter a password to authenticate you to the service. Many such scenarios are quite safe, particularly ones designed specifically for the Windows NT networking environment. These use techniques that avoid passing your password over the network in a manner that it can be captured by eavesdroppers. In short:

✓ Never enter your password unless you know the potential risks involved in the particular authentication scenario. When in doubt, ask your administrator.

✓ If you can select a password for a particular remote service, don't use one related to your NT logon password.

Trojan Horses—The Obscure Ones!

By simply viewing remote documents or downloaded documents, you can easily download programs that run on your system and may do damage. See the section that follows on such obscure intranet "vermin."

Your Workstation's Services

Apart from Trojan Horses and eavesdropping, the principal way remote sources attack your workstation is by requesting its services, perhaps exploiting some security weakness or by masquerading as a legitimate, remote source. For example, NT's file-sharing mechanism is just such a service. Most users aren't aware of the services that run on their own workstations and should not be charged with having to evaluate their security. However, be particularly wary if you install a program that provides services to other workstations. Check with your administrator first!

Secure Sockets Layer (SSL) and Certificates

Web browsers and other intranet programs may use a security technology called "SSL" or one of its closely related variants. These browsers clearly let you know when you are and are not in "secure mode." SSL gives you the following basic protections:

❖ It uses cryptographic technology to ensure that your communication cannot be eavesdropped or tampered. Its ciphers can be strongly configured and as such network attacks are no longer a serious threat.

❖ It can assure you that the remote site with which you are communicating is the site it purports to be, rather than a pretender. The SSL infrastructure uses cryptographic "certificates" to accomplish this. A certificate is a small piece of data loaded onto your system that describes a remote "certificate authority (CA)." CAs are trusted entities (like a company or widely recognized organization) that certify specific intranet sites by issuing the site its own certificate. Your browser obtains one or perhaps a few CA certificates in a trusted manner. Sometimes these are built into the browser, in which case you never even see them, and sometimes you or your administrator install them using a prescribed procedure. When your browser communicates with a remote site, the site presents its certificate and if it has been certified by one of your installed CAs, you are assured that the remote site is legitimate. Typically, your browser may warn you when the site's address, like "http://ajax.com," does not check against its certificate, the one issued to Ajax Corporation for its primary Web site at Ajax.com.

You should understand that a remote site is legitimate only to the extent you trust its authenticating CA to have conscientiously awarded the site its certificate, and that the remote site kept certain secret information about its certificate a secret. Although it's beyond the scope of most day-to-day users, you can read "Cryptography" in Chapter 9, The Internet and Intranets, for more detail on SSL and certificates.

Vermin in the Intranet Environment

Viruses, Trojan Horses, and related vermin (collectively, "malicious programs") are a particular concern in an intranet environment. With its ACLs, Windows NT is less prone to virus attack than systems without them, like Windows 95. Even so, there's seldom a good reason for not using commercial virus-scanning programs.

While many viruses arrive as Trojan Horse programs, a few are particularly insidious. Most users recognizing the dangers of downloading a program from a public bulletin board, but as a passive program it doesn't do anything until you run it, perhaps after you've scanned it for viruses. At least you can prepare yourself for its potential invasion. However, there are cases where malicious programs run unexpectedly.

Programs in Passive Documents

Some applications let you attach active elements (essentially programs) to a document that automatically run when someone simply views the document, perhaps unknown to the viewer. A recent "Word macro" virus furnishes a good example. Word lets the creator of a document attach a macro that runs when the document is opened. A Word macro can include actions like reading files and sending them across a network, all unseen by the reader.

The danger is that most users who know about Trojan Horses may not expect the simple act of viewing a document to trigger a part of the document to run invisibly as an active program. Such a loaded document could simply be offered on the intranet as one holding innocent information or be mailed directly to the target user.

For security's sake, these applications should give the recipient of a document options that control these automatic actions. For example, in Word you can hold down the shift key while opening a document to disable the macros that would otherwise run, and Word can now notify you before running these macros.

Sometimes you can get a separate program that simply "views" a full application's documents without running attached programs. These programs are particularly useful for browsers that automatically start them when you download a document with a particular suffix. For example, a Word viewer for *.DOC documents avoids the Word macro problem altogether.

> Maintain a constant vigilance for such programs. Make this a part of your checklist for introducing new programs onto your workstations.

WWW Applets

When you view a remote World Wide Web page that includes active "applets," like Java or Microsoft's ActiveX applets, your browser loads the applets onto your system, where they run as a program (essentially). Applets can gain considerable access to NT's basic system services and operations and may be able to do things like open files and transport them to remote locations unseen by you, the browser's user. (Note that ACL protection does no good as long as the person who runs the browser owns, or has "Change" permission access to, the items.)

Applet technologies differ in their capabilities. Java tends to be much more limited, and most browsers give Java almost no capabilities unless you direct them otherwise. For example, these browsers may let you confine Java applets to certain directory trees. Microsoft's ActiveX applets cannot be as strictly confined as Java applets and have almost unlimited access to your workstation. This makes them especially dangerous. Microsoft is currently proposing to sign these applets digitally which at least assures you that they run as their provider intends. However, malicious providers are still an enormous risk.

> Make sure you understand the browser's applet restrictions afforded by your browser. At the very least, try to restrict applications to specific directory trees that contain no critical data or programs.

A browser's standard configuration sets the applet's restricted access tree to the main browser directory that holds the browser itself and related programs. What's wrong with this picture? [18]

Summary

You should now be familiar with all your day-to-day security duties except managing ACLs:

❖ The Trusted Path is a major protection against malicious programs fooling you so they can use your capabilities behind your back, and also gives you the convenience of stopping runaway programs. You should now be familiar with all the actions you can do using the Trusted Path's Security window.

❖ Your administrator can impose lots of rules on how and when you change your account's password, including whether you can change it at all, when you are forced to change it at logon, its length, and whether or not you can reuse one of your previous passwords. Some of these can vary among accounts.

❖ While knowing when to change your password is important, it's critical to choose one that's appropriate to security. The secret is to practice a technique that gives you passwords that are appropriately hard to guess yet you can remember without writing them down. Have your administrator approve your technique.

❖ Administrators can place a number of restrictions on your account, including when it expires, the hours on certain days of the week it can be used, and the workstations on which it can be used for primary and secondary logons.

❖ Your account may need certain Rights on certain workstations that let you do administrative activities, like back up and restore other users' files.

❖ Power Users are like assistant administrators for a particular workstation. They have a few but not all the capabilities of a full administrator. Your administrator may make you a Power User for your own desktop workstation. If so, you need training from other chapters.

Quick Check:

✓ You walk up to a workstation and see the Security window. Someone has apparently already activated the Trusted Path. What do you do to start working? [19]

✓ A window that looks like the Security window unexpectedly appears, "The Trusted Path has been automatically activated by the system or your administrator, please…" What is your reaction? [20]

✓ How can NT's screen saver add security to your system? [21]

✓ You find a program that does something already done on the Security window more conveniently. Should you use it in place of the Security window version? [22]

✓ Is "As%$Rf^!Tgw" a good password? [23]

✓ Make up three good passwords. Are they hard to guess yet easy to remember?

✓ You can't do a primary logon at workstation **Y** in your domain. Are there circumstances under which you could log on elsewhere and access **Y**'s network share directories? [24]

A friend gives you a neat little program that lists passwords that are easy to remember, although you still use the Trusted Path to make the change. Is this program safe? Explain. [25]

Chapter 4

ACLs

Access Control Lists are the very basis for Windows NT security. They alone protect your data. We've talked a lot about authentication and passwords, and one of their major purposes is to support ACLs. It's an understatement to say that learning to use them correctly is important. This chapter presents a thorough, step-by-step explanation of ACLs, what they mean and how to use them. While we focus on files and directories, other objects have ACLs and we cover some of these in later chapters.

In This Chapter We Describe

Groups:

➡ Two kinds of groups (global and local)

➡ Some "special" groups built into Windows NT

➡ How to create your own groups

Basic ACLs for Files and Directories:

➡ How an ACL is made up of entries, each giving certain permissions to an account or group

➡ The basic **RWXDPO** permissions and how NT determines access based on the entries in the ACL

➡ How NT uses combinations of permissions (called "standard permission sets") that make your job easier

➡ How to use CREATOR OWNER to give permissions to a new item's creating account automatically

➡ How setting the ACL on a directory effectively sets the ACLs for the entire tree growing below it, except when you have a good reason to protect some of its items differently

➡ Setting up typical home and project directories

Special Topics:

➡ How to take ownership of files, protect network share directories with an ACL, and connect to remote shares under a different account

➡ Some tips for how applications use and interact with ACLs

Unless we instruct you otherwise, don't do the on-line exercises in this chapter as an administrator, specifically, as a member of the Administrators local group. This can cause some unexpected side effects.

Introduction

You can think of an ACL as a tag attached to each file and directory. Other objects, like shared printers, can have ACLs, but we focus on files and directories. Once you learn files and directories, using ACLs in other situations is a natural extension.

☞ Files + Directories = "Items"

Sometimes people use the term "file" to mean "file and/or directory." In this chapter, we don't. "File" means only a file—not a directory. We use "items" or "files and/or directories" when we refer to either or both.

An ACL controls which accounts can access the item to which the ACL is attached. It determines who can read, change, and delete data files; run programs; enter and list the contents of directories; and so forth. The ACL is not a part of the data of the item—it's separate and you see them as "properties" of files and directories.

Every item that has an ACL has an **owner**, the name of an account. (We might more properly call this the "owning account.") When you create an item, NT automatically attaches your current account as the owner. As owner, you can change the ACL any way you want. You can even change the ACL to let other accounts change the ACL or replace you as the item's owner. The ACL alone controls direct access to a file. The owner has no special access except as specifically allowed by the ACL. However, since a person who owns an item can change its ACL, they can give themselves any access permissions they want.

You're probably thinking, "Oh, no. I'm going to have to fiddle constantly with the ACL on each and every one of my files and directories." Don't worry. With a little planning on how you set up your directory ACLs, ACLs not only fully protect but require little day-to-day attention. You may go for weeks without having to change one.

Before ACLs, you (hopefully) organized your directories according to some logic. You can still use the same logic, but fold in one more important criteria: access by other accounts.

Example: Before ACLs, you may have kept all your reports in a single directory that you assume people who were interested read at their leisure. With ACLs you might well decide that you have two kinds or reports, ones for management and ones for everybody else. You now set up two directories and protect them differently. You might even decide on a third directory for old reports with tight permissions, reasoning that while your current reports are readily available to the appropriate parties, you are not keen on people rummaging through your outdated ones.

> The secret to no-hassle, secure ACLs is to organize your files into directories based in part on who should be permitted to access them and in what manner (read, read and write, and so forth).

Windows NT supports several kinds of disk formats, but only the new NTFS format has ACLs attached to each item. The traditional MS-DOS FAT and OS/2 HPFS formats have no per-item ACLs. Do all our exercises on NTFS.

☞ There may be restrictions on a file or directory in addition to and independent of the ACL. Throughout this chapter we make statements like, "If you have XYZ permission based on the ACL, you can read the file." Implicit in all these statements is the postscript "… other controls allowing."

Groups

An ACL can give specific access permissions to both individual user accounts and groups, so we start with a discussion of what groups are and how you manage them. A **group** is a named list of accounts. Although only administrators maintain some groups, regular users can create and maintain their own groups for use on their workstation. Groups give you the convenience of using a single name in place of a potentially long list of user accounts. More importantly, if you assign a certain capability to an group (like access to your files), when new members are added to the group they automatically gain that capability. There are two kinds of groups (local and global), as well as special built-in groups, although you will seldom care much about the distinction.

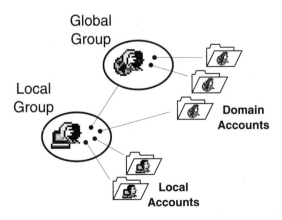

A **local group** is defined on a particular workstation and can be used only in ACLs on that workstation. A local group can include any user accounts and global groups visible from its workstation, but not other local groups. Both regular users and administrators can create local groups. The following figure is from the ACL window's Group Membership window. Study it carefully. It holds a global group, two domain accounts, and a local account. Note the different icons.

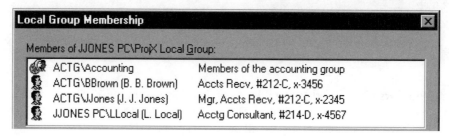

A Local Group on the JJONES PC Workstation

A **global group** is defined domainwide and is visible throughout its own domain and others based on the trust relationships. (The term "domain group" might be a better one, but we stick with what NT gives us.) Global groups include only user accounts from their own domain and only administrators can create them.

A Global Group from the ACTG Domain

Although there may be local groups of the same name on other workstations, they are separate lists of accounts and might well represent different sets of people used for different purposes. The key is that you can use each group only in ACLs on its own workstation, and so you never see two local groups of the same name in one ACL. While two global groups from different domains with the same name can appear in a single ACL, their names are prefixed by their domain (although NT sometimes omits the prefix from groups in the your account's domain).

Your domain account may be a member of several groups throughout your domain. (Some of which you may not even know about!) But it's a bit backward to think of the groups to which you belong as being "listed in your account." They aren't really listed in your account. Instead, your account name sits in various group definition lists wherever they sit on the network.

In summary, think of any group as a short name for a list of accounts. The distinction between local and global usually is not too important, except that local groups can be used only on the workstation on which they're created. We show you how to create local groups in "Creating Local Groups" later in this chapter. In "Special Groups," also later in this chapter, we present a few special groups, like one named Everyone that implicitly includes all accounts allowed on a workstation.

Basic ACLs for Files

ACLs on files are somewhat simpler than on directories, and so we start our presentation looking at files, then proceed to directories. The ACL is a property of a file or directory and you manage ACLs from the **Permissions** button on the Security property sheet. The following figure shows the ACL management window for a file. This window includes the name of the file and its owner, the ACL in the large box, and controls to modify the ACL:

Icon Menu: Properties→ Security→ {Permissions}

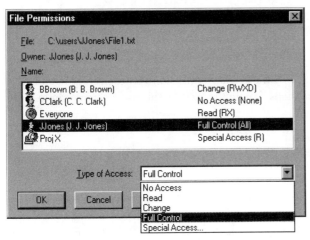

This ACL for a file named "FILE1.TXT" owned by JJones has five entries. Type of Access is used to select permissions for the highlighted entry.

An Example ACL for Files

An ACL is a list of **entries**. Each entry has the name of either a user account or a group, and a set of **permissions** that apply to that account or accounts in that group. The **ACL window** (which is titled Directory Permissions or File Permissions) lists the entries one per line and in alphabetic order. NT documents call an ACL entry the **access control entry** (**ACE**). In this window JJones owns the file and is represented by an entry in the ACL with "Full Control" permission. We also see accounts BBrown and CClark, a special entry for all accounts, named Everyone, and a local group named ProjX. Note especially the different icons. In this example, NT shows the local group prefixed by your workstation name, which is where the local group is defined, but omits the domain name before the global group. NT often omits a domain prefix when it's the same as your account. This is a short ACL with three entries. ACLs can have a large number of entries, although it's rare.

> **Creating working files**: We often ask you to create a file or folder in a folder. Whether you use Explorer or work from the desktop, you can easily create these using the *File→ New* menu sequence to create a "Text Document" or folder.
>
> While you can alternatively create some files elsewhere, and drag and drop them into the folder, if you create them on the same logical drive you *must* hold down the control key during the drag-and-drop to make sure you get a whole new copy of the file. Otherwise you are simply moving the file from one place on a drive to another and you won't see some of the effects we illustrate.
>
> **Perusing ACLs**: Create a file in your home directory. Working from a Desktop window or within Explorer, right-click the file's icon, call up its property sheet, select the *Security* page, and click the **Properties** button to view the file's ACL. Peruse the ACLs on a random selection of any files you can open. Avoid directories for now and don't change any ACLs yet.

☞ You may occasionally see "Account (or Group) Unknown" in place of an account or group name. Either this entry, once allowed on this workstation, is no longer allowed or a domain controller is off-line. If the latter, then the real names reappear when the controller comes on-line.

Permissions

The File Permissions window shows the **Basic Permissions** for each entry in parenthesis, like (**RWX**) or (**All**). Permissions denote the specific things a user can do to a file. They are listed in Table 4.1.

Table 4.1   Basic Permissions for Files

Read (R)	Read the data in the file.
Write (W)	Modify the data in the file, including appending and removing data.
Execute (X)	Run the program in the file. When used on files, **X** applies only to files that hold programs, usually *.EXE (executable) files. Files other than program files can have the **X** permission, but it has no effect.
Delete (D)	Delete the file. (You can delete a file without **D** if you have "Full Control" of its parent directory, but we discuss this later.)
Change Permissions (P)	Modify the ACL, but not change the owner.
Take Ownership (O)	Make your current account the owner. Does not change the ACL.

None of these implies any of the others. For example, "Write" alone does not allow reading. NT uses the special words "(**All**)" for all permissions and "No Access" for (**None**).

Viewing and Changing the ACL

If your account has **R, W,** or **X** permissions for a file or directory, you may view the ACL. However if you're the owner, you don't need any permissions—you can always view the ACL. The account who owns the item and any account with "Change Permissions" can change its ACL to anything they like.

The owner of the file has **P** permission implicitly, even though it's not shown. Therefore, an ACL may prevent the owner and users with **P** from directly accessing the file, but can't prevent them from changing the ACL, perhaps to allow themselves access. Also, users with **P** permission can give themselves **O** and then take ownership. The net result is that giving someone **O** or **P** alone lets them ursurp the other.

You seldom deal with Basic Permissions directly. Instead, for your convenience the ACL window presents a list of higher level sets of permissions listed in the *Type of Access* field. We call these the **standard permission sets**. Each is a name for a certain combination of Basic Permissions, which we list in parenthesis in Table 4.2.

Table 4.2 Standard Permission Sets for Files

No Access (None)	Use this to preclude all access to a file. (A file's name is actually kept in the parent directory, so even if you protect a file with "No Access," people may be able to see its name.)
Read (RX)	Lets people read but not change the file and, if it is a program file, lets them run it as a program.
Change (RWXD)	Allows all access to the file except changing its ACL or ownership.
Full Control (All)	Allows all possible file operations, **RWXDPO**. (There are only a few things users with "Full Control" can never do to a file. For example, you can never change a file's owner to an account other than your own.)
Special Access (…)	This special name lets you choose any other combination of the Basic Permissions—ones that you specifically construct. This custom set appears in parentheses. If you happen to construct one of the standard permission sets, NT uses the name for that set instead of "Special Access." When you select *Special Access…* or double-click an entry, NT shows you the window that you can then use to select a custom set of permissions

☞Whenever possible, use one of the standard permission sets instead of constructing a custom set.

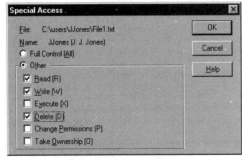

Setting "Special Access" Permissions

We can't overemphasize this advice. The problem is that you can see somewhat confusing behavior if you assign, for example, **R** without **X** or **W** without **R**. (Actually, there are few of these confusing cases for files, but rather more for directories.) The standard permission sets are "natural" combinations and usually work just fine. When you become an expert, you're allowed to improvise. We point out a few exceptions in later exercises.

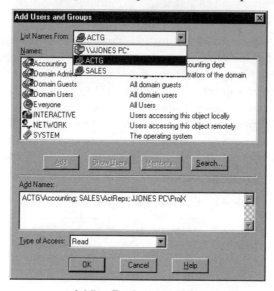

Adding Entries to an ACL

As you see in the following exercises, changing, adding and deleting entries is simple. The **Add** button lets you add one or more entries with the same permission set.

List Names From shows all the domains with users who are allowed on your workstations, as well as your workstation itself. If you choose a domain, NT shows you the global groups and domain accounts from that domain. If you choose your workstation, it shows only the local groups and accounts. (We haven't mentioned local accounts yet, but you seldom use them.) This figure shows names from the three possible sources.

We talk about the special groups like Power Users and Guests. Feel free to add them to ACLs in our exercises, but don't worry about who they are. Everyone is a special local group that implicitly includes all accounts, even those created after the ACL was defined. There are also some special grouplike entries, like NETWORK, that we discuss later.

By default NT shows only groups in this window. You must select the **Show Users** button to include user accounts in this list. This is NT's way of encouraging you to use groups instead of individual accounts where possible. Sound advice.

You can select several names from this list, using the **Add** button for each, then select a permission set and exit using **OK**. Use the **Members...** button to list the members of the selected group, a window we show earlier in the section "Groups." Use the **Search...** button to hunt for an account or group whose name you know.

These exercises familiarize you with the mechanics of managing file ACLs, even though we haven't talked about exactly how they allow access.

Exploring Basic Permission sets: Create at least three files in your home directory with which to work.

❑ Open one of their ACLs. Explore all the standard permission sets in the *Type of Access* field.

❑ Select an ACL entry and give it, successively, each of these permission sets and note which Basic Permissions (**RWXDPO**) they impart.

Exploring groups: Select one of your working files, open its ACL, and call up the Add Users and Groups window. Note the local and global icons. The rule of thumb is that any icon that contains planet earth is global. Others are local. Note the special groups like Everyone, INTERACTIVE, and NETWORK. We talk about these later.

❑ Examine all the options from *List Names From*. Can you guess what the names with the asterisk mean? [26]

❑ Use the **Members...** button to list the constituency of several groups, including the special groups we just mentioned. You can't show the members of some of these because they're special, predefined, built-in groups.

❑ Try the **Search...** button if you like, although you'll probably rarely use it. Note that the groups and accounts found through all your searches accumulate in the *Search Results* box and they are added to the ACL when you choose **Add**.

Changing ACLs: Now we do a series of exercises where you actually change the ACLs on your working files.

❑ Add a group and a user entry of your choice.

❑ Can you remove all the entries from an ACL?

❑ Add several entries at once with the same set of permissions. From the Add Users and Groups window repeatedly select an entry and click the **Add** button, then set *Type of Access*.

❑ From the main ACL window, double-click one of the entries to call up the Special Access window.

❑ Add each of the three following ACLs to your working files. (Some of these are unrealistic, but they're only for exercise.)

ACTG\Domain Users	Read (**RX**)
ACTG\Domain Admins	Change (**RWXD**)
ACTG\JJones	Full Control (**All**)
JJONES PC\Guests	No Access (**None**)
JJONES PC\Power Users	Full Control (**All**)

(continues)

ACTG\Domain Users	Read (**RX**)
ACTG\JJones	"
JJONES PC\Power Users	"
(add all three at once!)	
ACTG\Domain Users	Special Access (**RXD**)
ACTG\JJones	Special Access (**WXD**)
JJONES PC\Guests	Special Access (**P**)
JJONES PC\Power Users	Special Access (**RWXDPO**)

❑ Does setting all the "Special Access" permissions **RWXDPO** equate to "Full Control"? [27]

Prepare your home directory: For later exercises, it's important that you have **RWXDPO** access to your home directory instead of "Full Control." Although we haven't discussed setting the ACL on directories yet, it's similar to files. Just double-click the existing permission name for the applicable entry and select **RWXDPO**.

Changing the ACL on several files at once: Select two files with different ACLs and begin to change the ACL. Notice the scenario is a bit different, but you can nonetheless define a single ACL that is applied to each. The major difference is that you can't see any of the previous ACLs. Now change two files at once that begin with the same ACLs. Here you see the preexisting ACL.

(OPT) Prefixes that NT omits: Create an ACL with entries from your domain (ACTG) as well as from your workstation (JJONES PC). Make sure Everyone can read the file. Logged on as ACTG\JJones, open the ACL and note which domain/workstation name NT omits. For example, NT drops the "ACTG\" prefix from ACTG\JJones and prints simply "JJones." Now log on to a local account on JJONES PC and see which ones NT omits. (We haven't talked about local accounts yet, but you need to select JJONES PC in the logon window's *Domain* list and type the name and password of a local account. Use the Administrator account if you know the password.) This shows that NT omits the name prefix when it's the same as your account.

The "Mysteriously Disappearing Twin": There's an access type named *Special Access* (as opposed to *Special Access…*) that appears only after you've set a special access for an entry. Can you discover how it works? [28]

The Access Decision

When a person, through some program, attempts to access a file in any way, their account is checked against the file's ACL as follows: First, NT considers only (1) the ACL entry for the user account itself, if present, and (2) entries for groups of which that account is a member, if any. We call these the "applicable entries." All other entries are ignored and have no effect on the decision.

✓ If there are no applicable entries, access is denied.

✓ If *any one of* the applicable entries has the "No Access" permission, access is denied, regardless of any other entries that might otherwise allow it.

✓ Otherwise, all permissions are gathered from the applicable entries and this set as a whole determines access.

A few notes:

❖ When we say "an account **A** is a member of a group **Z**," the account could be a member of a global group **Y**, itself a member of local group **Z**. (We don't worry about any more combinations because only local groups can contain other groups, and then can hold only global groups.)

❖ Another way of looking at the successful part of the decision, the "gathering" of permissions, is that you get the Basic Permissions given to the total of all the groups that include your account. For example, you may pick up **R** through one entry and **W** through another.

❖ People don't access files—programs acting on their behalf access the files. Each program requests a particular combination of the Basic Permissions depending on what the program intends to do to the file. For example a word processor might attempt to open the file for at least reading and perhaps writing. It is these requested permissions that must be in the set gathered from the ACL.

❖ Before you can even attempt to access a file, you may need to wind your way through the file tree into the file's parent directory. Every directory through which you pass, including the file's parent directory, has an ACL that may deny you entry into the directory. Hence, a file's ancestral directories indirectly protect the file. In other words, giving somebody access to a file does no good if you deny them access to one of its parent directories. (Think of someone on the street giving you the key to a strongbox stored in their office where they work. Without a badge to get into the building and the key to their office, it does you little good.)

Consider the following ACL:

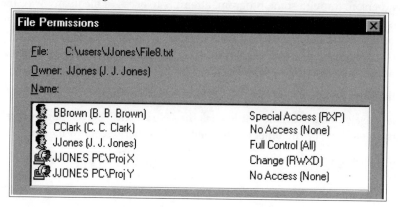

Neglecting the two groups (at the bottom) for a moment, BBrown gets **R**, **X**, and **P**; JJones gets all permissions; and CClark is denied access. Members of the ProjX group get **RWXD** and those in ProjY are precluded from accessing the file. Each line in the following table shows a situation when that user is a member of none, one, or both of the groups. For each line, list the permissions the user has. [29]

	ProjX	ProjY
BBrown		
BBrown	✓	
BBrown		✓
BBrown	✓	✓
JJones		
JJones	✓	
JJones	✓	
JJones	✓	
CClark		
CClark	✓	

❖ DDavis is a member of ProjX. What permissions do they have?

❖ In the preceding ACL, who can view the ACL? Who can change the ACL? Can JJones change the ACL if a member of ProjY? Does the CClark entry have any effect if CClark is not a member of either group? [30]

Consider the following ACL:

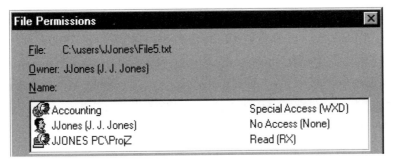

❖ In this example, the global group ACTG\Accounting is a member of the local group ProjZ. (1) Which permissions does BBrown receive as a member of ACTG\Accounting? (2) Which permissions does CClark get as a member of ProjZ but not Accounting? (3) Which permissions does JJones get as a member of ProjZ? (4) The file is owned by the local group administrators. Assuming they are not members of the groups in the ACL, which permissions do members of this group get? [31]

❖ A file is to be read, written, and deleted by JJones and BBrown and viewed by their group, ProjY. What ACL do you install? [32]

❖ Can you think of any overall ability someone gains when you give them "Take Ownership" that they don't get from "Change Permissions" alone? [33]

When you create a file, your account becomes the owner. The only way the owner can change is through a "Take Ownership" that we table until later.

Basic ACL tests: In these exercises you test ACLs by putting certain ACLs on one of your working files and then use Notepad to see if you can read or change it. Mostly, we want to convince you that they really work. We assume that JJones is your current account.

❏ In your home directory, create a working directory named AA and give its ACL the single entry for Everyone with "Change" permission. We haven't talked about setting the ACL on a directory yet, but it works a lot like for files. Create a working file named "FF.TXT" in AA.

❏ Set the ACL on FF.TXT with an entry for JJones and Everyone, "No Access" for both. Try to read, write, and delete the file. You fail.

- ❏ Give JJones **RWX**. Try to read and write the file. What does this illustrate? **[34]**

- ❏ Give JJones **R** and Everyone **WX**. Can you both read and write? What does this illustrate? **[35]**

- ❏ Give JJones **R** and Everyone **X**. Can you still both read and write?

- ❏ Give "No Access" to Everyone. Can you still see its name? Can you open its ACL? **[36]**

- ❏ Make sure your home directory ACL allows "Read" permission to Everyone. As a second user, can you see the FF.TXT? Can you open its ACL? **[37]**

- ❏ Continuing, logged on as JJones give all entries "Read" permission. As a second user, can you now open the ACL? **[38]**

- ❏ Logged on as JJones, delete AA.

Basic ACLs for Directories

A directory is an "object" separate from its files and subdirectories. Each directory has an ACL that controls access to the directory itself, for example reading the names of the directory's items and adding new items to the directory. Its ACL also controls whether users can even enter the directory and therefore indirectly protects all the items in the directory's tree.

> **Example**: Consider an analogy of a locked closet in a locked office with different keys for the office and closet. The lock on the office protects the office itself: its furniture and so forth. The lock on the closet protects its contents. Does the lock on the office protect the contents of the closet? Directly, no, but indirectly, yes, because you can't even try to enter the closet unless you have the key to the office. If your closet holds nothing more important than the office, you could leave the closet unlocked or you could set both locks to open with the same key.

The window that manages directory ACLs looks much like the one for files. The major difference is that each entry has *two* sets of permissions each (shown in parentheses).

The permissions in the left parentheses are the directory access permissions that control access to the directory itself, just like the single set of permissions in a file's ACL protects the file.

The file default permissions (right set) do not affect access to the directory. Instead, they're used only to determine the initial ACL of a file newly created in the directory. We table their discussion until later. Ignore them for now.

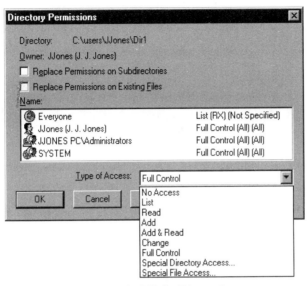

An Example ACL for Directories

Permissions and Basic Access

The same Basic Permissions we listed earlier for files protect directories in the same manner they affect files, but with a few nuances, as shown in Tables 4.3 and 4.4.

Table 4.3 Basic Permissions for Directories

Read (R)	Reads the names of the items in the directory. This does not let you read the data within those items or their attributes, like their ACL. NT denies many operations on an item if you can't read its parent directory to see its name. In other words, if you can't see an item's name (which is kept within its parent directory), you can't access the item at all, even if its ACL might otherwise allow it. Thus, each directory implicitly protects each item in the tree below it.
Write (W)	Creates new files and subdirectories in the directory. Your account becomes the owner and the item's initial ACL is determined by the parent directory's ACL, as we discuss later.
Execute (X)	Lets a program make a directory its working directory. For example, you need **X** to use the standard MS-DOS command "CD" to enter a directory. Also, the standard file open box that you see, for example when you save a document, also makes each directory you open its working directory, which **X** also allows. The **X** permission on directories can be a bit confusing. Follow this simple rule of thumb:
	☞ Do not use **X** without **R** or **W**; always use **X** with **R** or **W**. (These guidelines apply only to directories—not files.) In other words, among **R, W,** and **X,** use the combinations **RX, WX,** or **RWX**. NT's standard permission sets follow these guidelines. *(continues)*

Table 4.3 Basic Permissions for Directories *(continued)*

Delete (D)	Deletes the directory itself. However, to delete a directory you must be able to delete every item in the directory's tree and this is controlled by the ACL of each of those items. You don't need **W** or **D** to a directory to delete its items, but you need **D** permission to the items themselves.
Change Permissions (P)	The same as files, lets you arbitrarily modify the directory's ACL but not change the owner.
Take Ownership (O)	The same as files, makes your current account the owner. Does not change the directory's ACL.

The directory ACL window uses the same standard permission sets in the *Type of Access* field plus a few more that apply only to directories shown followed by the *"*"*:

Table 4.4 Standard Permission Sets for Directories

No Access (None)	Precludes all access to the directory's tree.
List[1] (RX)	Lets people view the names of the items in the directory and enter its subdirectories as their ACLs permit.
Read (RX)	Same as "List." (We see later why there's two standard sets with the same Basic Permissions.)
Add[1] (WX)	Lets you create new items in the directory, but not see the names of existing ones. Also lets you pass through the directory and into its subdirectories.
Add and Read[1] (RWX)	The same as "Add" except you can freely see the contents of the directory. The simple sum of "Add" and "Read."
Change (RWXD)	Gives you full access to the directory itself, but not the ability to change its ACL or owner. However, "Change" alone does not let you change or delete an item from the directory unless the item's ACL also allows it.
Full Control (All)	Effectively, all the Basic Permissions, plus: ☞ "Full Control" gives you a bit more power than the simple sum of all Basic Permissions. "Full Control" on a directory lets you delete any file or empty subdirectory regardless of that item's ACL. **RWXDPO** don't allow this unless you have "Delete" permission to the item itself. (This wrinkle satisfies a POSIX requirement.)
Special Directory Access (...)	Like "Special Access" for files, this names any other combination— ones that you specifically construct.
Special File Access (...)	Use this to specify a custom set of Basic Permissions for the file default ACL, which we cover later.

1. Unique to directories. Does not apply to files

Note that these follow our standard rules for using **X** with **R** and **W**. The access decision for directories is the same as for files, except of course that the Basic Permissions have a somewhat different meaning.

Exploring directory ACLs: Create a directory named Test in your home directory. Remove all its ACL entries except one for yourself and one for a second user, BBrown.

❏ Explore Test's standard permission sets. Set all the values. (Don't use *Special File Access...* yet because it has nothing to do with protecting the directory itself.)

❏ Give yourself "No Access" and BBrown "Read," then try to expand the directory. You can't.

❏ Now give yourself "Read" and try to create a working file in Test. Now give yourself "Change" permission to Test and try again. You should succeed this time.

❏ Now give yourself "Read" permission to Test and then "Change" to the file. (Make sure you do it in this order.) Now delete the file. This illustrates that you only need "Delete" permission to delete the item itself.

"Full Control" versus RWXDPO: For any working directory's ACL, use the *Type of Access* "Special Directory Access" to set **RWXDPO**. Back in the Directory Permissions window do you see "Full Control (**All**)" or "Special Access (**RWXDPO**)?" [39]

❏ Do *not* use *Replace Permissions on Existing Files* in this exercise. Give yourself "Read" to one of the files in Test. Now give yourself **RWXDPO** permissions to Test and try to delete the file. (Use the Delete key or move it to the Recycle Bin.) Now give yourself "Full Access" to Test and try to delete it. Explain. [40]

Discuss the advantage or disadvantage of **RWXDPO** versus "Full Control." [41]

ACL Wizard: NT has a "wizard" that lets you change the ACL on a directory to a few basic settings. It offers little additional functionality and is probably of little use to most seasoned users. However, you can check it out on the Wizard Manager, WIZMGR.EXE.

ACL Propagation: Protecting Trees

In this section we show how NT sets the ACL of a newly created file or directory from that of its parent directory. If you build a file tree without explicitly changing its items' ACLs, the root directory's ACL determines the ACLs of all the items in that tree. This lets you automatically protect an entire, growing tree by initially setting the ACL of its root directory.

This is an important NT metaphor because it frees you from the tedium of constantly tending the ACL of each and every file and directory you create. It's an essential one because you may not even know about some of the files your programs create on your behalf. Also, because non-NT systems (like Windows 95) connected to NT trees often can't set ACLs (they may not even know about them), these propagation features determine the ACLs of all the items they create.

Files Newly Created in a Directory

When you modify a directory's ACL you can set two sets of Basic Permissions for each entry: the directory access permissions that we just discussed (shown in the following figure, in parentheses on the left) and the **file default** permissions (same figure, right side). The standard permission set name that precedes them describes them both in a manner we describe shortly.

(The illustration on the left separates and aligns the permission sets for illustration. Most NT windows don't.) The file default permissions let you determine the ACL that NT applies to all newly created *files* within that directory. When NT creates a new file, it sets its ACL the same as its parent directory, but using the file default permissions only. When you look at a directory's ACL, mentally erase the directory access sets (on the left). What's left is essentially what's given to newly created files.

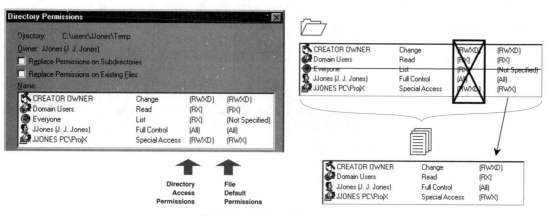

File Default Permissions

Exploring file defaults: Use the Test directory we've just created. Add several entries but not CREATOR OWNER. (It's special and we cover it later.) Give yourself "Full Control."

❑ For one of the entry's in Test's ACL, select each *Type of Access* and note which directory permissions and file default permissions the entry receives. Do you understand what these standard permission sets mean vis-à-vis the protection to the directory itself versus its newly created files?

❑ Create a new file in this directory. (**Note**: If you drag and drop a file from another directory on the same logical drive, hold down the Ctrl key to get a complete new copy, otherwise you don't see the effects we discuss.) Examine the file's ACL vis-à-vis that of the parent directory. Repeat this for a variety of ACLs on Test.

❑ Open the ACL on Test. Note that *Replace Permissions on Existing Files* is selected by default. What ACLs do existing files get if you use *Replace Permissions on Existing Files?* [42]

❑ When you change the ACL of a directory and don't check *Replace Permissions on Existing Files*, do ACLs on its existing files change? [43]

Many of the standard permission sets place the same permissions in both the directory access and file default sets. This is NT's way of encouraging you to protect new files the same as their parent directory, although you can certainly do otherwise if you have a good reason. Similarly, when you change a directory's ACL, NT replaces the permissions on its files because *Replace Permissions on Existing Files* is already selected.

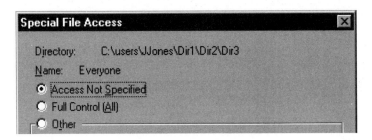

File defaults with "Not Specified": Use "Special File Access..." to set some of the entries in Test to "Not Specified" and others to something else. Create a new file. Describe its ACL.

As you can see, entries "Not Specified" are not included in the ACL of the new file. As we mentioned earlier, directories have standard permission sets that files don't, like "List" and "Add." When you select one of these, the file default permissions are tagged "Not Specified." In this case, NT omits that entry from the file's ACL. Therefore, "List" grants **RX** access to a directory without giving access to files within. "Read" additionally grants **RX** access to files.

> **More file default exercises**: Place an ACL on the Test directory with one entry for yourself and one for a second user, BBrown.
>
> ❏ **"Add" versus "Add and Read":** Give BBrown "Read" and yourself "Add." Can you see the contents of Test? Now create a file in Test. Does it succeed? Then give yourself "Add and Read," but *do not* select *Replace Permissions on Existing Files*. Create a second file. What's the difference between these two operations? **[44]**
>
> ☞ Use "Add" to let users add entries to a directory but not see its contents. Use "Add and Read" to let them also read its files.
>
> ❏ **"List" versus "Read":** Note that BBrown received "Read" permission to these new files. Now give BBrown "List" permission to Test but *do not* select *Replace Permissions on Existing Files*. Create a new file. What's the difference? **[45]**
>
> ❏ Log on as BBrown and confirm that while you can see the file's name, you cannot read its contents. Log back on as JJones.
>
> ☞ Use "List" to let users see the names of the directory's items, but not the contents of its files. Use "Read" to let them see both.
>
> **Creating files with empty ACLs**: Devise a directory ACL that attempts to place empty ACLs on new files. Test your scheme. What happens? **[46]**

CREATOR OWNER for Files

You can give permissions to the account that creates a file by adding the special CREATOR OWNER entry to the directory's ACL. It's not a real account and NT ignores it for access control. Rather, it's a special flag that NT uses when it constructs the ACL of a new file. The file default permissions you give to CREATOR OWNER are given to the account that creates a new file in the directory:

❖ If the creating account is already in the ACL of the new file, NT adds CREATOR OWNER's permissions to that account, which may expand that user's access.

❖ Otherwise, NT creates a new entry in the file's ACL for the creating account with CREATOR OWNER's file default permissions.

Demonstrating CREATOR OWNER: Empty Test then set its ACL with two entries: Everyone with "Add and Read," and CREATOR OWNER with "Full Control."

❑ Create a file in the directory. What happens to the CREATOR OWNER entry in the new file? [**47**]

❑ Add an entry to the directory's ACL for yourself (JJones) with only **RX** file default permissions. Give CREATOR OWNER the **WXD** file defaults. What do you expect your entry in a new file's ACL to be? Try it. [**48**]

❑ In Test, give CREATOR OWNER "No Access." Create a new file. Do you expect it to have "No Access" or **RX**? [**49**]

Use CREATOR OWNER when you want to give the creator permissions automatically. Remember that the account that creates a file can change its ACL and can always change the permissions it gets by default, so it may seem that technically you don't need CREATOR OWNER. However, there are some good reasons why you do:

❖ This is a convenience for creators. Usually, you intend the creator to have more permissions than others and you don't know beforehand who will create the file. CREATOR OWNER saves them the bother of manually changing the ACL.

❖ Some programs create "temp" files, usually in your working directory and almost always unnoticed. It's important for these files to be fully accessible by the program so you commonly give CREATOR OWNER "Full Control" or at least **RWXD**.

❖ Non-NT systems like Windows 95 can share NT file trees. These systems often don't even know about NT ACLs or have no provision for setting them on files and directories they create. CREATOR OWNER is important for giving the creator permissions to files they create.

☞ You'll find it common to give CREATOR OWNER "Full Control," since there's rarely a need to deny any permissions to the creator of a file. There's no security point to giving them any less. Because they are the owner, they can change the ACL to give themselves any permissions they want.

A quick summary of our progress so far:

✓ A directory ACL's directory access permissions protect the directory itself.

✓ Files newly created in a directory get a copy of its ACL, but with the file default permissions, except that entries with file defaults that are "Not Specified" are removed.

✓ The difference between "List" and "Read" is only in the file defaults and the same goes for "Add" versus "Add and Read."

✓ For newly created files, CREATOR OWNER's file default permissions in the directory's ACL augment the creator's permissions if they already have an entry in the

ACL. Otherwise NT creates a new entry for the creator with CREATOR OWNER's file default permissions.

✓ When you change a directory's ACL you have, by default, the option to *Replace Permissions on Existing Files*. This places the same ACL on its files as if they were created under the directory's new ACL.

Protecting Growing Trees

What ACL does NT give a newly created directory? Simple: that of its parent directory—unchanged. This means that whenever you set an ACL on a fresh, empty directory, you're arranging to give by default the same ACL to all the directories in its growing tree.

Create a small tree: Create a working directory named DirA in your home directory and place a few entries in its ACL. Include yourself with "Full Control" but omit CREATOR OWNER. Now create this directory tree. (Note that file F1 is in DirA and F2 is in DirD.)

Examine the ACL of each file and directory in this tree. You see how setting the ACL on DirA protected the whole tree identically? Of course, as you create a particular directory in this tree, you may want its ACL to be different. Just set the ACL after you create it and that ACL then propagates through its tree.

If you need to change the ACL of all directories in a tree rooted at a certain directory, use *Replace Permissions on Subdirectories:*

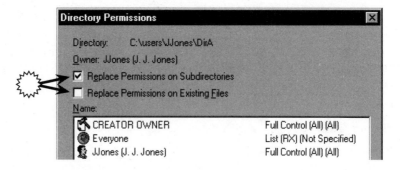

Replacing Directory ACLs throughout a Tree

This directs NT also to place this ACL on all directories in the tree below the current directory, assuming you have permission to change each. Files are not affected.

Recursively changing ACLs: In this exercise we recursively change directories, then files, and then both.

❏ Change the ACL on DirA to something distinctive, but use *Replace Permissions on Subdirectories*. Does it change only the subdirectories of DirA (Dir B1 and DirB2) or all the directories in the tree (like DirC and DirD)? [50]

❏ Again using DirA, choose a different, distinctive ACL and select only *Replace Permissions on Existing Files* (not subdirectories). Does this change only F1, or F2 also? Which new ACL do files receive? [51]

❏ Do the same exercise on DirA, again choosing a new, distinctive ACL, but select both the *Replace...* options. Now how extensive are the changes? [52]

CREATOR OWNER for Directories

CREATOR OWNER has much the same purpose and effect for directories as it does for files: the directory access permissions you put in the CREATOR OWNER entry are given to the user who creates a subdirectory. In addition, the CREATOR OWNER entry itself propagates unchanged into the ACL of new subdirectories. However, CREATOR OWNER creates a *new entry* (when the creating account is not already in the parent directory's ACL) and puts an asterisk after the directory access permissions for that entry, as shown in the following figure.

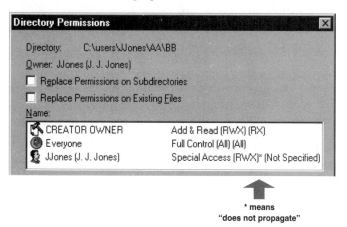

* means
"does not propagate"

CREATOR OWNER "*" Entries That Don't Propagate

The asterisk indicates that this entry is not passed on to subdirectories. In addition, NT sets the file default set to "Not Specified." For example in this ACL on directory BB, NT does not pass the JJones entry to directories created in BB. A few subtle points:

❖ Since the CREATOR OWNER entry itself propagates through the tree, a user constructing a subtree receives control of all its items via CREATOR OWNER *only* through CREATOR OWNER, not the asterisked entries it creates.

❖ This "one-level" limitation does not affect the case when CREATOR OWNER adds permissions to a preexisting entry for an account. Such entries as augmented by CREATOR OWNER propagate through the tree. In other words, any time you place a specific account in the ACL, it propagates normally. (In normal propagation, its permissions can be augmented by CREATOR OWNER.)

☞In short, when NT adds a new entry to a directory ACL via CREATOR OWNER, that entry does not further propagate to subdirectories.

Since CREATOR OWNER itself propagates through a directory's tree, there's no need for entries it creates in directories to also propagate.

Exploring CREATOR OWNER in directories and the "*": Create a directory named AA in your home directory and give it this ACL:

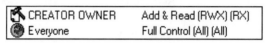

| CREATOR OWNER | Add & Read (RWX) (RX) |
| Everyone | Full Control (All) (All) |

❑ Create a subdirectory in AA named BB and examine its ACL. CREATOR OWNER created its JJones entry. Note that it's marked with "*" and has no file defaults even though the CREATOR OWNER in AA has **RX** file defaults.

❑ **Asterisked entries don't propagate...** Log on as BBrown and create a file F and a directory CC in BB. Note that the asterisked entry for JJones in BB does not propagate to F and CC. Asterisked entries don't propagate to new directories.

❑ **...unless you change them**. Still as BBrown, in directory BB change the permissions for the asterisked JJones entry to "Change." Is it still asterisked? Create a subdirectory DD and open its ACL. Did JJones propagate? **[53]**

❑ **Entries augmented by CREATOR OWNER are not asterisked**. Log back in as JJones and add a "Read" entry for yourself in AA. Create a subdirectory EE in AA and open EE's ACL. In this case, CREATOR OWNER only augments your preexisting JJones entry. Therefore, it is not asterisked and propagated. Try it.

❑ **Tidy up**: Delete AA.

This may seem confusing, but you need not understand this in detail. Like many of NT's security features it's a natural action that works automatically to help keep you out of trouble even if you don't fully understand the details. A quick recap:

✓ Except for the effects of CREATOR OWNER, NT gives a newly created directory the same ACL as its parent.

✓ If the creator of a new directory has an entry in the parent directory's ACL, CREATOR OWNER augments that entry just like for files. If there is no such entry, NT creates one that's asterisked and does not therefore propagate to subdirectories, and has the "Not Specified" file default permissions. In either case, the CREATOR OWNER entry is itself replicated unchanged to each new directory.

Setting up Your Home Directory

This subsection presents an extended ACL exercise where we set up your home directory with a number of special-purpose subdirectories. Your strategy is to be as stingy as possible, giving others minimal permissions to your files and directories. Logged on as JJones, enter your home directory and clean out all the working files and directories. (Alternately, you might want to do this exercise in a different directory as if it were your home directory.) Start out by assuming no one is to share your files and set up the directory's ACL accordingly. Which ACL did you use? [54] Create a file in JJones. Does it get the right permissions? Now we set up a variety of practical subdirectories.

☞Later on we explain why certain administrative entries should always be in ACLs you create (see "Special Groups" later in this chapter). However, we ignore them for now to keep things simple.

Public Reading Area

Create a subdirectory JJones\Public with contents everybody can read, but only you can create and change. Create a file in Public and check its ACL. Do you need to change the ACL on your home directory, JJones?

❑ Log on as another user and try to read and write the file, for example using Notepad, and delete it.

❑ Log back on as JJones and check your solution. [55]

DropBox

Now you decide to make a DropBox directory into which anyone can copy files, but where no one can read or change them. Create JJones\DropBox and set up its ACL.

❑ Log on as another user and copy a file into this directory, then try to enter DropBox to look at this new copy.

❑ Now check your solution. Do you need to change the ACL on your home directory? [56]

You might have put CREATOR OWNER on DropBox, perhaps with "Full Control." Is this proper? [57]

Notice that everyone can now see the *names* of the files and directories in your home directory (even if they can't read the files). What precautions should you take? [58]

If you don't like the idea of everyone seeing the names in your home directory, have your administrator set up directories like DropBox outside your home directory. For example, set up a common DropBox directory with a subdirectory for each user who wants one.

Private Working Area

Since everybody can see at least the names of the files in your home directory, set up a private working directory called Work inside JJones for your personal use only. Set its ACL accordingly. [59]

Collaboration Directory

You start writing a long-range planning document sharing authorship with BBrown. It's to be reviewed by CClark. Set up a directory called LRPlan that gives BBrown the ability to read, write, create, and delete items, and CClark the ability only to read. Specifically, when either you or BBrown create files, the creator is to have "Full Control" and the other two users "Read" only.

Create a file in LRPlan. (Don't create this file by dragging and dropping a file from the same logical disk. As we see later, if you move the file, it may not get a new ACL.) Does this file have the following ACL?

BBrown (B. B. Brown)	Read (RX)
CClark (C. C. Clark)	Read (RX)
JJones (J. J. Jones)	Special Access (All)

ACL on File in JJones\LRPlan Created by JJones

Log on as BBrown and create a new file in LRPlan. Is this its ACL?

BBrown (B. B. Brown)	Special Access (All)
CClark (C. C. Clark)	Read (RX)
JJones (J. J. Jones)	Read (RX)

ACL on File in JJones\LRPlan Created by BBrown

Check the ACL you put on LRPlan against our answer. [60]

Directory for Project X

If you don't already have one, create a local group called ProjX with members JJones, BBrown, and CClark. (See "Creating Local Groups" later in this chapter.) Create a directory of the same name in your home directory for use by that project. (On NT Server, you need to be an administrator to create this group.) Your access policy is:

❖ All members of the project are to be able to read anything inside the directory and create their own items, but should not have anything other than "Read" access to items other members create.

❖ You appoint BBrown as group administrator who is to have complete control over everything in the tree.

❖ You decide that in an emergency you may need complete access to the tree, but only by first changing the permissions.

Set up the ACL on ProjX accordingly. We show the correct ACL later because we don't want to tip you off too soon. Log on as CClark and create a file F1 in ProjX. Is its ACL as follows?

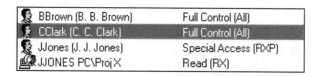

BBrown (B. B. Brown)	Full Control (All)
CClark (C. C. Clark)	Full Control (All)
JJones (J. J. Jones)	Special Access (RXP)
JJONES PC\ProjX	Read (RX)

ACL on JJones\ProjX\F1

❑ Log back on as JJones. Check your ACL for ProjX against our answer. [61]

❑ Create a subdirectory ProjX\Public where general project members have all permissions except "Take Ownership" and "Change." What's the proper ACL? [62]

❑ Create a directory ProjX\Manager under your own control. General project members can see what's there, but they can't change or add anything. Set its ACL and check it against our suggestion. [63]

❑ What ACL does NT place on a file in ProjX\Manager? Create one and check its ACL.

☞ It's almost universal to give CREATOR OWNER "Full Control." When you define who can create entries in a directory you need only give them "Add and Read," but use CREATOR OWNER to give them "Full Control" over items they create.

How would you set up a job-share situation where two coworkers have total access to each other's files, but from two different accounts? [64]

You have multiple accounts and need to set up your directory trees so that all your accounts have access by default. How might you do this? [65]

How could you set up a directory's ACL to let users create subdirectories yet limit their access to subdirectories they create? [66]

Summary

We started this section by saying default ACLs make your life easier, but we've covered a lot of detail. Is this really easier? When you reflect a bit, we think you'll agree it is. Look again at the window below to set the ACL on a directory.

☞ When you set the *Type of Access* for a particular entry, you select a single phrase, like "Read" or "Full Control," that you intend to apply not only to this directory, but to all the files and directories inside that directory and its entire subtree.

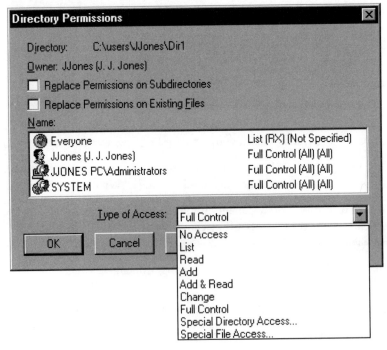

An Example ACL for Directories

Of course, if a tree rooted within some directory needs different protection, you set the ACL on that directory, in which case you're making the same blanket statement about its subtree.

This may help you appreciate the standard permission sets that apply to directories only. For example, "Add" lets you make the statement that you want someone to be able to add entries to a directory but not change its files. NT sets things up so this applies not only to this directory, but propagates through the entire tree by default.

To further appreciate the power of this scheme, think what you'd have to do if "Special Access" was all you had. It would be difficult to set all the right combinations while avoiding those that might confuse you and your coworkers.

Assorted ACL Topics

We finish our presentation of ACLs with several miscellaneous but nonetheless important topics.

In This Section We Describe

➡ Some special groups

➡ How to create local groups

➡ How to take ownership and how the Administrators group owns its items

➡ How ACLs on remote workstations include only entries visible on that workstation

➡ ACL "preservation" versus "reprotection," including the Backup program and NT directory replication

➡ How typical applications interact with ACLs

➡ Applying an ACL to a network share directory

➡ Properties and attributes

Special Groups

Windows NT has a few special, built-in groups. Some aren't really groups in the sense of being a specific list of accounts, but rather imply certain *kinds* of accounts.

Peruse the special groups: Open an ACL window and bring up the Add Users and Groups window. Use the **Members...** button to peruse the membership of the following groups as we discuss them.

Administrators and Domain Admins

Your most powerful administrators are members of the Administrators local group. Administrators are effectively all powerful and you can assume that administrators can do anything they want to your files and directories. For example, they can always take ownership of your files and directories, which lets them give themselves (or anyone else!) any permissions they like. Of course, this stamps the Administrators group as owner of the file, which even administrators can't then change.

Administrators may have a legitimate need to access your files and directories, and it's bothersome for both of you if they must take ownership to do so, since you have to take it back (assuming they've had the foresight to let you take it back when they changed the ACL). For this reason, it's common to give the local Administrators group "Full Access" to all your files and directories.

If you are concerned that this makes it too easy for administrators to change your files, you can give them less, but you should give them at least "List" permission to your directories. This lets them search through your trees to see what files are where. When they find something they need to fix, they may need to take ownership. This means you must take it back, but it also tells you they have changed something.

In any case, you and your administrators should agree on what you customarily give them. Do this before you start building your directory trees.

Everyone, Users, and Domain Users

There are three common groups you use frequently:

Everyone	implicitly includes all accounts	
Domain Users	*usually* holds all the accounts in the workstation's domain	
Users	a local group, *usually* holds all local accounts plus Domain Users	

All the accounts implicitly included in Everyone are nonetheless valid accounts, and people can't use them without being logged on by NT. Think of Everyone as "every user properly authenticated into an active, valid account."

Administrators can change the membership of Domain Users and Users. For example, they might include in Users the Domain Users groups from all the domains allowed on this workstation. In this case, Users is roughly equivalent to Everyone.

Ask your administrator who, by policy, they include in Users. Verify by viewing its members while adding the Users group to an ACL.

Guests

The Guests group cannot be deleted but its membership can be changed. Administrators determine how it's used and who's in it. Guests is intended for the occasional or miscellaneous users lumped together for access control. Don't put Guests in your ACL unless you understand how administrators determine its membership.

INTERACTIVE and NETWORK

 INTERACTIVE implicitly includes only the account that's currently logged on to your workstation (primary logon). Hence, it's the workstation's current user.

 NETWORK implicitly includes accounts accessing a workstation from the network (secondary logon). These two groups cannot be deleted from NT nor can their implied membership be changed.

Example: You want to prevent users at remote workstations from accessing a directory. Add the NETWORK group with "No Access" to its ACL. This is the way you'll typically use these groups.

Could you accomplish the same protection by allowing access only through the INTERACTIVE group? [67]

You want to give local users "Change," but remote users only "Read." Can you do this? [68]

SYSTEM

 Refers to the NT system itself, including its many services. It's generally safe to give "Full Control" to SYSTEM.

☞ It's standard practice to give SYSTEM "Full Control" on all your files and directories. Without this, some system services may not be able to do their job. *However*, you can alternatively restrict access to your personal files and relax it only when some service complains.

Power Users

Power Users have some administrative capabilities on their workstation. If one has created your account, you may want to give the same access you afford Administrators. Because a Power User created your account, if they really want to, they can give you a new password then log on as you and access all your files anyway. Of course you'd be tipped off by the different password, but they could access your files nonetheless.

Operators

Backup Operators are the ones who use the Backup program to back up and restore files throughout the workstation's drives. You don't need to give Backup Operators access permission to your files because their backups and restores override ACLs. You may see other Operator groups but won't likely use them.

Like all groups, these special groups are with respect to the workstation that holds the current ACL. For example, Domain Users in an ACL in a remote domain refers to that remote domain's users. Also, while all these appear in the ACL window's group lists, some (like INTERACTIVE) are not real groups and you may not see them in other places that list groups. Some final advice about all groups:

> People who use a particular group in their ACLs must have the same understanding of who are (and who are not) members as of those who maintain the group's membership. Don't use a group unless you clearly understand who's in it and, often more importantly, who might be added later, perhaps without your timely knowledge.

Creating Local Groups

User Manager

The administrative tool User Manager is a good way to explore groups. When you start it up, you see the list of users and groups visible from your current workstation.

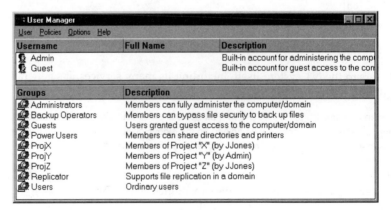

User Manager

While anyone can peruse this window, only administrators or the creator of a group can expand a group by double-clicking it.

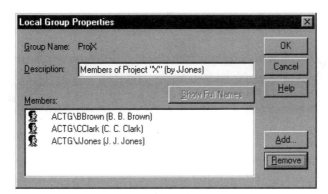

User Manager: User→ Properties..

Add members to a group using a window similar to the ACL window shown on the following page. Access the window as shown here.

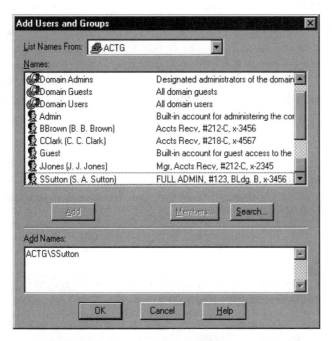

User Manager: User→ New Local Group...→ {Add...}

Deleting members is straightforward. Create local groups for the convenience of you and your close coworkers. (Only administrator's can create global groups.) When you strategically populate your ACLs with these groups, a change in membership grants (or precludes) access to those files automatically.

> When you grant a group access permission to your files and directories, you're implicitly letting the user who created the group pass that access on to others, since they can add accounts to the group.

Name and describe your groups clearly so there's no confusion as to their membership. "Group Z: A few misc people" is bad; "SAS Staff: Personal Staff to S. A. Sutton, President (SSutton)" is fine. Don't use the same name as any visible global group. It's even better to choose a name that's unique among global and local groups across your network, even though this is hard to ensure.

Example: A site institutes a policy that regular users prefix the group names they create with their initials and include their account name in parentheses in its description, as above.

You or your cohorts can create local groups of the same name and intent on each of several workstations. Keep their memberships in sync. If their use propagates widely, ask your administrator to make a global group to take their place. Although everyone must adjust their ACLs manually, both groups can coexist during the transition. (During transition, you can just make the local groups have the global group as their only member.)

☞Choose group names carefully. You can't rename them!

> **Building some local groups**: Create a few local groups and populate them with a variety of users and other groups. (Don't worry about creating too many. You can easily delete them.)
>
> ❑ Try to add one of your local groups as a member of another. What happens? [69]
>
> ❑ (OPT) As administrator, can you add to the special groups: Everyone, INTERACTIVE, and NETWORK? [70]
>
> **Residue from deleted groups**: Create a file or directory and add one of your new local groups to its ACL. Delete the group then examine the ACL. Is the group still there? [71]
>
> Create a new group with exactly the same name as the one you just deleted. No need to add any members. Check the ACL again. Has the group reappeared? [72]

A new, earnest Windows NT manager in an architectural company decides to start life on NT with a variety of groups for future use:

Engineers
Partners
Secretaries
BS, MS, PhD   Three groups for people with certain degrees.
Benefits   People on the benefits committee they chair.
A-K, L-Z   Two groups for people based on their last initial.
Men, Women
Others

Are these useful groups? [73] The moral:

☞ It's often better to create groups only as the need arises.

You want to restrict access tightly to certain printers because they're expensive. (Each NT printer has an ACL.) You decide that only managers should be able to submit jobs to these so you create a group called Managers and use it to control access to these printers. Is this a sound choice? [74]

Pick an institution (like an office, manufacturer, military installation, bank, university, or intergalactic space station) and define some useful global and local groups. (This makes a good team exercise.) [75]

If you want to explore groups further, read the "User Groups" section in Chapter 7, Managing Groups and Accounts.

Taking Ownership

An account that has the "Take Ownership" (O) permission for a file or directory can make itself the owner. Use the **Take Ownership** button from the Security property sheet:

Icon Menu: Properties→ Security→ {Ownership}

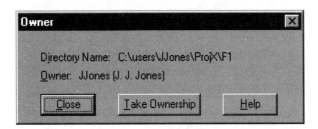

Your account becomes the owner of the item. While you don't get any special permissions to access the file or directory itself, as owner you can change the ACL to give yourself any permissions you like. No one, not even administrators, can change the owner of an item to an account other than their own (at least using standard NT utilities). Once you take ownership, you can't give it back.

One of the NT Rights gives an account the ability to take ownership of any file or directory. Full administrators usually have this Right and can take ownership of your items. However, having taken ownership, even full administrators can't make anyone else the owner (at least using standard NT utilities).

When users from the Administrators group take ownership, this group becomes the owner. This is the only case when the owner of an item is a group. Effectively, each file and directory created by a full administrator is equally accessible and owned by all administrators.

Taking ownership: Do an exercise from two different accounts. Experiment with the O permission so that each account can take ownership from the other, back and forth.

(OPT) **Administrative ownership**: Log on as a full administrator. Create a file or directory and observe its owner. Take ownership of a preexisting file or directory and again observe its owner.

Visibility: ACLs in Remote Directories

Which accounts and groups can you include in an ACL that's on another workstation, usually when you connect to one of its network share directories? Although we've broached this before, the basic rule is a simple one:

☞ An ACL can include any account or groups visible from (allowed on) *its own workstation:*

❖ local accounts and local groups

❖ domain accounts and global groups from the workstation's domain

❖ domain accounts and global groups from other visible domains, *regardless* of the workstation at which you are physically working

For example, if you log on to a workstation **Y** and connect to a network share directory on **Z**, the entries you can add to **Z**'s ACLs are those visible from **Z**—not workstation **Y** or your account's domain. But you don't really need to remember these rules because Windows NT shows you only allowed accounts and groups in its lists. As a rule of thumb, NT omits the domain prefix when it's the same as your account's domain, but shows it otherwise. Consider the following two windows. Both are from ACTG\JJones's ACL windows on JJONES PC and could occur during the same logon session. The first shows what you can add to an ACL on a local file, as shown in the figure on the following page.

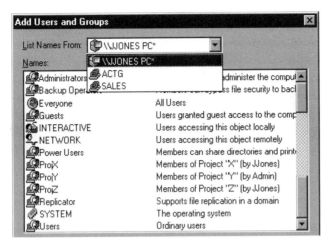

ACL Groups for Local File on JJONES PC

You can choose local accounts and groups from JJONES PC (shown in this window) or domain accounts and global groups from ACTG and SALES. However, you can't add local groups or accounts from the ACTG or SALES domains because they can't be used on JJONES PC. NT doesn't even show these when you select ACTG or SALES.

The second figure shows what you can add to an ACL on a remote file on the local domain server, ACTG-SERV. First note that listing names from JJONES PC is not even an option here, since its local items are not allowed on ACTG-SERV. We've selected the items from the ACTG domain, which include all the groups and accounts defined on ACTG-SERV, even local ones.

These two windows show no group or account in common. While you see, for example, the name "Users" in each window, each is a different, local group: one on JJONES PC and the other on ACTG-SERV. (The tip-off: Each has a different description in this example.)

Perhaps the biggest potential confusion is that yours and another workstation may each have a local group of the same name but with a different intent, or with a poorly coordinated membership. This is complicated by the fact that regular users can create their own groups.

Example: Two local groups named Bob's Group are created on different workstations with names that are the same by coincidence. They represent unrelated sets of users, friends of two different Bob's. When working with files from both workstations, you might easily get the two confused, giving one access to files intended only for the other.

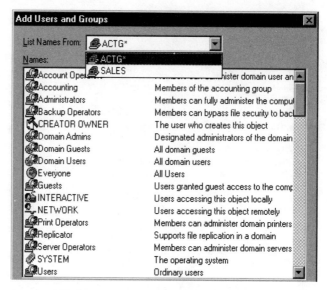

ACL Groups for File on Server ACTG-SERV

Example: Two groups of the same name are created on different workstations but for the same purpose. However, while the membership list on one is kept up to date, the other becomes badly outdated. Poor practice!

There can be similar name conflicts between a global and a local group, but since you see them both listed, you're more likely to notice ambiguities, and only administrators can create global groups. It's still bad practice to have a global and a local group of the same name. As we see later, similar cautions apply to local accounts, but they are more sparsely used and, because they're guarded by passwords, are less of a potential problem.

The perspective within a domain: Select a file on your local workstation and a second for another workstation in the same domain. While adding an ACL to a file from each, compare the lists of users and groups for differences. Check the membership of common local groups like Administrators and Power Users.

(OPT) **Two groups—same name**: To further illustrate, create two local groups of the same name but with different descriptions on two workstations. Again, add an ACL to each and note that these really are two separate groups.

Working across domains poses no special problems. Mainly, you might see some domains in which you don't normally work. Because the names you can use in an ACL are the ones visible from the ACL's workstation, if that workstation is in a different domain it may see yet other domains that you don't see from your usual domain.

> You connect to a workstation in some other domain using your domain account. Can you always add names from your account's domain to its ACLs? [76]

> **Perspective across domains**: Open one ACL window for your local workstation and a second in another domain. While adding an ACL to a file from each, compare the lists of users and groups for differences.

Connecting to Share Directories under Another Account

Windows NT offers you a special service where you can connect to a network share directory under an account of a different name than your own, providing you know the password. The purpose is to let you access a workstation that does not allow your current account, but where you have another account with a different name. To connect to a network drive, select the *Map...* option from My Computer's icon window:

Icon Menu: Map Network Drive...

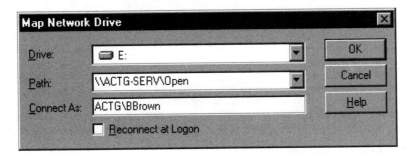

The *Connect As* field lets you connect to a remote resource under a different account. You can use a simple account name on the remote workstation, like BBrown, or a domain account visible from the remote workstation, like ACTG\BBrown. (If you enter an unprefixed name like BBrown, NT matches to any remote account it can find with the same name. Sometimes you may have to prefix a local account name with its workstation name.)

If your current password (the password for the account under which you're currently logged on) is different than that of the account you request, you are asked for the new account's password:

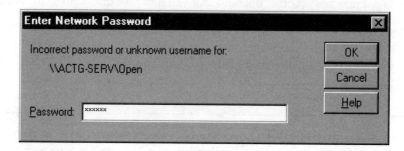

As you should expect by now, the capabilities of the new account you name govern your access to items in this share directory.

Connecting under another account: As a first option, log on to one account, say ACTG\JJones, and connect to a share directory on your domain server under a second account, say BBrown. If this fails, as a second option log on to your usual account (JJones) and connect to a directory on your own workstation as a different user, like ACTG\BBrown. It's most interesting if your "connect as" account has a different password. Create a file or directory under the share directory and examine its owner.

Copying and Moving

If you place a carefully crafted ACL on a file then copy it to another location, does the copy have the same ACL as the original? It depends on the program. Because it's the program's responsibility to do so, only programs that support Windows NT's ACLs might do so. We call this **preserving** the ACL. The alternative to preserving the ACL is that the copied item gets the ACL given to new items created in the destination directory. We call this **reprotecting** the item.

For example, many programs both copy and move files and directories, including their trees. "Copy" creates a new copy, leaving the original unchanged; while "move" deletes the original. Items you move or copy are reprotected with one small exception: when you move an item within the same logical disk; for example, from one place on drive D to another.

☞ Generally, when you copy an item it gets reprotected, getting the default ACL in the destination directory. Think of this analogy: When you move your valuables from one safe to another, they become protected by the new safe's combination.

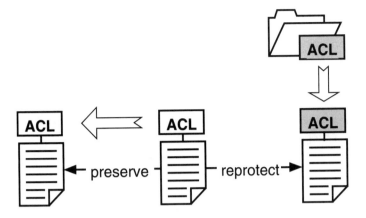

Your directories protect their newly added items with the default scheme you build into their ACLs. When you put something into a directory, even when it's moved from somewhere else, you should expect the protection of the new directory to apply, whether more restrictive or less. Consider the case when you copy a file into a network share directory that has a stronger ACL than the file. NT reprotects and applies the new, stronger ACL to the file. It may well be that the file needs stronger protection because it's now exposed to the network, whereas before it was not. Preserving the ACL is not in the interests of security in this case.

Of course, you could counter that moving it to a less strongly protected directory weakens it. You could also point out that you might *expect* the ACL to be copied. But when you create a new file in a directory, you expect it to get the default ACL. Isn't making a new copy in a directory creating a new file? It's hard to say whether reprotection or preservation is more secure. Just be aware of this issue.

Preserving the ACL may not be possible in a network environment. We've seen that different workstations can allow different accounts and groups. The entry names in an ACL on one workstation may not exist on another and vice versa. How could a program possibly preserve the ACL faithfully when it moves a file from one to the other?

When you start using a new program that copies or moves items, check which strategy it uses.

Reprotection: Create two directories IN and NE in your home directory. Give IN's ACL an entry for INTERACTIVE with "Read" and yourself with "Full Control." Give NE's an entry for NETWORK with "Read" and yourself with "Full Control." This makes it easy to distinguish the two ACLs.

❏ Create a file in one then copy it to the second. For example, hold down the Ctrl key while dragging the file to the second directory. Is the ACL preserved or reprotected? [77]

❏ Do the same exercise but *move* the file. Is it preserved or reprotected? [78]

❏ Create a small directory tree in one of these directories and copy the whole tree to the other. Is the whole tree reprotected? [79]

❏ Now copy a file to another logical disk. Is it preserved or reprotected? [80]

(OPT) Explore your applications: Using one of your favorite applications, create a document and give its file an ACL different than its directory's default. Now edit the document, make some changes, and *Save as...* to a different name in the same directory. Is it preserved or reprotected? Try a few other applications.

(OPT) Traditional MS-DOS commands: Test MS-DOS commands like "COPY," "XCOPY," and "MOVE." Preserve or reprotect? [81]

ACLs and Shortcuts

You can create a shortcut to almost any file or directory you can see, even if you don't have access to it. Shortcuts have their own ACL. In order to access a shortcut's target, you need "Read" access to the shortcut itself in addition to whatever access permissions the target's ACL requires. In other words, making a shortcut does not circumvent the target's ACL. Because of this, there are few reasons for restricting "Read" access to a shortcut.

Shortcuts: Use Notepad to create two files "No.txt" and "Read.txt." Preclude all access from the first and allow only "Read" to the second.

❏ Create shortcuts for both and confirm that the original ACLs still govern access.

❏ Preclude access to the shortcut to Read.txt. Now try to open the file.

Think of a shortcut as a special file that just holds the path name of its target. The system only needs to read the shortcut file itself, then proceeds to open the target as it would if you had named the target directly.

Backups and Replication

Windows NT has a standard backup and restore program called Backup. Members of the Backup Operators group can use this program to back up and restore any files on the system regardless of their ACLs. The Backup program overrides the ACL protections for these users when backing up and restoring. Other users can use Backup, but only under the control of the ACLs. They can't back up files they can't normally read, or restore files to directories where they can't write. The Backup program saves ACLs when it creates a backup tape. Upon restore, it either preserves the original ACLs or reprotects the files, at your option.

Backup

Select *Restore File Permissions* (see figure on next page) to preserve, or leave it blank to reprotect. If you make a tape on one computer and restore it on another, some of the groups or accounts in the ACLs on the tape may not be allowed on the destination. If so, these entries may be omitted from the restored ACLs.

☞ In this case, you may wish to forego the *Restore File Permissions* option and reprotect instead.

Backup: Operations→ Restore…

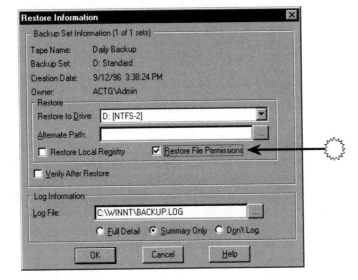

You can back up and restore remote share directories (that is, back up and restore on the same computer, but deal with a remote share directory), and in this case the ACL entries are fully restored.

The Backup program has another important security option. If you check *Restrict Access...* on the Backup Options window, then your account name is saved on the backup tape:

Backup: Operations→ Backup...

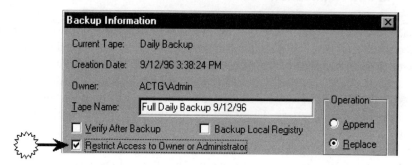

Choose *Restrict Access...* to limit to yourself or an administrator those who can restore from the backup. The Backup program restores such tapes only when run from your account or members of the Administrators or Backup Operators groups. This prevents other users from reading your backup tapes using the Backup program. It does not, however, prevent them from attempting to peruse your tapes using other programs.

> **Exploring the Backup program**: Demonstrate these features by using Backup for some simple backup and restore operations.

NT lets an administrator designate certain directories on NT Server to be automatically replicated to certain other workstations, either NT Server or Workstation. They are said to be exported from the controller and imported onto the other workstations. Every few minutes the replicator service automatically synchronizes the destination and updates the import-side files and directories as necessary. NT preserves the ACLs (including the owner) on replicated directory trees.

Applications and ACLs

Most of the programs you acquire for Windows NT probably don't know about ACLs, at least for the short term. Their designers did not make a specific provision for dealing with ACLs. Windows NT accommodates these programs nonetheless, mainly because default ACLs ensure that the files these program create get a proper ACL, at least to the extent you set up your directory trees correctly. However, there are a few situations around which you need to work. We don't mention specific commercial programs, but use hypothetical ones instead.

Temporary Files

Many programs create temporary files for their own internal use. You seldom see these because the program deletes them before it exits. Mostly you see them when the program meets an unexpected demise and leaves cryptically named files lying about. Two situations arise when a directory's ACL prevents the program from creating a temporary file:

> **Example**: A spreadsheet program ABC always creates a temporary file in the same directory as the file it opens. If you're in a directory where you can't create new files, the program fails when you try to open the file because it can't create the temporary file.

> **Example**: A word processor XYZ does something similar, but only creates the temporary file when you instruct it to update the file (often "save") the file on which you're working. While you may still have the temporary file problem like ABC, it's not so bad because you can usually create files in a directory, which has files you can change.

Temporary files can pose a security problem. Programs often keep an image of your work in a temporary file, for example to help you recover changed work. If the temporary file is not adequately protected, people may be able to read it and see something you don't intend them to see. They may even be able to change the temporary file which could indirectly change the document on which you're working! There are two common cases, both with good workarounds:

❖ Suppose the program creates the temporary file in the same directory as the file on which you're working. Since the actual and the temporary files are in the same directory, they're created with the same ACL. As long as you don't manually make the original file's ACL more restrictive, the temporary file is adequately protected.

❖ Suppose the program creates the temporary file in a common directory on the system, perhaps used only by this application. There's a surefire fix in the following question:

What ACL would you give a directory used exclusively for temporary files? (This is tricky!) **[82]**

If you were the designer of a new program, how would you avoid problems with temporary files? **[83]**

Programs That Change the Unexpected

Suppose you use a text editor named "XYEDIT" and when you direct it to save a file to which you knew you had "Write" permission, it gave you a "Can't write" error. What you may never have noticed is that when XYEDIT writes ("saves") a file, it also changes the name of the file in the parent directory, changing it to upper case. It may be in a directory where it can write the file but not its name, which is protected within the parent directory.

File Shifting

A graphics program "GRAPH" works such that when you use it to modify a file, it creates a whole new file. Internally, it creates a new file with a temporary name, writes it, deletes the original file, then renames the new file giving it the original name. You would not likely notice this level of detail. However, as we now know, the new file may have a different ACL than the original and it could be less restrictive. This poses a potential security problem. Of course, we hope the company that develops GRAPH makes it smart about NT ACLs so that the program can ensure that the ACL on the new file is the same as the old.

☞ This is yet another argument for sticking with the ACL a file gets by default when first created. Or, at least don't make its ACL more restrictive.

In summary, what you need to do to protect yourself depends on the programs you use, but it's often impractical to find out which problems may crop up. Windows NT helps you avoid these problems by encouraging the ACL practices we've talked about in this chapter:

✓ Plan your directory trees so that each directory keeps out users who have no business there.

✓ When possible, use the standard permission sets (in *Type of Access*) instead of custom sets.

✓ Set up file default permissions so that the files' original default ACLs need rarely be changed.

✓ Seek applications that are savvy about NT's ACLs.

ACLs for Network Share Directories

When someone shares a directory to the network, NT attaches an ACL to the shared directory's tree as a whole. We call this the **share ACL**. (Only Power Users and administrators can share a directory.) When accessed from the network, NT enforces the share ACL independent of and in addition to the ACLs on its individual files or directories. One must pass both the share ACL as well as the individual items' ACLs. Another way of looking at this is that the share ACL imposes absolute restrictions on the whole shared directory tree no matter how it grows through time. You initially set a share ACL when you make its directory tree available on the network from the Sharing page on its property sheet:

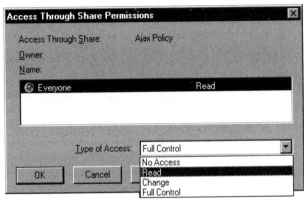

Icon Menu: Properties→ Sharing → {Permissions...}

You can change the share ACL on an existing share with this same window. The share ACL has the same form and function as the file ACLs and you manage it similarly. You select one of the following four permission set names:

Full Control Places no restrictions on access

Change Like "Full Control" but prohibits changing the item's ACL and taking ownership

Read Like "Change" but prohibits operations that modify files or directories, including their attributes

No Access Prohibits all access

In our example we've made sure no remote user can modify any aspect of the shared directory tree. You can also limit the number of simultaneous users, but this is more a performance than a security control. Notice our emphasis on what the ACL *prohibits* rather than what it allows. This is the nature and philosophy of share ACLs, since what they appear to allow can be prohibited by the per-item ACL. There's no way to view the share ACL of directories you access across the network, and only Power Users and administrators can view the ACL on locally shared directories.

As a fine point, the directory at the root of a shared tree has its own personal ACL just like all other directories. The share ACL is separate and limits the root directory's ACL and its entire tree. Network share directories on logical disks formatted with other than NTFS have a share ACL that is their only ACL protection.

☞The share ACL affects access only through the network file-sharing mechanism. It does not restrict your access to your workstation's own local files or directories, even when they are within a local, shared directory tree.

> **Testing a share ACL**: You need to be in the Power User, Server Operators, or Administrators local group to do this exercise. Let's assume your account is a Power User.
>
> ❏ From its property sheet, share your home directory to the network giving Everyone "Read" permission.
>
> ❏ Open this directory through Network Neighborhood. Because this new window uses the network share mechanism, just as if the share directory were on another workstation, the share ACL governs access to your home directory through this window.
>
> ❏ Create a file in your home directory in your original window and make sure you have full access to it. Now try to delete the file from the second window. Does the share ACL prevent this? [84] (Just to check, delete the file from the original window.)

You may be tempted to set the share ACL to "Full Control" and let the individual ACLs alone control access. However, it's more secure to keep the share ACL as restrictive as possible. People who create items in the tree can open them to anyone, but a share ACL can prevent them from giving access permissions that the share ACL precludes.

☞ From your perspective as a regular user, share ACLs mean that when you access a file or directory on another workstation you may not get some of the permissions its ACL seems to grant you.

> In the figure on page 105, we've made sure that people remotely accessing the directory tree cannot modify its items or their attributes, but we've not given the Administrators or SYSTEM groups "Full Control," as is customary. Have we made a mistake? [85]
>
> You create a network share with all permissions for Everyone. Someone says that no matter what they do they just can't access or perhaps ever find your share. What's the likely problem? [86]
>
> (**OPT**) A workstation advertises a network share directory that's inside a second directory tree it advertises. When someone accesses a file in the inner directory, which share ACLs apply? [87]

> (**OPT**) You want to prevent BBrown from changing anything when remotely accessing one of your share directories. Rather than putting BBrown in the share ACL with "Read" access, you instead put BBrown with "Read" in the ACL of the directory on which the share is based. Your theory is that since BBrown must pass through this directory to get to the rest of the tree, you've prevented BBrown from changing items in the whole tree. Is your reasoning correct? [88]

Properties and Attributes

Files and directories have attributes other than the ones we've discussed, for example the ones you see on the General window of the property sheet.

Icon Menu: Properties→ General

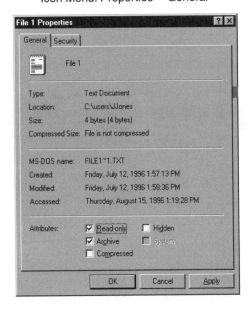

As a rule of thumb, you can query an item's properties if you can see its name, but change its properties only if you can write it. You may be accustomed to using the Read-Only property. It can prevent accidental erasures, but is not a strong security feature.

> If security is your concern, use the ACL to keep an item from being changed or deleted—not Read Only.

> **Exploring properties**: Set a file so that Everyone has "No Access." Look at its properties. Try to change them.
>
> **Testing the Read-Only property**: Give a file an ACL that allows "Full Control" but set its "Read-Only" property. Try to delete the file from another account. What happens? [89]

Diskettes, FAT, and HPFS

On Windows NT each of your logical disks (A:, C:, D:, and so forth), including those shared from other workstations, has one of three formats: FAT, the long-time MS-DOS standard; HPFS, introduced in OS/2; and the native NT format called NTFS, which is endemic to Windows NT. Only NTFS has an ACL on each file and directory. The other two have no ACLs at all, although share ACLs apply to all formats. Obviously, security-sensitive sites minimize the use of FAT and HPFS. However, diskette ("floppy") drives, like A:, can be only FAT. Items copied from a diskette to an NTFS drive gain ACLs under NT's default mechanism, but this is a "safe" operation. Other media, like optical media, may or may not support the NTFS format.

Beware: Items you create on diskettes and FAT logical drives have no ACL. When in doubt about whether a logical drive has ACLs, try to view an ACL from an item on the drive. You won't be able to!

Summary

Groups

❖ A group is a named list of user accounts. Although local groups can include global groups, they ultimately expand to a list of user accounts. Use groups in ACLs to grant permissions to a group as a whole. Users later added to the group automatically gain the access previously given to the group.

❖ Administrators create global groups, which are allowed throughout a domain and all domains that trust it. Regular users can create local groups, although they can be used only on the workstation on which they were created.

Basic ACLs

❖ The ACL is the main protection mechanism on Windows NT. It can be applied to files and directories, printers, network share directory trees, and several other objects.

❖ Each ACL is a list of entries sometimes called access control entries, or ACEs. Each entry names a user or group and specifies its permissions. The groups and accounts that you can add to an ACL are those visible from (allowed onto) the workstation that holds the ACL. Hence, remote ACLs may present you with a different list than local ones.

❖ Each ACL has an owning account that can arbitrarily change the ACL. When you create an item, you become its owner and can therefore set its ACL to anything you like. Any account with "Take Ownership" permission to an item can commandeer it, becoming its new owner with all the accompanying capabilities.

❖ Basic access permissions are "Read," "Write," "Execute," "Delete," "Change Permissions," and "Take Ownership." However, the ACL window gives you named combinations called "standard permission sets" (or "Access Types") that are easier to use. These names differ a bit between the various items ACLs protect (files, directories, printers, and so forth). NT encourages you to use these standard sets instead of custom combinations of the Basic Permissions whenever practical.

❖ The ACL on a directory: (1) determines the ACL placed on files created in that directory, which we call the file default ACL, and (2) propagates unchanged to newly created subdirectories, except for the effects of CREATOR OWNER. In this manner, the ACL you place on a directory propagates to both files and directories throughout the entire directory tree rooted in that directory, unless of course you change the ACLs of specific items.

❖ You can also give special permissions to whoever creates such an item using the CREATOR OWNER entry in the directory ACL.

Special ACL Topics

❖ NT defines a number of special groups that you might frequently use, like Everyone and Users. It also has a special administrative group named Administrators that you can use to give administrators emergency access to your files. You can use the special groups INTERACTIVE and NETWORK to control access based on whether the user is primarily logged on to the workstation or is accessing it remotely.

❖ It's common to give SYSTEM and the local group Administrators "Full Control" to all your files and directories, but check with your administrator.

❖ Shortcuts are a separate file with their own ACL. To access the target file or directory, you need "Read" access to the shortcut file itself as well as access permissions through the target's ACL.

❖ You can connect to a network share directory under an account different than your current one, providing you know the password. Your access to its contents is through this new account.

❖ Some NT interfaces and applications *reprotect* an item that's copied by giving it the default ACL in the destination directory. This is as opposed to keeping the ACL unchanged, or *preserving* it, which is not feasible in network cases. The Backup program and NT Directory Replication are examples of programs that preserve the ACL.

❖ Many applications are not specifically designed to handle NT's ACLs. Although their use is not necessarily unsecure, you need to watch out for a few things, like the application's use of temporary files, programs that change items you don't expect, and applications that create a whole new file with an ACL that may be different from the original when you "save." Your best protection is to set up directory trees that use only default ACLs.

❖ You can apply an ACL to a network share directory that protects the entire shared tree in addition to the ACLs on each item in the tree. This is the only ACL protection for disk formats other than NT's native disk format, NTFS, since they have no per-item ACL. Keep the share ACL as restrictive as possible.

❖ Traditional MS-DOS file and directory properties, like the Read-Only property, are not strong security protections like the ACL.

Quick Check:

✓ Which are the more flexible and why: local or global groups? [90]

✓ Could a global group be allowed outside its domain on a workstation that does not allow one of the group's member accounts? [91]

✓ You're a member of two groups. One has "Full Control" in an ACL and the other has "No Access." Which permissions does this ACL grant? [92]

✓ A coworker calls global groups "domain groups" instead. Is their term a poor one? [93]

✓ There are two local groups of the same name but on different workstations in your domain. Are they the same group? Do you ever see them in the same ACL? [94]

✓ No one has "Delete" (**D**) access to a file. Can the file be deleted (without changing the ACL)? [95]

✓ What's the difference between the built-in groups Domain Users, Users, and Everyone? [96]

✓ What is your most likely use of CREATOR OWNER? [97]

✓ You connect to a network share directory of another workstation you've never accessed before. While adding entries to its ACLs you see domains of which you've never heard. Is this okay? What's the situation here? [98]

✓ You carefully craft many ACLs in a directory tree, then move the whole tree to another location. What happens to your ACLs? [99]

Chapter 5

Special Situations

Local Accounts and Matching

This section describes local accounts that are used relatively rarely in full domain environments. It also presents a related topic: how NT "matches" the account you present to a remote workstation when your account is not allowed there. Despite the length of this section, these topics are quite transparent and require little attention on your part.

In This Section We Describe

➡ How NT matches your current account to a remote account when you access a workstation outside your normal domain environment

➡ What happens when the two passwords differ

➡ Matching to the default Guest account

As we've mentioned before, there are two kinds of accounts on Windows NT: **domain accounts** and **local accounts**. A domain account is allowed on workstations throughout the domain in which it's defined, and possibly others. Domain controllers keep a single copy of each domain account. By contrast, a local account is kept on an individual workstation (whether by a domain controller or not) and can be used only on that workstation. Although a domain account has a few more security controls, they hold essentially the same information and NT uses them for the same basic purpose.

We've talked primarily about domain accounts because in a pure NT domain environment you seldom use local accounts. Our suggestion is to forget about local accounts and skip this section unless you are put into one of the situations that use them.

Using a Remote Local Account

Suppose you need to log on to, or more likely, need remote services from a workstation named "BETA" in another domain that does not allow your current account. (Technically, that other domain does not "trust" your domain.) The typical solution is for an administrator to give you a local account on BETA that has the same name as your regular domain account. When you request a service from BETA, because it doesn't allow your current account, it "matches" your account's name and password against its local accounts. BETA says, in effect, "Although your account is not allowed on this workstation, I'll give you services under one of my local accounts if I can find one with the same name and password." It matches your original account name with an account of its own.

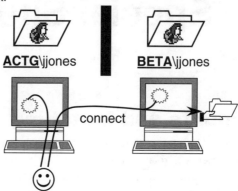

This matching is mostly invisible to you. Since your remote actions on BETA are under the same user name (for example, JJones), at a higher level it may appear as if you're working under the same account on both workstations. From a day-to-day perspective you don't see anything particularly unique about this situation.

Only one JJones account is visible on each of the two workstations. When you place your local account name in an ACL on BETA, it's not your domain account. Although they are technically different accounts, they represent the same person—you. For example, suppose you log on to your customary workstation in ACTG as ACTG\JJones and connect to BETA. The following figure illustrates the ACL from two different files: the top on BETA and the bottom on your current workstation, JJONES PC.

A Remote ACL

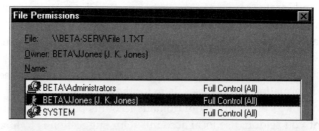

A Local ACL

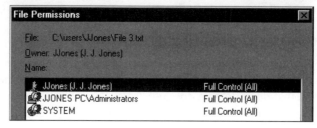

ACLs Using Local and Remote Matching Accounts

On BETA the local account under which you're working is spelled out as BETA\JJones, while on your local workstation it's your usual domain account ACTG\JJones. (NT omits the prefix.) If you look closely, you see that the administrator on BETA has your wrong middle initial. Proof that these are two different accounts!

These are different accounts and must be maintained separately. For example, they can have different account parameters, like password expiration times. Mostly, this means you must update your password on each local account. However, as we saw earlier you can do this from a single workstation.

The password differences get to the heart of the disadvantage of local accounts: you need a separate account on every workstation from which you need services. The resulting proliferation of accounts becomes an administrative headache that may also inconvenience you. Twenty users at twenty personal workstations with universal access means four hundred separate accounts across the network that somebody must maintain. Situations like this are also ripe for security problems.

Two matched accounts of the same name may have different passwords. If so, browsing windows ask you for the password of the account visible on the remote host:

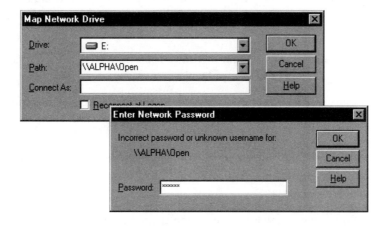

They also ask this when the name doesn't even match. However, other scenarios don't ask—they just deny your request.

Having different passwords in your various local accounts can be a useful security feature, but is a lot to remember. And then there's the Trusted Path issue:

Matching a remote, local account: You need a local account on another workstation that does not allow your domain account. It can be either a domain controller in a domain named BETA that does not trust yours or an NT Workstation named "BETA." Set up a local account with your name (JJones) but a different password and account description. *(continues)*

❑ Log onto your normal account ACTG\JJones. Then, from the Network Neighborhood expand a shared directory on BETA. Because your passwords are different, you have to enter your account and password on BETA.

❑ Open an ACL on each workstation and seek your user name, for example in the Add Users and Groups window. Note that there's different descriptive text for each (at least, if the accounts have been set up with this subtle difference). This is evidence that they are really separate accounts. Note also that your remote account is likely prefixed with the remote domain name.

❑ Create a local and remote directory and examine their owner. In both cases you see "JJones," which at a higher level you can consider to be the same user—you!

Local accounts on domain controllers are sometimes prefixed by the domain name. Local accounts on nondomain controllers are often prefixed by workstation name. Except for keeping the passwords and other account parameters in sync, they really do look like the same account in day-to-day use.

Can the remote, local account name become visible on your local workstation by virtue of being included in a group? **[100]**

Can you think of a situation when you might be able to gain the capabilities of someone else's local account that happens to have the same name as yours? **[101]**

Consider the situation in the windows presented earlier where BETA\Users and JJONES PC\Users appear in their respective ACLs. Do you expect these to have the same membership? **[102]**

Entering the remote password is not via the Trusted Path. Is this safe? **[103]**

Other Local Account Scenarios

There are a few other cases where you might encounter local accounts.

Peer NT Networks

An administrator can configure NT Workstations to participate in a **workgroup** instead of a domain. Domain accounts (and global groups) cannot be used on these workstations. (They're not even visible). This means you need a local account on the workstation to log on to it and to request its services from elsewhere on the network. In this situation primary logon to a local account is similar to a domain account, except you can specify no domain in the logon window. As long as your work remains local to the workstation (you don't use any network services), your logon session is identical to a domain logon.

You may even have networks where all NT Workstations are in workgroups. These "peer NT" networks can still provide rich client-server environments. In many respects day-to-day life is similar to the domain environment, but peer NT networks don't have the power and scale of a domain-based network. Each workstation maintains its own local account for each account it allows, so if you regularly access a dozen workstations, there's a dozen accounts for you strewn around the network. If peer networks are large, keeping a given user's accounts synchronized across the network can become intractable.

The Remote Access Server (discussed later) is often used under a workgroup scenario.

Accessing a Remote Domain Account

There's a rare variation on the remote local account. If you're logged on to a local account on an NT Workstation not participating in domains, a domain controller grants your secondary logon if it can match any of its accounts against your local account name.

Matching to the Guest Account

Whenever NT matches a secondary logon against its local accounts, if it can't find an account of the same name and the Guest account is active and has a blank password, it matches to the Guest account. It, of course, performs its services locally under its Guest account. For example, NT makes Guest the owner of all objects you create, and everyone else that uses Guest! If Guest has a password that's not blank, NT considers this a match of the account name but not the password, and may prompt you for the Guest password.

Summary

A quick synopsis of matching and local accounts:

❖ If you encounter local accounts at all, it's usually when you request a service from a workstation that does not allow your domain account or is not participating in NT domains.

❖ In this case the remote workstation tries to "match" your local account name and password to one of its own accounts. If it finds an account that has the same name but a different password, sometimes NT asks you for the password of the server's account. Other times it denies the request.

❖ When a proper match occurs, your actions on the remote workstation are under that remote matching account. For example, it's that account that goes into ACLs on the remote files and directories. However, it's the same account *name* you're using on the client, so there's little opportunity for confusion. The key here is that you don't see your original and the matched account in the same ACL because the two accounts are never visible simultaneously from either workstation.

❖ If the server cannot match your account name, it may log you on as the Guest user, depending on how the server's administrator has set up its Guest account.

❖ If you use local accounts, typically through one of these scenarios, you may need to maintain their passwords separately. Whether or not they should be the same is a trade-off between security and convenience. Check with your administrator.

❖ Among a community of NT Workstations not participating in domains, all remote services are done via this account matching.

This leads us to the summary statement that any NT Workstation can service any other NT Workstation on the network either through domain participation, which is preferred, or by setting up a local account on the server. One thing is constant: a Windows NT Workstation never provides services unless it can determine a suitable account with a password match, even if it's the generic Guest account which can be set up to match any request.

After this discussion you may be a little confused, but on a properly administered network it's not as bad as it may seem. Administrators should prevent the situation where you can see both your domain account and a local account of the same name together, for example in the same ACL. Instead, they should arrange that you always see just one or the other. Since they both have the same name and they both refer to you, on a working basis, you can ignore the technicality that they're separate accounts, although they have separate passwords and you may want to keep them the same unless security warrants otherwise.

Using the Remote Access Service

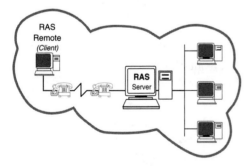

Windows NT's optional RAS lets you work from an NT computer remote from a LAN by dialing into a RAS server on the LAN. There are several kinds of connections you can use including regular modem-to-modem dial-in or connecting across the Internet using Point-to-Point Tunneling Protocol (PPTP). Once you do this, your computer is effectively a part of the RAS server's LAN. You can browse the LAN and connect to its hosts' shared resources, security permitting. (One minor caveat is that the RAS server administrator may prevent you from accessing the LAN, leaving you with access only to the RAS server's resources.) In this section we cover the pertinent RAS security topics. You can check any of your system documentation for general advice on using RAS.

Dial-Up
Networking

The Dial-up Networking icon on your desktop lets you not only initiate and close a RAS connection but also configure RAS phone books. There are a few important security parameters for each phone book entry, as shown in the figure below. When you are connecting to a Windows NT RAS server use *Microsoft encrypted authentication* for maximum security. That, and its companion, *Accept only encrypted authentication*, ensure your passwords are never passed across the connection to the RAS server unencrypted where they could potentially be stolen. (A securely configured Windows NT RAS server usually requires Microsoft encrypted authentication even if you don't require it from the client side.)

Dial-up Networking: {More}→ Edit entry...→ Security

When using Microsoft encrypted authentication, choose *Require data encryption* to ensure that your RAS client only connects in a mode where its data traffic to the RAS server is encrypted. This prevents malicious people from eavesdropping on your traffic and, to a large extent, prevents them from maliciously changing it. (The current "40-bit key" encryption is of moderate strength, but can be broken by someone with a little time and money. See "Cipher Keys and their Distribution" in Chapter 9, The Internet and Intranets, for a little background on this topic, although you don't need to understand it to use RAS.) The RAS server may require this of your client anyway, but by setting this parameter you force this mode when you deem such protection prudent, for example when you are connecting via the Internet where eavesdropping and interception are relatively easy.

RAS often connects during your session if you attempt something that requires remote services and it is not already connected. You can select *Use current username and password*, which directs your RAS client to use the user name and password presented at logon for RAS connection during your session. This option not only makes it easier for most of your RAS connection scenarios, but keeps you from typing your password during your session, which is not through the Trusted Path. You may also be asked by certain scenarios to save your password, as in the figure on the next page.

119

If you so select, then later automatic reestablishment of the RAS connection uses this name and password. This is also a good idea, although the former technique is generally more useful when you always use RAS under your logon identity. You can direct RAS to forget this password from the Security page using the **Unsave password** button.

Your local workstation can be configured to be a member of one of the LAN's domains or not, and your interactions are a little different for these two cases.

Stand-alone Workstation

If your workstation is not a member of a domain, then you must log on using one of its local accounts. (The logon window does not even present you with any domain options.) This scenario is just like the peer NT networks we discussed earlier in "Other Local Account Scenarios." When you connect to a RAS server, or after having connected to the LAN you request any of its resources (like network share directories), your local account and password are matched against the accounts visible on the server that's servicing your request. Many scenarios preset your local logon name and password by default, and in many cases you can specify alternates. For example, RAS lets you specify an alternate and you can connect to network share directories under a "connect as" account.

Your administrator typically provides you with accounts of the same name as your local account on all the remote locations you need to access. If you keep the passwords the same among these accounts, then for all practical purposes it looks like you work with a single account. This setup is typical when you use RAS only occasionally.

Domain Membership

Once connected through RAS to a LAN, your workstation can be placed in a domain just like any other workstation on the network. In this case, you would typically log on to your workstation using one of the domain accounts. The logon window now lets you name a domain and gives you the option of automatically establishing the RAS link.

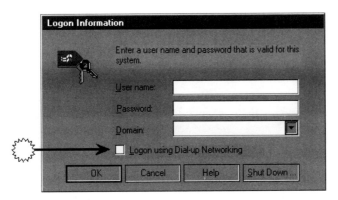

Establishing the RAS Link at Logon

If you choose a domain account (the normal case), then the RAS link must already be established, or you must select *Logon using Dial-up Networking*, which first establishes the RAS link then logs you on. (The link may be already established at this point and if so you need not establish it.) As long as the RAS link is active, you are fully a member of your domain just as if your workstation were physically connected to the LAN. For example, you can add domain users and groups to the ACLs on your workstation. The remote NT Workstation saves its recent logons and can log them on if RAS or the domain server is not available, just as it does for a workstation connected directly to the LAN.

While this scenario is the "fullest" use of domains, the only minor drawback is that the RAS link needs to be active for many local activities, like managing ACLs. (ACL access control is fully active, just that you can't see the names of domain entries in the ACL.) Of course, you can always reestablish the link (indeed, NT often starts the scenario automatically). And if you seldom need domain resources anyway, this is no significant drawback.

In summary, using RAS is straightforward. Your main obligation is to configure the Security window we presented earlier for each phone book entry.

Windows 95

Windows 95 is the successor to Windows for Workgroups and is positioned between WFW and Windows NT. While more powerful than WFW, it is still short of Windows NT in power, features, and, most important, security. Windows 95 includes many security features and is quite flexible in the way it interfaces with a number of operating environments, including WFW, Novell networking, and Windows NT. One of its particular strengths is that it integrates more fully with the NT domain environment than its predecessors. You can almost think of it as a "light" version of NT Workstation.

In this section we discuss the security aspects of using Windows 95 workstations in the Windows NT domain environment. Administrators should note that we present Windows 95 administrative issues in Chapter 10, Subsystems and Other Security Features.

In This Section We Describe

➥ Logging on to the domain environment

➥ Sharing directories and printers using "user-level sharing"

➥ Changing your password, protected screen savers, accessing other workstations, and administrative restrictions on your Windows 95 environment

Overview

There are many parameters your administrator can set to control your Windows 95 security environment. In the presentation that follows we assume it is set up to maximize its integration into the NT domain environment and that your administrator places certain, basic limitations on your Windows 95 environment. (We show administrators how to do this in Chapter 10, Subsystems and Other Security Features.) Windows 95 positions itself as a network client similarly to Windows NT Workstation and from the user's perspective the two are quite similar. Hence our discussion often compares the two.

The most significant security difference is that Windows 95 supports only the FAT file system that does not have ACLs on its files and directories. This means that any user (or their malicious programs) on a Windows 95 workstation can change any of its files. Because all local security controls are kept and enforced in local files, any user (or program) can arbitrarily disable any security controls Windows 95 attempts to enforce. Windows 95 also does not have a Trusted Path, so malicious programs can also easily capture your passwords. But do not despair. If your environment is prone to these threats, your administrator should have installed NT Workstation instead of Windows 95!

When set up as we recommend, a Windows 95 computer appears to be a member of a domain in much the same way that Windows NT Workstations are members of domains. For example, browsers see a Windows 95 workstation as a member of its domain in browse lists. Like NT Workstation, you must log on to Windows 95 and log off when you complete your work. When you log on to Windows 95, you must present an NT account usually from the workstation's home domain. Hence, all Windows 95 users work from an NT domain account. One significant difference is that you can log on to any domain from a Windows 95 workstation, while NT Workstation restricts you to the workstation's domain or one it trusts.

Selected users can share Windows 95 directories and printers on the network. There are two ways that Windows 95 controls remote hosts' access to its shares. The first, called **share-level security**, extends the WFW legacy and attaches optional passwords to each share. The second, called **user-level security**, attaches ACLs to its network shares instead of passwords, much like NT. Administrators configure each Windows 95 computer with either share-level or user-level security, and we assume the latter because it's specifically targeted to the NT domain environment.

Your administrator defines the users and groups you can place in share ACLs. Typically these will be from a specific domain and domains it trusts for each Windows 95 computer. In this sense Windows 95 is almost identical to NT Workstation. Unlike NT, however, Windows 95 can further attach ACLs to directories (although not files) within a share. Note, however, that these ACLs only protect access from remote hosts—not programs on the sharing system.

Logging on and Off

You must log on to Windows 95, presenting an account and password from the domain in which the Windows 95 computer is a member. The system first presents the logon banner (at your administrator's option) and then the standard logon window:

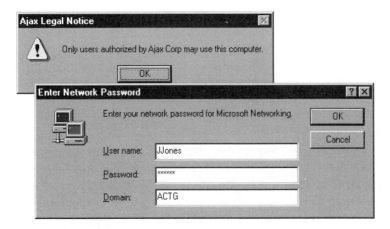

Unseen to you, when you successfully log on to a domain account, Windows 95 also logs you on to Windows 95 itself. In effect there are two accounts with your user name, one is a domain account that is used for all your networking activities and the other is a Windows 95 account used for local activities. If your Windows 95 password is the same as your domain password (the normal situation), Windows 95 invisibly logs you on to Windows 95. Otherwise, it then presents you with the Windows 95 logon window:

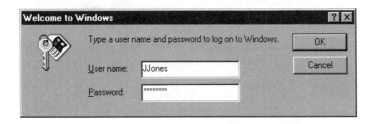

Your Windows 95 account is little used when your workstation is fully set up for NT domains. Its main use is a holdover from WFW where it protects your list of share-level security passwords, which we assume are not used in favor of user-level (ACL) security in the NT environment.

Like NT, you should log out when you are done using the computer. Choose the *Shut Down...* option from the *Start* menu. All of the options with which you are presented log you out except *Restart computer in MS-DOS mode*. This option doesn't really log you out, although you have to log on if you subsequently reenter Windows. Usually you shut down or simply log out (the first or last options). You can alternately press the Control, Alt, and Delete keys and follow the simple instructions, although they only let you shut down the computer.

You can log on to an account from any domain on the network for which you know an account name and password. This is broader than Windows NT where you can only log on to domains trusted by your workstation's home domain. However, the ACL user and group names available on your workstation are always taken from your workstation's home domain (at least under our assumed configuration). Although Windows 95 domain membership is not quite the same as on NT Workstation, it's close and you need not worry about the small differences.

Changing Your Passwords

Passwords

Use the Passwords control panel to change the password for your domain and/or Windows 95 account. You normally keep these the same. To change both at once, select the **Change Windows Password** button and then the *Microsoft Networking* check box on the next screen. You must then type your current password and the new one twice. This figure shows this scenario with the **Details** button selected:

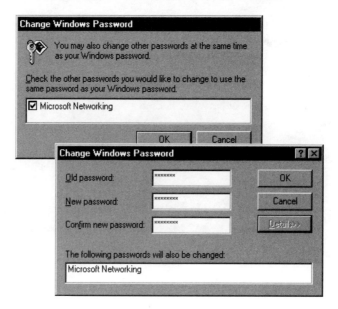

Note that both NT and Windows 95 can impose restrictions on new passwords and you cannot choose one that's not allowed by either. While you can use this control panel to change only one of your two passwords, we recommend against it. (It's not so much a security issue as one of convenience. There is, at best, a weak security justification for having separate passwords.)

Sharing Directories and Printers

Users who are permitted can share directories to the network for access by any compatible client, most notably Windows 95 and NT. As in NT, you share one of your directories through the *Sharing* page of its properties:

Like NT, you can grant specific access permissions to user accounts and/or groups from a specific NT domain or a domain that it trusts. There are two standard access permission sets:

❖ **Read-Only** lets others peruse the contents of the directory and read all of its files, but they can't modify the directory, or the contents or attributes of its files in any manner.

❖ **Full Access** lets them additionally modify, create, and delete files or directories.

The share ACL access decision is a little different than NT's. If the accessing user is in the ACL, than only those permissions apply. Otherwise, the user gets the sum of the permissions from all the groups of which they are a member, or if they are a member of none of the groups they get no access. For example, in the above figure JJones has Read-Only even if a member of ProjX. If BBrown is a member of ProjX and ProjY, BBrown gets Full

Access. Unlike NT share ACLs, there's no "No Access" permission, which means you can't exclude users who would otherwise gain access through their group membership. The detailed access permissions are shown in the following window:

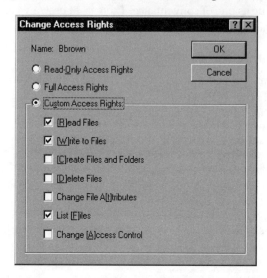

These rights are mostly self explanatory. "Attributes" refers to the traditional DOS file protections: Read-Only, Hidden, and so forth. (See "Properties and Attributes" in Chapter 4, ACLs.) List Files lets you see a directory's entries. Change Access Control is not used.

You can select a custom set of these access permissions, but few combinations are useful. For example, **RWF** would seem to let others browse the directory, and read and modify its files but not delete or create new files or directories. However, the problem with this particular combination is that many applications modify a file by creating a new copy then deleting the original, which doesn't work under **RWF**. List Files (**F**) alone lets users peruse your directory tree without reading its files, but this is seldom useful. Like NT ACLs, it's better to stick with the standard permission sets.

Unlike NT shares, in Windows 95 you can give each directory within the shared directory tree its one unique ACL via the *Sharing* page of its Properties window. For example, suppose we chose a directory (RESTR) inside the one presented in the window on the previous page (OPEN) and removed ProjX, as we did in the window shown at the top of the next page.

Note that even though you can freely change its ACL, you do not generally share the directory because it's already shared as a part of its enclosing tree. Note the window notations "Already shared via C:\OPEN" and *Not Shared*. Files have no ACLs. Instead, each file is protected by its parent directory's ACL.

Directories that have no share ACL appear to have the ACL of their nearest parent that has one, so this window always shows you an ACL. Of course if you change the parent's share ACL, all its descendants that have no ACL implicitly change. When you change an ACL on a directory, if any of its subdirectories has its own ACL, the system gives you the option shown in the second figure on the following page.

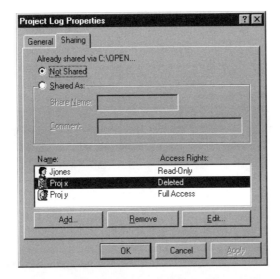

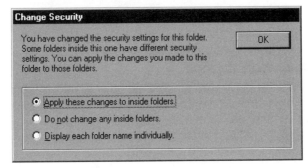

If you choose the first option the entries you just changed, added, or deleted are correspondingly changed, added, or deleted in all descendent directories with their own ACL. The last option lets you interactively apply the changes.

Finally, share ACLs never restrict access to files on your own workstation. You always have full access to all files and directories (except of course for the DOS Read-Only and its sibling restrictions, which can be overridden).

Exploring Share ACLs: Create a folder with a few layers of subfolders and share it on the network.

❑ Change its share ACL and verify that the ACLs on all its descendent directories have effectively changed.

❑ Change the ACL on one of the descendent directories. Change the main share directory ACL and select the *Display each folder…* option. Note which folders it presents.

127

Password-Protected Screen Savers

Like NT, your screen saver can be password protected. Unlike NT (and wisely for Windows 95) you unlock it with a password different than your account's password. Instead, you choose an unlocking password when you select the *Password* option. Use the *Screen Saver* page of the properties of the desktop background.

Protect your work by setting up password locking, although you can use a fairly simple password. *But* don't use your domain account password to unlock your screen!

Why did we make the "wise" comment above and why should you not use your domain password? (Both have the same answer.) [104]

You can share your local printers just like your directories. Each shared printer has an ACL but the only access permission is Full Access.

Accessing Other Workstations

You can access share directories and printers on other Windows 95 and NT Workstations where your logon domain account determines your access permissions. You cannot access Windows 95 shares that are password protected (share-level access), although we assume share-level access is not in use in the full domain environment we describe.

Restrictions

Your administrator typically restricts several of your Windows 95 operations, for example, access to the Network control panel. Windows 95 usually shows you a nice little message when you attempt to use a restricted service, although in other cases menu options or tabbed pages are simply absent. Just be aware that your system may not supply all the operations in your Windows 95 documentation. If these restrictions present a problem, contact your administrator. They may be able to relax them for your account.

Windows for Workgroups

The Microsoft Windows for Workgroups product is a software extension to Windows that lets you share resources with other workstations in much the same way you share them under Windows NT. While WFW workstations can share information independent of Windows NT, WFW is fully compatible with Windows NT and can access NT's shared resources. In this section we discuss the security aspects of using WFW workstations to access NT Servers. Administrators should note that we present WFW administrative issues in Chapter 10, Subsystems and Other Security Features.

In This Section We Describe

➤ Briefly, how WFW security features work

➤ How to access NT resources from WFW

➤ How you or your WFW administrator can increase network security by requiring WFW to authenticate your account in an NT domain

➤ How NT workgroup participants access WFW network-shared resources

WFW Background

Log On/Off

While a complete description of WFW and its native security features is beyond our scope, a little background is in order. Any WFW user may create accounts, assigning each account an initial password. Thereafter, anyone who knows the current password for an account may change the password. Anyone can start up a WFW workstation and use its local resources, even making them available to other workstations, without any sort of logon. However, you must *log on* before WFW lets you access remote resources on a network, independent of the kind of remote workstation you wish to access (WFW, Windows NT, and so forth). You can log on at any time using the Log On/Off networking utility or the Network control panel that we show later.

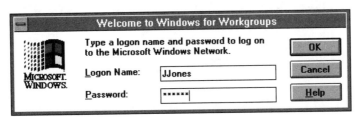

Logging on to WFW

Network

If you type a new name and password, WFW creates a new account. WFW automatically presents you the opportunity to log on when you attempt a network access if you're not already logged on. The Network control panel also lets any user control various networking parameters: the workstation's name and its current workgroup, and the WFW account name presented in logon windows by default, as shown in the figure on the next page.

The Network Program (from Control Panel)

There's a button for changing an account's password and for recording events that we discuss later. The **Startup** button produces several security-related items:

If you select *Log On at Startup,* WFW presents you with the logon window when you start Windows. Because you can cancel the logon and proceed directly to Windows, this is a convenience and not a security enforcement. We talk about the Enterprise Networking options later.

WFW workstations view the network grouped into **workgroups** that look like NT domains in browser listings. A WFW workgroup is a convenience for users in that browsing and other windows expand the workstation's workgroup by default. While browsers list domains as well as WFW workgroups, they show domains as if they were a workgroup.

There are no security barriers between workgroups and any user can switch a WFW workstation to become a member of any workgroup on the network. They can even select a domain as their workgroup, but this gives no special capabilities in the domain and it's not correct to think of them as being a member of the domain like NT Workstations. Membership in the WFW world means only that WFW expands by default the selected workgroup or domain in the browsing windows.

WFW does not have the security features of Windows NT nor the base on which to build them. While NT's critical resources are protected by ACLs, WFW's are not because WFW file systems have no ACLs. Malicious programs are unrestricted on WFW and can modify any software on the system, steal passwords, and so forth.

Accessing an NT Server

You can access an NT Server if your WFW account name matches an account name on the server. If your WFW password is the same as the password on the server, connecting to network share directories on the server requires no special interaction. Unseen by you, WFW presents your WFW name and password to the server for secondary logon each time you make such a request. However, if the passwords are different, programs like File Manager ask you for the password of the server account. This is like connecting to an NT Workstation under a matched account.

Authentication in an NT Domain

If you select *Log On to Windows NT...* on the Startup Settings window, WFW authenticates you in a Windows NT domain as a part of its standard WFW logon. After your WFW logon window (top window following), WFW shows the Domain Logon window, where you select the domain and the password you wish to present (middle window):

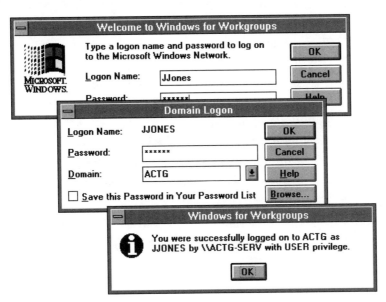

WFW Logon with Domain Authentication and Confirmation

The domain must have an account with this password with the name that is the same as your WFW account. If you elect to *Save this Password...* WFW remembers this domain password and thereafter automatically authenticates you in the domain without even showing the Domain Logon window. However, your WFW administrator may prevent this option from appearing in this window. The administrator may even configure WFW so that this domain logon serves in place of the normal WFW logon and you don't see the WFW logon window at all. The *Don't Display Message...* on the Startup Settings window determines whether or not WFW informs you when it authenticates you in the domain (bottom window, previous page).

Why authenticate in a domain? First, if your WFW and NT passwords are different, once WFW authenticates you with the NT Server, you don't have to enter your NT password each time you connect to and request other resources from the server. This is a convenience. Second, WFW's local logon does not succeed unless the domain authentication also succeeds. And of course, if the WFW logon fails, you can't access the network. This is an important security control because it prevents WFW users from accessing the network unless they have a valid account on a Windows NT domain. It's so important, that WFW administrators can force the domain logon as if you had selected *Log On to Windows NT....*

The **Set Password** button lets you change the password in your domain account on an NT Workstation. There's a bit of a danger here because WFW is not as secure as Windows NT and has no Trusted Path. Changing your domain password from an NT Workstation is much safer. Of course, any time you type a password from WFW there's more danger that it can be captured than on NT.

In summary, the most secure and convenient way to work on WFW in a Windows NT environment is:

✓ Establish a WFW account of the same name as the account on an NT domain controller under which you wish to work.

✓ Give your WFW account a password that, we advise, is different from the NT's account password and as least as hard to guess.

✓ On the Startup Settings window, select *Log On to Windows NT...* and, at your option, *Log On at Startup* and *Don't Display Message....*

✓ The first time you use the Domain Logon window, if *Save this Password...* is present use it at your discretion, although there are security issues involved that you should discuss with your administrator. See our summary on the next page.

✓ It's considerably safer to change your domain password from a Windows NT Workstation rather than using the **Set Password** button on WFW's Startup Settings window.

> **Practicing on WFW**: Most of these features are straightforward. If you want to practice, set up an account (either a domain or a local account) on an NT Server on your network that has the same name as your logon name on WFW. Set up different passwords. You can then exercise everything we've discussed.

WFW and NT Workstations in Workgroups

You can access any NT Workstation participating in workgroups (as opposed to domains) if your WFW account name matches an account on the NT Workstation. Just like connecting to an NT Server, if the passwords are different File Manager asks you for the password of the NT account.

> **Accessing NT Workstations**: You can illustrate this by disabling the *Log On to Windows NT…* option on the Startup Settings window on the Network control panel. (Make sure your WFW administrator has not independently required domain logon. See the section "Administering WFW" in Chapter 10, Subsystems and Other Security Features.) You need an account on the NT Workstation that has the same name as your WFW account. Use File Manager to connect to a share directory on NT. It should succeed, providing you have access to that network share directory and your administrator has not otherwise prevented this operation.

If you're logged on to an NT Workstation that's a member of a workgroup, you can access the resources of a WFW workstation much as you would from another WFW workstation. Because each shared resource on a WFW workstation may be protected by one or more passwords, the system may ask you for a password when you attempt to access a WFW resource. For example, when you connect to a share directory on WFW, one password may give you Read-Only while another gives you Full Access. The person who makes a WFW resource available usually chooses the passwords and you need to get the passwords from them.

Summary

❖ You must log on to a WFW account before you can access the network at all.

❖ In order to access a remote NT Server or Workstation from WFW you need an account on the NT system that's the same name as your WFW account and to which you know the password.

❖ You or your WFW administrator can force WFW to perform a domain authentication as a part of its own logon scenario. If your WFW account name exists on the domain server and you know its password, this authentication succeeds. If it fails,

WFW logon fails and you can't access the network. In this manner, you can't access the network without a domain account. WFW administrators concerned about security often require domain authentication.

❖ WFW can open a shared resource, like a network share directory, to NT Workstations providing the NT user knows the password WFW uses to protect that resource.

The most important caution to keep in mind when working from WFW to Windows NT is your selection of passwords:

❖ Whether or not WFW saves your domain password via *Save this Password...* is an important security issue (called "password caching"). WFW has no ACLs to protect its local storage of passwords (although they're encrypted locally), so some regard it a risk to store domain passwords on WFW and would choose not to do so. However, WFW also has no Trusted Path, so perhaps it's safer to enter only a domain password once when you first start up the system. This is a difficult trade-off and you should discuss it with your administrator. Your administrator can prevent password caching and if so, *Save this Password...* does not appear in the Domain Logon window.

❖ If you use password caching, your WFW local password in effect protects your domain account, since anyone who knows your WFW password can access your capabilities in that domain without knowing the domain account's password. For this reason, your WFW password should always be at least as strong as your domain password.

❖ While you can change your domain account's password from WFW, it's not as safe as doing it on NT itself.

If you use password caching, make your WFW password as strong as your domain account's password and never use a "blank" WFW password.

PART II

Administration

Chapter 6

Planning Domains

This chapter marks our transition into system administration. If you're a regular user, you need these topics only to the extent you've been granted administrativelike capabilities. If you are a Power User or Server Operator you need only the topics in Chapter 7, Managing Groups and Accounts. If you're fulfilling one of the other NT Server Operator roles, there are no required sections. However, users with even limited administrative capabilities can benefit from a general reading of this part. If you're a regular user that's particularly hardy, the chapters that follow can enhance your understanding of Windows NT security. We also transition from our previous vantage point, Windows NT Workstation, to the NT Server, where most administration is done. However, NT Server security is largely a superset of NT Workstation and the differences are small.

The focus of this chapter is the broadest and most fundamental we address: how to structure your domain environment for security (although there are several other criteria for this structure).

In This Chapter We Describe

➥ The different kinds of administrators, their scope, and how they get their power

➥ The criteria you need to subdivide your network into domains effectively, with lots of examples

➥ How to help keep your domain relationships simple by using local accounts for exceptional cases

➥ How to establish and dissolve trust relationships between domains

   Prerequisite: You should have read all the preceding chapters in preparation for the ones that follow. We generally don't repeat our earlier discussions.

What Is Security "Administration"?

We've often used the term "administrator" generically. It actually covers a variety of users with differing power. We call the most powerful administrator a full administrator. They

137

have almost unlimited power within one or more domains, and control who become other administrators within that same scope.

How Administrators Get Their Power

All administrators gain their power through their account. Just as we learned that "account" is more accurate than "user" in describing the system's security controls, "account" is also more accurate than "administrator." However, we continue to say that "an administrator can" when we should more precisely say "an administrative account can" Administrative accounts get their power mostly by membership in certain, built-in local groups that in turn get their capabilities in part from their identity and in part from Rights assigned to these groups. We talk more about the details later.

Domain Operators and Power Users

Domain operators ("operators") are special administrators that have some subset of full administrative capabilities. There are four kinds of operators, each targeted to a particular set of operational, day-to-day activities on the domain controllers:

- ❖ **Account Operators** create and manage the domain accounts and groups, but can't perform any other security duties.

- ❖ **Server Operators** manage the domain controller's day-to-day operations except security (for example, shutting down the server and changing the time).

- ❖ **Backup Operators** mainly do backups and restores. They have no security-relevant duties other than observing commonsense backup procedures.

- ❖ **Print Operators** control access to printers by making them available on the network.

Full administrators have complete control over operators, and operators can't expand their own power. A **Power User** is a sort of administrator whose power is on par with operators, but exists only on NT Workstations.

Most administrators also work day to day doing things not directly related to administration. Except for perhaps Power Users, it's a good security idea for administrators to do nonadministrative tasks from a nonadministrative account. Use your administrative account only for administration. Get a "regular" account for your day-to-day work.

What Is the Administrator's Scope?

While it's natural for an administrator to control a single domain, it's also common for them to control more than one. They can also be limited to specific workstations. It depends on how the network's administrators decide to carve up the network pie. At least in the beginning, they must cooperate to lay the subdivision of responsibilities.

Are They Trusted?

Within their scope, full administrators are implicitly and totally trusted. While there are some security controls, full administrators who want to skirt the rules can do almost anything they want—undetected. While an administrator's powers may be confined to certain domains or workstations, it's never a good idea to make a person an administrator unless you trust them not to circumvent maliciously any bounds on their power. Operators and Power Users are a bit different. Their capabilities are quite limited.

While the firewalls we place around administrators and operators certainly help to prevent malicious actions, they are perhaps more important in confining them to areas in which they've been properly trained and to avoid the "too-many-cooks-spoil-the-broth" syndrome, where confusion and lack of coordination among too many people with overlapping duties leads to security fissures in the system.

Master Jugglers

Mostly, administrators are master jugglers, planning and constantly riding the network security range, training and working with users, and securely integrating new functionality into the networking environment. Before you do any of these you need to write a site security policy and procedures document, which we talk briefly about in Chapter 12, Summary and Checklist. In the following chapters, we walk you through all your security duties:

- ❖ Defining your domains up front
- ❖ Planning your networkwide administrative scheme
- ❖ Managing accounts and groups, including some initial security decisions as well as day-to-day management
- ❖ Security auditing
- ❖ Protecting the TCB
- ❖ Tending the security aspects of various subsystems

We repeat an earlier statement that there are many important parts of system administration that we don't include in our definition of "security." Although we can't quarrel with an observation that they have some indirect impact on the general security of the environment, our targets are the mainline features important to combat the threats we discussed in Chapter 1.

> **Prerequisite**: Although not strictly necessary, it helps if you know the basics of the User Manager, Server Manager, and Event Viewer.

Planning Domains

Give considerable thought to how you structure your domain environment because once you establish domain trust relationships, they're hard to dissolve. There are no hard-and-fast rules, but there are a number of security and other criteria that you must use your judgment to apply.

Trust Relationships

Trust relationships between domains allow domain accounts and global groups from one domain to be visible from and allowed into other domains. Consider the security importance of our example domains:

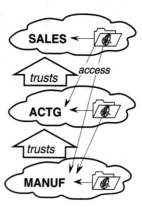

MANUF   Manufacturing is our least-sensitive domain that holds data pertaining to our production process. We deem that accounts (users) from ACTG and SALES are trustworthy in MANUF and have legitimate reasons for being there.

ACTG   Accounting is our medium-sensitive domain, holding the day-to-day information on accounts payable and receivable, payroll, and so forth. While we don't trust MANUF accounts inside ACTG in general, we trust users from SALES, who have a legitimate reason for accessing ACTG workstations.

SALES   This is our most-protected domain. It contains important data on customers, negotiations, and sales figures. Because of its importance, we do not allow other domains into SALES.

We enforce these constraints by precluding ACTG and MANUF users from the SALES domains, and MANUF from ACTG. The trust relationships are shown in the figure above.

☞ If we set up ACTG to trust SALES, then SALES's domain accounts and global groups are allowed in ACTG. Think of rephrasing "ACTG trusts SALES" to "ACTG allows users from SALES."

In addition to the local accounts and accounts from its own domain, a workstation allows all the accounts and global groups from domains its own domain trusts.

The basic trust relationship is inherently one-way. For example, when ACTG trusts SALES, while SALES users are allowed in ACTG, the reverse is not true. Of course, we can set up two domains to trust each other, in which case all users in both are allowed in each.

The trust relationship does not pass through. For example, suppose MANUF does not trust SALES. In this case, MANUF trusts ACTG who in turn trusts SALES. However, this does not mean MANUF trusts SALES. Trust does not "pass through." (Our mathematical friends might say, "Trust is not transitive." Nice phrase, isn't it?)

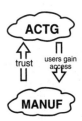

One end can't force a relationship; it takes administrative power in both domains to let one domain trust another, even one way.

"Access" works in the opposite direction of "trust." Because MANUF trusts ACTG, users in ACTG "gain access" to MANUF. While these two expressions are compatible, their "arrows" run in opposite directions.

Security Criteria for Domains

Your network may have many workstations, dozens to hundreds or even more. If you have more than about a dozen, you should consider dividing the network into domains. If you have more than a few dozen, domains are important. Subdividing your network into domains is partly a consideration of the user accounts on the network and which workstations those accounts use on a regular basis. The operational guideline is that each user should be much more likely to share resources with accounts in their own domain than in others. If each person uses a single workstation, like one on each person's desk, defining your domains is easier. Where workstations are shared among accounts, it's a bit harder. The major *security* considerations for grouping accounts and workstations into domains are as follows:

Domains as Security Boundaries

Domains form natural security barriers, largely by precluding the very existence of users (accounts) who should not have access to a domain's resources and data.

☞ Trust is a way to completely disallow network accounts into a domain, which protects that domain's data and other resources.

Example: The domain security criterion is most often the handling of sensitive data. You decide to group all your high-level managers into a single domain that has access to all other domains, but gives access to none. In other words, all other domains trust the management domain, but it trusts none. This domain structure protects managers' sensitive data while allowing them easy access to other domains.

Example: A small university engineering department has a single domain. However, a group named GAMMA in the department is doing particularly sensitive research and has its own security administrator. GAMMA should be given its own domain for security reasons.

What trust relations do you establish for GAMMA? [105]

Example: A circuit court sets ups a computer network for use by defense, prosecution, and judicial staffs with a domain for each with appropriate trust relationships.

How would you set up these trust relationships? [106]

Example: A company might group its domains into PUBLIC, INTERNAL and SECRET domains to protect its nonsensitive, moderate, and highly sensitive information.

What are the trust relationships? [107]

Remember that just because an account has access to another domain, ACLs still protect individual resources. In theory you don't need domains to enforce access to resources. One large domain with carefully tended ACLs is quite secure. But ACL mistakes can be made. The domain is a natural security boundary that you should use when it doesn't conflict strongly with other criteria. Because you can always set up matching local accounts to let particular users access any workstation (discussed later), you need not worry about domains precluding these exceptional cases.

Administration and Security

It's natural for a component of a large organization to want to manage its own piece of the network, usually its own workstations. Domains are natural administrative lairs where an administrator can be given control of one, or perhaps a few, domains. Each domain can set itself apart from administration by the others, making it capable of being administered by nobody outside the domain. Each could further allow certain outside administrators to act as domain administrator, perhaps people who are designated as administrators over several domains or even the whole network. Similarly, some domain structures let you further centralize administration for many domains, just like the domain itself centralizes administration for a group of workstations. Local administrators can be more in tune with the day-to-day security needs of a domain and are therefore better positioned to defend the domain.

Example: A company has nine different divisions spread over three sites. They decide on a domain for each division, averaging twenty-three workstations each. Each division gets a few administrators for its own domain. There are also a few administrators for all the divisions (domains) at each site, and a few administrators for all domains—the whole network. We can't really be sure what the trust relationship should be. It depends on what kind of data the domains handle.

User Convenience and Security

Many NT windows list items from the account's and/or the workstation's domain expanded by default so selecting network resources is quick and easy. It's most convenient to select these. To see items from other domains you have to do something extra, although seldom more than a few mouse clicks. You'd like to minimize these alternatives across your user community. Also, you'd like to limit the length of the lists presented to a user. Trying to add a new account to an ACL from a list of hundreds can be a little frustrating, even though NT alphabetizes the lists. In short, if people don't usually work with other workstations, they shouldn't be bothered by seeing them on a regular basis.

> **Example:** All the students in a large college dormitory could share a single domain but browser lists could have hundreds of entries! Better to subdivide by floor. In this example, each domain might trust all others.

Perhaps the only real security issue here is the use of the broad, inclusive groups, like Domain Users. Breaking a huge list of accounts into several domains is best when the domains form a natural ACL group entry via groups like Domain Users. For example, in our college dormitory division by floor (assuming a strong floor social structure) is better than an alphabetical grouping (A–G, and so forth) because this is more useful for access control.

Most large organizations subdivide into smaller organizations that may further subdivide until you get to partitions that are small enough to be domains. This sort of organizational chart domain criteria is the most natural. Of course, it may be legitimate for two such partitions to inhabit the same domain if they share resources frequently, like research and advanced projects.

Once you decide on the domain layout, having carefully considered each of these criteria, you then go about defining global groups in each domain and the conventions for who administers what, both of which we cover in later sections. You also need to deal with special situations, mostly accounts that need access to domains that do not allow their domain account. You handle these with local accounts as we discuss in the next subsection.

> The major security criteria is that when "**A** *does not trust* **B**," user accounts in **B** can never have access to **A**'s resources. **B**'s accounts are not allowed in **A** and we well know that NT performs services only for allowed accounts.

> How would you set up the trust relationships for the two example domains we haven't discussed, personnel (PERS) and research (RESCH)? **[108]**
>
> Because sales information is quite sensitive, we've decided, for security reasons, that employees in MANUF are not allowed access to SALES. But can sales information leak to the MANUF domain? **[109]**

"Matching" and Local Accounts

Many domain scenarios involve special cases where a particular account needs the services of a workstation in another domain, but such a setup is contrary to your general trust relationship policy. Rather than trying to bend the domain structure in unnatural directions, it's often better to handle them with separate, matching accounts. Matching accounts let you design cleaner domain structures. Recall that the idea of a matching account is simple:

☞ Secondary Logon "Name Matching." When NT performs a secondary logon, it may not recognize the client's account, either because it's a local account on the client or an account from a domain not allowed on the server. When this happens, NT looks for any account allowed on the server workstation that has the same name (like JJones) and password. If NT finds one, it allows the logon, and the client's actions on the server are governed by the matched account. If the passwords are different, many scenarios ask the user for the password in the matched account.

First we look at using a local account on the server and how aspects of local accounts make them useful in handling exceptional cases. Suppose a domain account MANUF\PLine needs to access data in the SALES domain. For example, PLine might be a production manager that anticipates future capacity and needs to read a sales projection database in the SALES domain, normally forbidden to MANUF accounts. It's not necessary to establish a trust relationship from SALES to MANUF. Just set up a local account named "PLine" on the appropriate workstation in SALES, which could be either an NT Workstation or Server. Now MANUF\PLine can gain ready access to that workstation in SALES under their matching local account named "PLine."

Of course you must set up a local PLine account on each workstation in SALES to which PLine needs access. PLine must maintain the password for each such account but can do so from any workstation.

> As administrator, discuss the security aspects of having the two passwords be the same versus different. **[110]**

So far we've allowed PLine access to specific workstations in SALES, not the SALES domain in general. You could have alternatively established a domain account

SALES\PLine on a domain controller in SALES. The MANUF\PLine account now matches SALES\PLine in SALES.

The local account presents tighter security because it allows PLine access only to specific workstations, but it can become a maintenance headache if you need to maintain the local account on many workstations.

☞ Typically, use a *local* account on a domain controller when you want to give matched access only to the controller—not the other workstations in the domain.

Primary and secondary logon requests are often bundled and passed to an appropriate domain controller for authentication. You don't see these details, but this image may help you understand the whole trust scheme and matching accounts. The two common scenarios are:

❖ A workstation in domain ACTG gets a primary or secondary logon request for the account SALES\TTorn. Because ACTG trusts SALES, the request that includes the user's name and password gets forwarded to the SALES domain controller. The workstation waits for a yes/no response and allows or disallows the logon accordingly.

❖ By contrast, a workstation in ACTG gets a secondary logon request for MANUF\PLine. Because ACTG doesn't trust MANUF, the workstation tries to match PLine against one of its local accounts and, that failing, denies the logon.

Example Domain Models

We now consider several multidomain scenarios, some of which are a little impractical but nonetheless instructive. While you may opt for one of these, you might also construct your own, hopefully from ideas they demonstrate.

Strict Separation

In the simple scenario shown here, no domain trusts any other. This highly segregates a network. You can provide cross-domain access via matching accounts, but you want to minimize this because it's inconvenient.

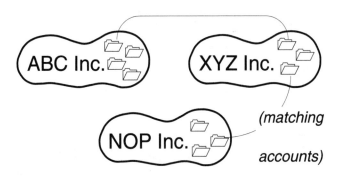

145

An "incubator" building houses several small, unrelated startup companies and provides them a building wide Windows NT network. Each company gets its own domain and no domain trusts any other. Because it's easy to *add* new trust relationships, the strictly separated domains can be easily combined later.

If an incubator company (domain), Bright Paints, decides to let JeffVet Veterinary Clinic temporarily use their color laser printer, Bright can set up a local account for users in JeffVet. Bright can set password controls on this account appropriate to its own environment and independent of the security in JeffVet. Bright might even prevent JeffVet users from changing their Bright passwords, leaving Bright administrators to change them—securely!

Two companies in the incubator might need to share their domain environments if they need to share resources frequently. Similarly, a single company could inhabit several domains with any trust relationship scheme among those domains they like. In both cases, domains that establish trust relationships must agree and they can't impose their agreements on the other startup companies.

Suppose the building management provides a centralized backup service for certain workstations throughout the building. Each such workstation could set up a local account to be used by the backup service or they could create a central incubator domain that all trust.

Master Domain

In this simple, natural scenario there's a single MASTER domain that all others trust, but no other trust relationships exist. (A "MASTER" domain is not a specific NT feature, just a name we give to this example scheme.) In this scheme you typically define all accounts in the MASTER domain, giving a central point for account control. The MASTER could also house frequently used global services. Since all accounts are in a single domain, global groups are simpler because they can hold any combination of accounts. (See "Multidomain Global Groups" in Chapter 7, Managing Groups and Accounts.) The administrative scheme is also simpler. As always, you can use local accounts for the special cases.

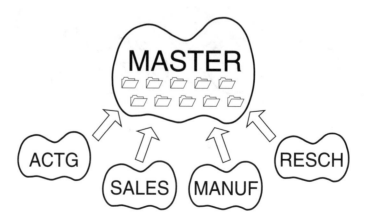

Each domain can still exercise a degree of autonomy to establish and control its own resources. For example, you could define accounts in these domains for use strictly inside the domain, although you don't want this to be a substitute for what should be a new MASTER domain account. Probably the biggest operational drawback is when individual domain administrators (in the event you create them) add local capabilities that should be available through the MASTER domain instead.

Complete Trust

In this scenario, each domain trusts each of the others. This means the sum total of accounts and global groups in all the domains is allowed in each. You might use this when your goal is only for the user browsing convenience we discussed earlier or perhaps when there is no central administrative responsibility. It's also useful when most users need at least occasional access to resources throughout the network. You could still set up networkwide and per-domain administrators. Global

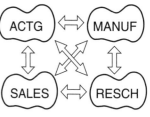

group administration is perhaps the biggest disadvantage because no global group can hold accounts from more than its own domain. Our college dormitory is a good candidate for this model.

A Segregated, Highly Secure Workstation

This is not so much a general scenario as a way to augment any of the other scenarios. Suppose you want to highly segregate a workstation for security reasons, strictly limiting the accounts that access the workstation, imposing a uniformly strong degree of security (like password controls and auditing), and limiting administration to a few local logons, especially where the network security as a whole is not so strict. You might make this workstation a domain of one workstation running NT Server and limit access from other domains through a few local accounts. This is security in its extreme. However, we repeat

selected, matching accounts

an earlier comment that any workstation can be made tightly secure by proper ACL management and you probably won't use domains this radically. Still, if you segregate in this manner *and* tightly control ACLs, you maximize security. Our RESEARCH domain might be a good candidate for this technique.

As you can see, planning your domains and accounts is a multidimensional task. Develop your strategy early and carefully. The best test of your scheme is to map out all accounts (global and local), global groups, and shared resources, then look at the network from the vantage of each account to see if its user can access the resources they need and are kept from the ones they're not allowed to access.

Consider a CENTRAL domain that trusts each of the other "subject" domains. When might this be useful? [111]

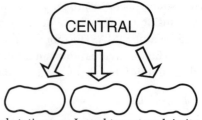

Which is the natural direction of trust between a "service" domain and a set of its "client" domains? [112]

Someone says, "I have two major server workstations, so I need to put each in its own domain." Absent any other reasons, is this necessary? [113]

Of what use are two domains that trust one another, as opposed to having a single domain? [114]

Managing Trust Relationships

User Manager for Domains

Establishing a trust relationship is easy but requires the cooperation of administrators in both domains. Both administrators agree on a secret phrase, a password (not to be confused with an account password), used to establish and maintain the trust relationship. Each administrator uses the User Manager for Domains on their primary domain controller. In our example MANUF is to trust ACTG. First, the administrator on ACTG allows MANUF to trust ACTG by setting up the following path:

User Manager: Policies→ Trust Relationships…

From the Domain to Be Trusted

You must enter a password that the administrator on MANUF uses when they complete the trust relationship, as illustrated by:

User Manager: Policies→ Trust Relationships…

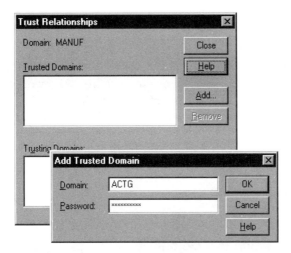

From the Domain That Trusts

Of course, the domains could be set to trust each other, which means you have to do the same operation in reverse. It can take a few minutes before new trust relationships take effect. You can use this interface remotely to manage any other domain in which you can be secondarily logged on as an administrator in that domain, and if so you can establish the relationship from one location. **Hint**: This window is a good way to see who trusts whom.

While you can delete trust relationships by removing entries from this window, it's not a good idea. Deleting a domain relationship means that all references to domains no longer visible, like in ACLs, become invalid. NT does not automatically delete these "unknown accounts" and they become deadwood, albeit harmless. (If you again establish the trust relationships, they reappear as valid entries.)

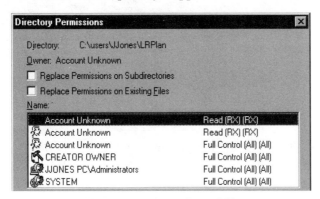

Unknown Accounts in an ACL

Carefully plan your trust relationships. Although adding new ones is easy, re-moving them is troublesome.

Establishing a trust relationship: Establish a trust relationship from one domain to another, as in the figure on the previous page. Test this by opening an ACL in each domain and trying to observe the other domain. (You may have to wait several minutes before newly defined trust relationships actually take effect.)

You may need to do this exercise by first breaking the relationship between two domains then reestablishing it. This causes no problems if you don't do much between the breaking and reestablishing. Before reestablishing, wait several minutes after the break and check that the relationship no longer exists.

Adding a Workstation to a Domain

Network Server

Server Manager lists the workstations in a domain. The Add Computer to Domain window is your first step in adding a new one:

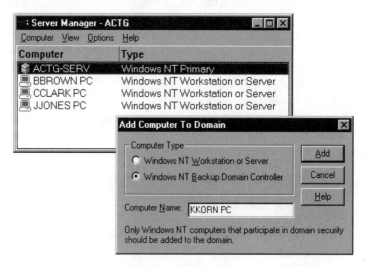

Server Manager: Computer→ Add to Domain...

Second, from the workstation's Network control panel select the **Change** button and enter the domain name, as shown in the figure on the next page:

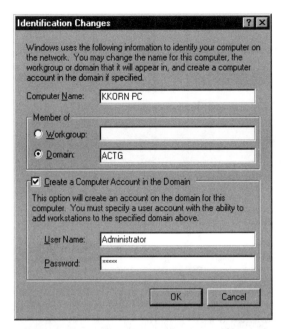

Network Control Panel: Identification→ {Change}

The workstation is now a member of the domain, although it may take a few minutes for this to percolate through the browser windows. Alternately, you can omit the first step and do the entire process on the workstation by using the *Create a Computer Account in the Domain* option. Enter an administrator account and password from the domain. NT also gives you the opportunity to join a domain when you install NT onto a new workstation.

Adding and removing a domain workstation: Use these techniques to remove and/or install a workstation from domains. Check via the browsing windows. (Remember that you may have to wait a while to see the results. You can hasten the process by restarting both the workstation and controller.) It does no harm to move a workstation among domains, as long as it ends up in its original domain.

What problems might you encounter if you remove a workstation from a domain in which that it has long been a member? [115]

> **Explore Server Manager**: Server Manager is a powerful program for day-to-day administration. Explore it if you like. You can do little harm on an experimental network. In particular, note that you can change the ACL of a network share directory using *Computer→ Shared Directories...→ {Properties...}→ {Permissions...}*.

Summary

❖ Full administrators are all powerful but only in their scope (normally one or more domains, but perhaps only a single workstation). They define and control all other administrative users. Operators have limited power in certain operational areas, but cannot expand their own power. Most operators are defined only on NT Server. Power Users are like operators of a single workstation, and a person is often made a Power User on their own desktop workstation.

❖ Planning domains is a balance between user convenience (keeping browsing lists short and pertinent), security (domains are natural, strong security boundaries even between administration), and administration (the domain is an excellent scope for an administrator).

❖ The essence of "**A** trusts **B**" is that **B**'s domain accounts are allowed (usable, visible) in **A**. Trust relationships are not transitive: If **A** trusts **B** and **B** trusts **C**, **A** does not trust **C**. You must explicitly make **A** trust **C**.

❖ Establishing new trust relationships is easy and free of side effects. Dissolving a trust relationship is nettlesome, mostly because you leave straggling, cross-domain references.

Chapter 7

Managing Groups and Accounts

We now turn to the task of managing accounts and domains, including those for administrative users. While the mechanics are quite simple, for maximum security you need to carefully plan the "balance" among your user security policies, as well as the way you structure your hierarchy of administrators. We give many examples.

In This Chapter We Describe

Groups:

➡ Administrative criteria for defining and naming groups, especially global groups

➡ How to set up groups to hold accounts from more than one domain

Accounts:

➡ The many security controls in an account, how they interact, and the trade-offs you make

➡ The "Rights Policy"

➡ How to control who administers what in networks small to large.

NT's term for the collection of user accounts and group definitions on a computer is the "Security Accounts Manager (SAM) database."

User Groups

Your group strategy is just as important as that for domains and accounts. It is part and parcel of your network structure and bears considerable planning. We've already covered groups from the regular user's vantage point and we now turn to some special aspects of their administration. Plan the groups that populate your network early. Administrators from different domains may need to coordinate, and it's a good idea to develop sitewide policies for who's in the special groups. We defer our discussion of administrative groups until the "Administrative Access" section because they're at the heart of the network's administrative scenario.

Groups Defined

To recap, a group is a named list of user accounts. There are two basic kinds. A **global group** is kept on a domain controller, can hold only user accounts from its own domain (not other groups), and is visible throughout the domain and all domains that trust it. Only administrators create global groups. A **local group** is kept on a workstation and is visible only on that workstation. It can hold local accounts, and domain accounts and global groups, but can't hold other local groups. Both administrators and regular users create local groups.

If an account is a member of a global group that's a member of a local group, the system considers the account to be "a member of" the local group, indirectly. Even though a local group can contain global groups, we can still think of any group as a list of accounts, some directly named, some indirectly named through other groups. Note that group nesting never goes deeper than a local group containing a global group. This gives you a degree of flexibility while keeping things simple. You can use User Manager to list the set of groups to which an account belongs, but this lists only the groups visible from your workstation.

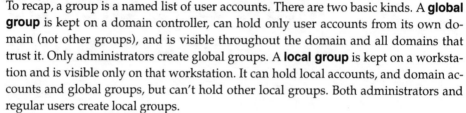

User Manager: User→ Properties...

There could be other groups not visible on this workstation that also include this account, typically local groups on other workstations. Don't think of the groups to which an account belongs as a list that's kept "inside the account." Instead, view groups as lists of account names kept around the network independent of accounts.

You can delete a group, which implicitly removes it from all ACLs and other groups, but once deleted you can't resurrect it, even though you can create a new one with the same name. NT stores groups internally as a special numeric "ID." For example, it's the ID that's kept inside an ACL, not the name. When NT shows you an ACL, it just fetches the current name for the group's ID. If you delete a group, then create another of the same name, they have different IDs. Even though they have the same name, they are not the same group in that the new group has a fresh set of members and does not automatically appear in ACLs that held the old one. Also, you can't rename a group.

We discussed the mechanics for creating a local group in "Creating Local Groups" in Chapter 4, ACLs. Global group management is similar.

> **Creating a global group**: From NT Server, use User Manager for Domains to create a new global group. Try to include groups and accounts from other domains. (You can't.)

You can't delete a group if any of its members are using it as a Primary group. See the exercise when we discuss adding groups to an account in "General Security Controls," later in the chapter.

Who Can Create Groups?

Administrators can create both local and global groups, and can manage and delete all groups except those that can never be removed from NT. Account Operators can do the same, except they can't usurp administrative powers by modifying the membership of other administrative groups.

Power Users and members of the local group Users or the global group Domain Users can all create local groups, but can change and delete only the ones they've created. Power Users can also modify the membership of certain predefined groups, including Users, Power Users, and Guests.

Windows NT fastidiously prevents people from expanding their administrative capabilities by adding themselves (or their friends) to more powerful administrative groups. However, they can create more administrators like themselves. For example, Power Users can create other Power Users on their own workstation.

If you remove a regular user's account from the Users group, that user can't create local groups. This is a little drastic, because groups are a great feature designed hand in hand with ACLs, which are the easiest to use when their entries are predominantly groups.

Criteria for Groups

How do you decide which groups are appropriate for your site? Remember that the value of a group is not just shorthand for a list of accounts, but that when you add new members to a group they automatically gain (or are denied!) access to the various ACLs around the network. A few other reasons to create a group follow.

Access Control

Because groups are mostly used in ACLs for access control, in some sense there's no reason to create a group before some user is ready to add the group to an ACL, although a little forethought never hurts.

Access to Programs

This is a special use of ACLs. You may want to control who can run certain programs. It's natural to create special groups and then use the groups to grant access through the programs' ACLs. (In small-scale cases, you could just use accounts themselves in the ACL.)

> **Example**: An inventory program works on a common database. The program was not written for security, so that everyone who runs the program can modify the single inventory database. (Perhaps it is assumed that only authorized people have access to the computer on which it runs.) This is a good place to use a group named, perhaps, Inventory Control.

> **Example**: As a matter of policy, you may want to prevent certain users from creating their own programs. You could create a Programmers group and allow only its members access to various programming tools (compilers, linkers, and so forth). Of course, people could import their own tools, but this helps.

> **Example**: You install special network security hardware and it comes with a program that lets you turn it on and off and otherwise set its parameters. You should only let members of the appropriate administrator's group access the program.

The latter illustrates that, at least for administrative tools, it's better to use an existing administrative group when the activities fall within their duties.

Remember that if you need to protect the data that a certain program uses, for example the inventory database we mentioned, you need to protect the data itself. Simply preventing people from running the program doesn't mean they can't use other programs to modify the database files directly. In our example, make sure this common inventory database is owned by a trustworthy user and allows only the group Inventory Control to access the data.

Conversely, access to programs doesn't necessarily give one access to data created by that program. When JJones creates a spreadsheet file it gets an ACL appropriate to JJones use. Let's assume it allows access only to JJones. If BBrown runs the same program, it doesn't, by virtue of running the program, gain access to JJones' spreadsheet file.

Administrative Capabilities

Sometimes you empower groups with certain administrative capabilities. We discuss this extensively in the "Administrative Access" section later in this chapter, but you may also want to create small-scale groups that act as administrators for a particular task or group.

Example: You create a large directory tree for general use by many accounts. You'd like a few of the users to act as administrators for this tree with complete control over its contents. Create an appropriate group and arrange for all ACLs to grant this group "Full Control."

Aid for Selecting Multiple Accounts

As we see later you may need to make a certain change to a whole group of accounts at once. One of the ways you can select accounts is by membership in a group. You might create groups solely for this purpose.

Example: You decide to place all users in one of three groups of logon hours: Work Hours, Extended Hours, and All Hours. If your site becomes busy, you can easily extend the hours of these groups as a whole.

Rights

It's common practice to associate Rights, which often represent administrative capabilities, with groups. However, NT has a standard policy for allocating Rights that you seldom change, so you probably won't create groups for Rights allocation.

Example: NT requires a special Right to log on directly to a domain controller. Although administrators are set up with this Right, you may want to create a new group, Controller Logons, for others you trust to do so.

Resource Use

Remember that ACLs control things other than files and directories, like printers.

Example: You buy an expensive color printer that you don't want just anybody to use ($$). Create a group Jasper Color Laser, with the users you trust to use it wisely.

Profiles

We don't cover user profiles in depth because they have little security relevance, but they can also be based on group membership.

One of the disadvantages of all but the first of the above points (ACLs) is that such groups clutter up users' ACL group lists with groups that they'd probably never select because these groups are not designed for access control.

Hints for Defining Groups

Name them descriptively. Make the name as descriptive as you can. Project Anaconda is better than PJA; Visiting Researchers is better then Misc. ("Misc" is terrible because it's not at all intuitive who might be in the group.) Because you can't rename a group, choose its name carefully.

Describe them well. Recall that each group has a description and you should give each the best description you can. Make it clear who the members are. For example, "Visiting researchers not on staff" is better than "Created by John."

Don't surprise anyone. You don't want a user to add a group to an ACL then sometime later find someone added to the group that this user would not have expected. Once you create a group, don't change its intended membership without ample warning to all who might use the group. If you change your criteria for who's in the group, other users may need to adjust their ACLs.

> **Example**: A certain project "X" has both internal staff and external consultants who work off site. It's appropriate to include all in a ProjX group. The description should indicate that it includes consultants who work off site. Alternately, you might create a separate group for the consultants, judging that you may want to limit their access to less than the whole group.

> **Example**: You now decide to add select customers to ProjX. Give advance notice! You may be better advised to create a new group for these customers and add them selectively to ACLs.

Avoid same names—different intent. It's usually a poor practice to have two groups on the network with the same name but completely different intent. It's just plain confusing. There are two common exceptions. The first is a group clearly understood to have different members on different workstations, like Power Users. A second is when no user could ever work with them both.

It is okay to have two groups of the same name on different workstations or in different domains (usually local groups) if you intend them to have the same membership policy. You might even purposely make their membership a little different. For example, there may be accounts on one workstation, and in a local group there, that don't exist on another workstation where you have a group of the same name and intent. However, even this can be a bit confusing because users giving access to the group (or more important, denying it) might reasonably expect all members be included.

> Regular users and Power Users might create their own groups and are unlikely to coordinate the names. Regularly cruise the network and/or your security log looking for conflicts, such as two local groups of the same name but entirely different intent.

Develop site policies and advertise them. While some groups are inherently local or confined to a domain, many are visible from wider venues. Develop a consistent, sitewide group policy, especially for common groups like Users and Guests.

> Critique these group names and descriptions, and whether they seem useful. [116]
>
> | | |
> |---|---|
> | **Students** | Students at Riverland College |
> | **Group A** | Members of the Athena project |
> | **Tall People** | Those significantly over average height |
> | **VIPs** | Important people |
> | **Pat's Friends** | Friends of Pat Penache |
> | **Mail Room** | Mail room personnel |

Special Groups

We've already discussed some of the special groups (in the "Special Groups" section in Chapter 4, ACLs), but here are some notes for administrators on a few of them.

Users and Domain Users

The global group Domain Users typically holds all the accounts in the workstation's domain. When you add a new domain account, NT automatically adds it to Domain Users. NT's default is that the Users local group on each workstation holds the Domain Users group, plus all local accounts. (When you create a new local account NT adds it automatically to the Users group.)

Only members of Users (or Domain Users) can create local groups. Membership in Everyone (which is implicit) or Guests alone does not let you create local groups. For this reason, you might remove users if you don't want them to create local groups.

☞ Your best bet is to support NT's intent for these groups. You may want to extend the Users local group to include users from other domains by including the Domain Users global group.

Guests and Domain Guests

The Guests group is built-in but its membership is up to you. Guests do not have the special capabilities of Users. For example, with membership in Guests alone one cannot create local groups, as can members of Users.

Domain Guests is by convention a member of all the local Guests groups and is therefore a simpler way to include a set of domain accounts in the Guests groups throughout a domain. You could extend the local Guests groups to include Domain Guests from other domains, just like you could for Users and Domain Users.

Example: You might have a list of user accounts who regularly use a server's resources and you set up the ACLs for them specifically, and perhaps give each a personal working area in the directory tree. You might consider Guests a specific list of other, occasional users to whom you grant access as a whole. For example, you might confine Guests to a common area of the directory tree or prevent them from using certain printers.

cases:

The Guest *account* implies a lack of authentication, that you may not know who's really using it. (See "The Guest Account" later in this chapter). The Guests *group* is different. People in the Guests group are properly authenticated (except, of course, for the Guest user). The Guests group can be useful even if you disable the Guest account.

Multidomain Global Groups

Global groups are the simplest to maintain because there's only one definition for an entire domain, but they hold only accounts from their own domain. What if you need a centralized group definition for users from multiple domains? The solution is a local group that you place on all applicable workstations. While you could define the group as the list of domain accounts, it's common to create a global group in each domain that holds the actual domain accounts, then include all these global groups in the local group:

Example: An administrator may want the local group Users to include all accounts from all domains allowed on the workstation. Recall that the Domain Users global group typically includes all the accounts in the domain. The administrator can therefore add the Domain Users global groups from all visible domains to the Users local group on each workstation.

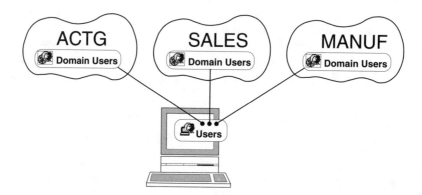

Example: You could extend the Users/Domain Users example for the employees of a company. Define an Employees local group on all workstations that includes the Domain Employees global groups from all visible domains. You might do the same with managers or partners.

☞ Since these populate each workstation, it's useful to define them up front.

A primary advantage to this scheme is that domain administrators can add to the relatively few global groups without having to change the local group on each workstation.

While you could make the local group name the same as the global, this can be confusing because you see them both in the same listing. It's a good idea to follow the Users/Domain Users example.

Summary

❖ There are several reasons to create groups, but the most important security criterion is for use in ACLs.

❖ It's essential that users understand a group's intended membership when they give the group access to their files. Name and describe the groups clearly, always with the goal of delineating its membership. Don't surprise anyone.

❖ Groups to hold users from multiple domains must be local groups, preferably that include only global groups named similarly, like Users and Domain Users.

The local Users group on an NT Workstation named "ZZZ" includes the global group Domain Users, which in turn includes a local account on the domain controller. Therefore, a local account on the controller is an indirect member of a local group on another workstation. But we've said that local accounts are strictly confined to their own workstation, the domain controller in this case. Does this situation allow a local account on the controller onto another workstation, ZZZ? [117]

Accounts

By now you should thoroughly appreciate how Windows NT security depends on accounts. NT does almost nothing except on behalf of accounts and always requires password authentication for those accounts.

Names and Ownership

We've already introduced the two basic kinds of accounts: global and local. Only domain controllers hold domain accounts and NT allows them throughout the domain and others that trust it. Any NT workstation can hold local accounts, but they're allowed only on that workstation. However, because NT matches local account names during secondary logons, it can appear as if a local account spans several workstations.

The great asset of NT domain account administration is that it's done centrally, in a single database with networkwide influence. This not only eases the burden of administration, but helps eliminate fissures in network security. Domain accounts are key to centralized administration and should be the basis for your entire network. As we've seen earlier, local accounts are occasionally quite useful. Because you can use them to let any workstation on the network serve any user, they let you handle special cases without affecting the overall simplicity of the domain structure.

Accounts are almost always created for individuals. Otherwise, you don't know whom to hold accountable for the account's actions. This holds for administrators also. Administrators should work through personal accounts that gain their power mainly by their membership in certain groups, like the built-in Operators groups. The only common exception is an emergency Administrator account on each workstation.

On the flip side, it's okay for one person to have more than one account. For example, administrators shouldn't do their day-to-day, nonadministrative duties under an administrative account. While you can give regular users more than one regular account, it can become quite inconvenient and it's unlikely you'll find much use for this.

You almost always name the account after the user: JJones, BBrown, or (in small offices or for important people) Chris. You may want to name administrative accounts distinctively, like JJones-Admin. The system makes no distinction based on case. For example, to NT, JJONES and JJones are the same name. NT often shows the full name alongside the account name so account names like Chris K. Walker are redundant.

As a final note, domain controllers store domain accounts and, in the normal course of events, it's the controllers who authenticate domain users for NT Workstations. You might be concerned that you can't use a domain account for logon when its controllers are "down." Each NT Workstation remembers recent logons and can often log users on even when the domain controllers are indisposed.

General Security Controls

The User Manager's main window is your home base for managing an account:

User Manager Main Window

The User Properties window gives an overall view of an account:

User Manager: User→ Properties...

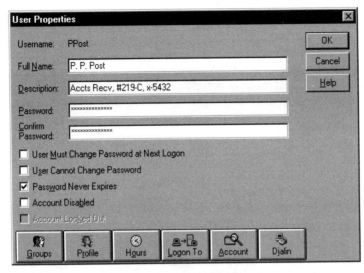

Main Account Window

You create a new account with a similar window. The *Username, Full Name, Description*, and *Password* fields are obvious.

Creating a new account: Create a user account with *User→ New User....* Experiment with the fields in this window. Leave the account open for the following exercises.

Always give a new account a good password, even if you intend the user to change it.

The next group concerns password control. Passwords are at the heart of security on almost all modern systems. They're also often the source of controversy. Ultimately, their correct use is a "people issue" and this makes it difficult. Much of the advice we gave to regular users in Chapter 3, Your Working Environment, applies to your job as administrator, and we don't generally repeat it here. First we present the separate password controls, then discuss their combined use in a later section.

User Must Change...

If you set this, the logon scenario forces the user not only to present their current password, but to define a new one before they're next allowed to begin their session. Set this anytime you think it's a good idea for a user to change their password. Because some sites don't like the idea of an administrator knowing a user's password, they often set this whenever the administrator defines a password for the user. In this spirit, NT even sets *User must change...* automatically when you change an account's password from the User Properties window, although you can reset it. (See our notes on *Users must log on in order to change password* in "Account Policy," discussed later.)

User Cannot Change...

This prevents users from changing their passwords, mostly to accommodate sites where administrators alone assign passwords. (You also typically use it for the Guest account.)

Password Never Expires

As we see later, you can declare passwords older than a certain age to be "expired." When an account has an expired password, either the user can't log on at all and you must assign them a new password or they can log on but must immediately change their password before they can continue. Select this option to exempt the account from password expiration. (See also our notes on *Users must log on in order to change password* in "Account Policy," discussed later.)

Account Locked Out

Use this to unlock an account locked by the Account Lockout feature we discuss later.

Groups

This shows all visible groups that include the account as a *direct* member. It does not include indirect membership. For example, this user is a member of a global group (Accounting) which in turn could be a member of a local group (Financial). In this case, NT doesn't show Financial in the *Member* list. You can add (remove) this account to (from) any group by moving the group names between the lists.

The account may be a member of other groups on the network that are not visible on this workstation, and of course they aren't listed here. The Primary group affects POSIX applications and is also used by NT's Services for Macintosh. Think of it as their "main" group.

> ☞ It's a bit backward to think of the groups to which this account belongs as being "listed or held in the account." NT defines groups by a list of accounts kept with each group name. This account window is just a handy way to focus on groups visible from this workstation that currently include this account.

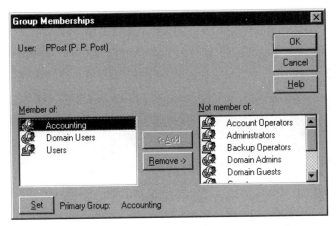

User Manager: User→ Properties...→ {Groups}

Managing groups: Add and remove some groups. Try to remove all groups. What happens? [118]

Hours[1]

The Logon Hours window (shown at the top of the next page) prevents primary and secondary logons during certain periods of each day of the week. For example, if the user is logged on when time passes into a restricted period, they can no longer establish remote services because this requires a secondary logon. If you so specify in the server's Account Policy, NT cancels the services provided by the domain controller when the user passes into a prohibited period. Logon hour restrictions do not affect the account's local workstation activities if the account is already logged on when time enters a prohibited period. NT does not force users to log off. In summary, NT does not allow primary or secondary logons during prohibited hours and you can instruct the domain controller to cancel its services to remote user sessions when they enter these hours. However, you can't log them off their workstations or close their other network connections.

Logon Hours: Practice setting the logon hours. Select a rectangle of boxes and click **Allow** or **Disallow**. If you feel industrious, test our description of this feature, but you need to do it "on the hour" (or change the system clock).

---

1. NT Server only—not NT Workstation.

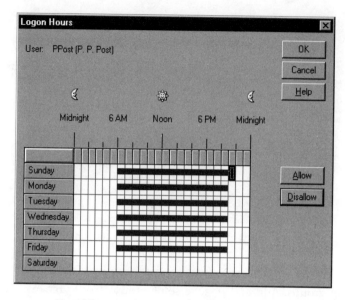

User Manager: User→ Properties...→ {Hours}

Logon To

Use this to restrict primary logons to specific workstations on the network. Enter the unprefixed names of the workstations, which can be any workstation on the network regardless of its domain affiliation. Be careful not to misspell the name—you get no error message if you do. (There may be other restrictions that still prevent logons to the workstations you name here.)

User Manager: User→ Properties...→ {Logon To}

☞This restricts only primary logon—not secondary.

Each workstation's Rights Policy controls the accounts or groups that can perform primary and/or secondary logons to that workstation. (See "The Rights Policy" later in this chapter.) The Rights Policy is a broader, more fundamental control over who can use a workstation and need not be set in each account. Also, if you need to limit access but need more than the number allowed by the Logon Workstations window, use the Rights Policy, although you must set the policy on each disallowed workstation.

Account[1]

This determines when the account expires, if ever. NT does not delete an expired account and you can reactivate an account by setting a new expiration date. This is a good way to review periodically accounts seldom used. Expire them and see who complains. From this window you can also select whether the account is local or global, although you seldom switch an account from one type to the other.

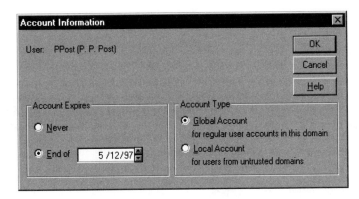

User Manager: User→ Properties...→ {Account}

Dialin

Determines whether this account can be used for remote access, for example, through Remote Access Services (see "RAS and PPTP" in Chapter 9, The Internet and Intranets). This is enforced on the dial-in server when a remote client remotely accesses the server using this account. If you select a callback option, the dial-in service hangs up the remote client and calls it back. You can either let the remote used specify the callback number or set a fixed number. You can also set these permissions using the Remote Access Admin program.

☞This is obviously an important parameter. Allow dial-in only to those who are actively using it. Use a preset callback number for maximum security.

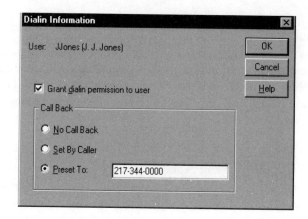

User Manager: User→ Properties...→ {Dialin}

Profile[1]

The user's profile has little relevance except that the home directory and logon script files need proper ACLs. We cover these topics later.

Most of these windows are self-evident and there's little discussion to add. We suggest that logon hours may be more useful for operational than security reasons. While prohibiting logons to an account outside its user's "normal" hours is to some degree a deterrent, the other NT security controls are strong without it. Also, the times people need access outside these hours are often critical, like that report due in the morning. Security that precludes these situations generates resentment and work-arounds ("Can't use your account? Use mine. Here's my password.") Carefully weigh what you gain by restricting logon hours.

The logon workstation limits are more significant. If ACLs are properly maintained on a workstation, anyone should be allowed to log on with little fear of compromise. However, some workstations may have file systems without ACLs and you must limit logons to protect them. Even with full ACL protection, it's poor security practice to let a user log on to a workstation where they have no business. Remember that this feature prevents only primary logons—not secondary. Hence, while they can't sit down and directly log on to that workstation, they may be able to access its network share directories.

As a subtle point, NT performs a secondary logon only the first time a workstation connects to a workstation, so account restrictions like logon hours and disable don't apply to connections after the first one in the account's logon session.

The Account Policy

The User Manager's Account Policy window, shown on the top of the next page, sets parameters that apply to all accounts on a particular workstation.

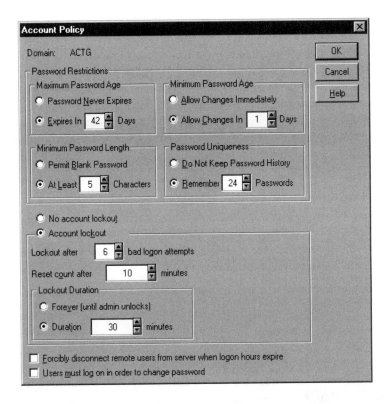

The Account Policy, Accessed via User Manager: Policies→ Account...

Minimum Length

Administrators set the minimum-length password that user's may choose. A length of 0 is called the "blank password." The axiom of the password art is simple: the longer the password the harder it is to guess; but, the harder it is to remember, the more likely it's written down. If you trust people to write it down in a safe place, make 'em long. Unfortunately the bottom of mouse pads and keyboards are popular. If you force long, random passwords, like "agtse%1hSG" or even "latpijutpo," they write 'em down. Guaranteed. And writing down a password frequently compromises it. Studies show that people have trouble remembering sequences of more than six or seven items, so you'd like to make this minimum no longer. We discuss later the trade-off between minimum length and other factors.

Maximum Age

NT deems passwords older than the maximum age "expired." When a user logs on, NT checks the age of the password against the current maximum age. If the password is older, it's expired. For example, if you set the maximum age at five days then all passwords older than five days are considered expired when their users attempt to log on. For this to affect an account you must turn off the *Password Never Expires* option.

Security lore cites the need to change passwords regularly. One reason is that it neutralizes stolen passwords. However, a stolen password can do lot of damage in a short time, especially if the thief understands it doesn't last long. Perhaps a better reason is to neutralize passwords that people have "loaned" to others. You can't do much about the short-term use of loaner password, but the person who loans a password probably keeps an eye on its short-term use. Regular changes prevent long-term abuse to which the lender is less diligent. In short, expiration is a useful but modest security feature.

Password Uniqueness

You can direct NT to "remember" the most recent passwords for each account and to not accept a new password that's on this list. This helps prevent users from switching among a small set of their favorite passwords. There's no point is enforcing uniqueness unless you also set a minimum age as well.

☞There are few reasons not to enforce password uniqueness. If you select the maximum list size and a minimum age (see below) of one or two days, you'll ensure uniqueness for all but the most obstinate users.

Minimum Age

If you enforce password uniqueness, you should worry about a user who quickly creates a series of new passwords to clear the list, then picks an old favorite. You help thwart this by setting a minimum age. Once a user selects a legitimate password, they can't change it for the "minimum age" time.

Users Must Log on in Order to Change Password

Users with expired passwords cannot log on at all if you select *Users must log on in order to change password*. Presumably an administrator must then give them a new password. If you don't select this option, they can log on with an expired password but NT immediately forces them to change their password before they continue. A better phrase is: "Fail authentication if password expired."

Forcibly Disconnect Remote Users from Server When Logon Hours Expire

If you choose *Forcibly disconnect remote users from server when logon hours expire*, when an account has services outstanding at this domain controller when time passes into one of the account's restricted periods, the controller suspends these services. For example, if you have connected to a network share directory on the controller you can no longer access the drive. NT's Messenger Service warns users several times shortly before NT suspends such services.

Account Lockout

This feature thwarts one user trying to guess another user's password (say PPost's) by repeatedly trying to log on as PPost. You can tell NT to lock PPost's account after this happens the number times you set in *Lockout after*, which we call the "locking threshold." The period you set in *Reset count after* is called the "reset time." When a period of time equal to reset time passes with no more attempts, the count of failures is reset to 0.

The lock is applied to the account itself, not the workstation. Others can log on to a workstation where a user has just locked their account, and having locked their account from one workstation a user is locked out of all workstations.

We recommend you use account lockout, but select values reasonable for your site. Users often take several tries to log on, so set the locking threshold at about five or six. Setting it lower doesn't gain much security. What's the chance that someone can guess a password in six versus three tries? Probably not much. You can set the reset time quite high because it does not encumber legitimate use of the system. (See also the accentuated "obscure lockout effect" below.)

> With what overall frequency can a good penetrator try to guess a password without locking the account? [119]

As this exercise highlights, the combination of threshold and reset time determine the degree of protection against guessing passwords. This feature slows down the overall rate at which one user can try to guess another's passwords. Even modest settings can nonetheless slow the rates dramatically. If you choose higher thresholds, choose proportionally higher reset times to ensure the same level of protection.

Once the account locks, you can have it automatically unlock after the time you set in *Duration* or leave it solely to an administrator to unlock it. In either case, an administrator can always unlock an account by deselecting *Account Locked Out* on the account's main window.

An obvious problem is that one user can use this feature to lock another user out of their account. Counter this by setting the lockout duration to some reasonable value, perhaps thirty minutes.

Failed secondary logon attempts also trigger lockout. The secondary failures come when NT attempts to match the remote client's account to one of its own of the same name and password.

☞ One obscure side effect is that there are cases where, if the two matching accounts have different passwords, a user can lock a remote account without actually (mis-) typing the password at all. For example, suppose you attempt to expand another workstation in the Network Neighborhood of a browsing window and that workstation has a matching account with a different password. This triggers several (usually three) remote logon attempts. These "expansion failures" count toward lockout.

Lockout and the Local Administrator Account

As a precaution, NT never locks the Administrator local account. However, this also leaves this critical account unprotected by lockout. Your best defense is to give this account a long, random password and then only use it in exceptional cases. Day-to-day administration can be done from administrative accounts (like JJones-Admin) with membership in the local Administrators groups, which are subject to lockout protection. You should almost always deny RAS access capabilities to the Administrator account. For added protection, you can remove the Right to "access this computer from the network" from the Administrator account (this also denies RAS access), which helps thwart password guessing except from the keyboard. (The notable exception is that the Internet Information Server allows remote access to accounts denied this Right.)

Your Password Policy

Some common issues in developing your password policy are discussed in the following pages.

User versus Administrator Defined

Weak passwords come from untrained or obstinate users. While NT's controls do all they reasonably can, a determined user can partially circumvent the intent of any rule. For example, if you require a long password, they can write them down or choose "aaaaaaaaaaaaaa." If you require eight-deep uniqueness, they'll keep a list or cycle a counter at the end of their password, like "jjones06." You may have worked on systems that prohibited simplistic passwords, like dictionary words. While these prevent naive users from picking something bad, they're trivial to thwart. NT has no such password screeners.

If you don't trust certain users, the only way to ensure good passwords is to assign them yourself. Then your only worry is that the users might write one down. You could work with each user to select a new password. Perhaps they make it up and you approve it. Let them try it out several times in your presence. With confidence, maybe they won't jot it down after you leave the room.

On the flip side, some sites decry the case where an administrator knows other users' passwords. However, full administrators can do pretty much anything undetected. A user that thinks they can keep a determined and clever administrator out of their files is mistaken. The decision as to who changes passwords is yours. Weigh it carefully.

"Loaned" Passwords

People should not loan their passwords to others. This sounds obvious, but unfortunately it's often inevitable. Your job is to minimize it and to do that you must know where it's being done. Your best bet is to impress strongly on your users not to loan their passwords, but to tell you if, in rare cases, they must. Figure out why they did it and fix the problem. If you penalize them for loaning their password when they deem they have no other choice, they won't tell you and you can't fix the underlying problem.

A Password's "Space"

NT protects passwords carefully, so your main worry is that one user might guess another's password by attempting to log on as the user or change the user's old password. How likely is this? The length of the password and the rate at which it can be guessed determine the probability it can be guessed in a certain time frame. The strength of a given password selection technique depends first on the total number of combinations it can generate, or its "space." For example, six-character passwords chosen at random from lowercase alphabetic characters can produce 26^6 unique combinations, or about 300 million. The chances of guessing that in even a few hundred tries is probably less than the computer melting into a heap of slag as you try. But suppose you select six-character pronounceable passwords, like "latpit" or "yiptop." This scheme's space is only $(21^3) \times (5^2)$, or about 230,000. Still not bad.

The strength of a password scheme also depends on characteristics that can make it easier to guess. The phrase scheme we proposed to regular users in Chapter 3, Your Working Environment, concatenates the first three letters of the words in a four-word phrase to produce a twelve-character password. If the twelve characters are random, the space is astronomical. (Pun intended.) But they're not random. The average user might select from only a vocabulary of, say roughly one thousand words, so an alphabet of one thousand items taken four at a time yields 10^7, or ten million. Still pretty strong, and easy to remember! But we're not done yet. Users probably tend to choose easy words like "big" or standard colors like "red," and this makes the phrase and therefore its password easier to guess and reduces their effective space. We could go further, but just remember that "raw space" calculations alone are not the yardstick by which to measure a password's strength.

Password Space and Guessing Frequency

The size of a password's space and your lockout strategy are intertwined. Ultimately, your quantitative concern should be the probability that a penetrator, guessing as fast as lockout allows, can guess a target password in a given time period. For example, your site policy may be a one-in-one thousand chance in one hour of guessing. Suppose lockout limits the attempt rate to ten guesses an hour. This means a penetrator can get ten guesses in your one-hour target period. Therefore, the password's space should be at least ten thousand.

Strong Passwords for Powerful Users

Accounts with a lot of power, usually administrators, need stronger passwords. Remember that the Administrator account is not protected by password lockout. Fortunately, these people are more trustworthy and can select strong passwords.

Duplicate Passwords and the Trusted Path

When you set up multiple local accounts for the same user, they can have different passwords. Should they? Security discourages using the same passwords on different workstations, but the main risk is when one workstation is much less secure than the others. If all are equally secure, and we should include physical security in this case, identical passwords are not so bad.

The problem with different passwords in local accounts is that when NT asks the user for the password during secondary logon, it does not use the Trusted Path. In a strong Trusted Path implementation the system never asks for something like a password except through the Trusted Path. Fortunately, in NT the choice is yours and the user's. If you deem this isolated lack of Trusted Path a danger, keep the passwords the same.

Forcing a Password Change

It's a good idea to make users change their password when you extend their capabilities, for example if you add them to Operator groups or even new, regular User groups. In this way, others who knew the old password don't gain the new capabilities.

Internal Password Threats

Our discussion has focused on the threat of one person guessing another's password or finding it written down. Internal attacks also threaten passwords. For example, NT sends encrypted passwords across the network. Penetrators connected to the network might capture the encrypted password and apply cryptanalysis techniques to recover the password. Obsessively long passwords, for example fourteen-character random sequences like "2Fkw&dTh9*jeC!" greatly reduce this threat.

The question is: Should you force such passwords to counter such internal attacks? First, note that NT itself does not encrypt data on the network (except passwords), so network taps can do considerable damage without your password. Second, it's the system's responsibility to use sufficiently strong techniques to protect your password both on the system and in transit, where "system" includes Windows NT and any security hardware or software add-ons. The obvious downside to such long passwords is that they will be written down. In the end, it depends on whether you consider network taps or written passwords a greater threat, and this depends on factors like the physical accessibility of your network and your workplace.

> **Example**: Your company inhabits a single building with an all-NT network that you're confident no one can "tap into." You scrupulously avoid untrusted programs that might harbor malicious code. The physical environment is quite open within the building and the company has a strong policy that employees not know each other's password. In this case, written passwords are the greater threat. Passwords that are relatively short and easily remembered are appropriate.

> **Example**: An employee working at home uses the Internet to connect to your company NT network. You trust this employee to keep written home passwords well hidden. Random, fourteen-character passwords are in order.

> **Counterpoint:** Implicit in this scenario is that you don't trust the Internet. (With good cause!) Even with these long passwords, all the employee's data traffic can

be freely viewed by elements on the Internet. You might therefore decide to incorporate an add-on product that encrypts data transported on the Internet. In this case, the encrypted passwords are now quite safe on the network and the need for obsessive password space has vanished.

Consider the technique of using the first letters of a five-word phrase, like "dtlsg" for "Dump Truck Lost Smelly Garbage." What is its space and are there characteristics that could help someone guessing? [**120**]

Make up two widely different password schemes of roughly the same "first-glance" strength. Then estimate the password space of each and compare them.

Some applications may keep their own passwords. We caution users not to use an NT account password for these applications. Why? [**121**]

Our discussion may lead to a conclusion that all administrators eventually rediscover:

You can lead a user to the trough of strong passwords, but you can't make them drink. Most of NT's security rests on passwords, and passwords rest on human nature. Work with, not against, that nature.

The Mechanics of Managing Accounts

We've already learned the basics of changing an account. Now we present some of the higher level techniques.

Template Accounts

Setting up a dummy account to use as a template is particularly handy. Set all its parameters except the password and disable it so no one can log on to it. When you want to create a new account with approximately the same parameters, highlight the name of the template account and select *User→ Copy*. NT gives you a normal window for a new account, as shown at the top of the next page.

The fields on this window that don't normally replicate to new accounts are cleared, and some of the check boxes are set or reset for convenience. However, all the parameters set by the buttons along the bottom remain unchanged from the template. Unless you give the new account a password, it has the "blank" password and is set up so the user must change the password at first logon.

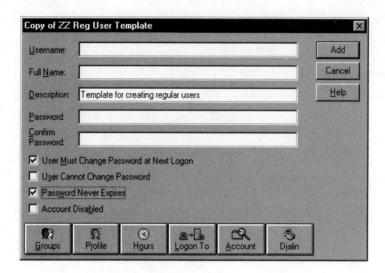

User Manager: User→ Copy

Hint: NT lists templates among real users when people add users to ACLs. You might want to start templates names with something like "ZZ" to put them at the end of the list where they are least in the way.

Creating an account template: Make a template for "normal" users. Carefully consider all its parameters. Then use it to create two new accounts. You need not leave the Template window to create the second account. Give one a password. Note which boxes are automatically checked.

☞When you create a new account *without* a template, User Manager automatically adds the account to Users or Domain Users. It does not do this when you use a template account.

Setting up the Home Directory

Most accounts have a working directory for their activities, often in the standard NT USERS directory. You need to create the directory yourself and set up its initial ACL. Create an entry giving the new owner "Full Control" and add any other site-standard entries. In short, set up the ACL in the "proper" manner for your system so that the new owner need not change it. Cite the home directory in the Profile window. When the new owner first logs on, they should take ownership of the directory and, if they want, adjust its ACL.

Hint: Give the user **RXO** permissions only. This means they can't create items until they take ownership and set up the home directory's ACL properly. Otherwise, they might forget to take ownership.

Setting up new users: Set up home directories for these two new accounts in the USERS directory. Set their ACLs properly. Define each account's home directory using the **Profile** button using a full path name, like E:\USERS\JJones. Log on as each of them. (Do you have to select a new password?) As the new user, take ownership of the directory and see if you should change its ACL.

Changing Multiple Accounts

You can change several accounts at once, setting some properties in each while leaving other properties different. For example, you may want to change the logon hours of a whole set of accounts. There are two ways to select multiple accounts. From the User Manager's main window, select more than one account using any standard technique (for example, using the Shift or Ctrl keys as you select accounts with your mouse). You can also use the Select User window to select or deselect whole groups of users:

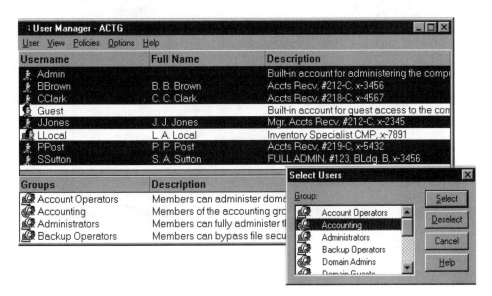

User Manager: User→ Select Users...

When you select a group from this window, its members are either added to ones already selected in (**Select**) or removed from (**Deselect**) the main User Manager window (in the background in this figure). Of course, when you return to the main window, you can use the Control key and your mouse to further select or deselect accounts. Note that group membership in this case is only *direct* membership. For example, if you select a local group, members of any global groups in that local group are not selected or deselected.

Hint: You often want to clear all selected accounts before calling up *Select Users*. Simply select any one of the *groups* on the main window.

Hint: The best way to select all users is by selecting the Users group, but beware that this may select template accounts also.

Selecting multiple accounts: Exercise all the points we just discussed, but there's no need to do anything other than select accounts for now.

After you select multiple groups, *User→ Properties...* calls up an account window that is a little different from a single account:

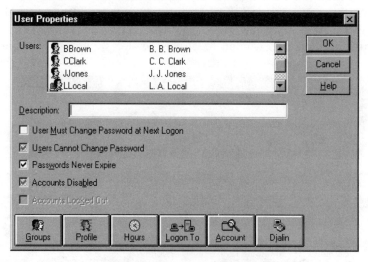

Property Window for Multiple Accounts (User Manager: User→ Properties...)

This window omits fields that make no sense to change for multiple accounts at once, like the user's real name and password. Check boxes are either:

☐ Item is not selected in all accounts
▨ Item is selected in some but not all accounts
☑ Item is selected in all accounts

You can cycle through these options by repeatedly clicking the box. If after doing so you leave it gray, the accounts are not changed in regard to that item. The Group

Memberships window (from the **Groups** button) is analogous to the form for a single account, but works a bit differently.

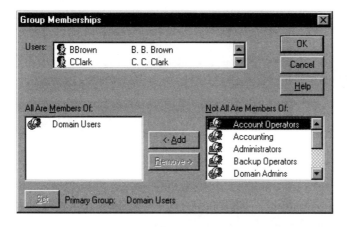

Setting Groups for Multiple Accounts (User Manager: User→ Properties...→ {Groups})

The left list shows groups to which all belong, the right list shows all other groups (of which some of the accounts may be direct members). If you **Remove** a group from the left list, all of the accounts are removed from that group. If you **Add** a group to the left list, all accounts are added to that group. The rest of the button windows are straightforward, but there's a few small exceptions we explore in the following exercise:

Changing multiple accounts: Create three identical accounts from one of your templates. Give the middle one a completely different set of parameters. Explore changing all the parameters to all three at once, noting what happens when there are differences.

Disabling, Renaming, and Deleting

You can disable an account by setting the *Account Disabled* field on its main window. This prevents future logons, although it does not forcibly log off the user. If you want to make doubly sure an account can't be used, give it a random password.

Like groups, you can delete accounts, which implicitly removes them from all ACLs and groups. Select one or more accounts then use *User→ Delete*. Once deleted you can't resurrect the account, even though you can create a new one with the same name. NT stores accounts internally as a special numeric ID. It's the ID that's kept, for example, inside an ACL, not the name. When NT shows you an ACL, it just fetches the current name for the ID.

NT ensures that no two accounts you ever create have the same ID. If you delete an account, then create another of the same name, they have different IDs. Even though they have the same name, they are not the same account in that the new account does not automatically appear in ACLs that held the old one.

You can easily rename an account with *User→ Rename....* Its name in each ACL in which it's used automatically changes and from that point on people see the new name in various NT lists of accounts (although it may take some remote workstations a little while to catch up).

> Can you guess how this "automatic change" takes place? [**122**]

Similarly, NT's Backup program stores the internal IDs, so it always restores ACLs with the latest names. However, if an ID on a backup tape has been deleted from the system, NT restores the ACL without that entry.

> **Deleting accounts**: Delete all the accounts you just created. Check the ACLs of the two home directories you've set up. What's there? [**123**] Delete these directories.

Managing Accounts in Other Domains

Only accounts in the local Administrators or Server Operators groups get the full power of User Manager. You can use User Manager to create or maintain domain accounts in any other domain that you can secondarily log on to as an administrator. Use *User→ Select Domain* to make your choice.

Wizards

NT has a few wizards that let you create new groups and accounts. They offer little additional functionality and are of little use to most seasoned administrators. However, you can check them out on the Wizard Manager, WIZMGR.EXE.

The Guest Account

There's a built-in account named Guest that you can't delete. It's a local account on NT Workstation and a global account on NT Server. During secondary logons, if the Guest password is blank, NT automatically logs you in to the Guest account if it can't find the account name you present. However, if the Guest password is not blank you still have to be logged in as Guest.

NT does not treat Guest specially during primary logon. That is, it does not substitute Guest when it can't find the account you request. If you log on to Guest, you must present its current password.

It's common to assign Guest the null password, but you don't have to. If you assign it a password, you can control who can use the account through the distribution of its password. The major reservation about Guest is that it's antithetical to authentication where NT always "knows" the individual who is using the system. Guest circumvents this.

If you have a guest on your system, it's easy enough to give them their own personal account. Disable the Guest account unless you have a good reason to use it, for example networking programs that use it, and are willing to accept its lack of authentication. You may also want to remove it from the Users group.

The Guests *group* is a little different. It does not suffer from a lack of authentication since the account using it is properly authenticated. You may well use the Guests group. For example, you might give your guest's new personal account membership in Guests.

Make sure your users understand your policy for the Guest account and Guests group.

Should you let someone logged on as Guest change the password? [124]

Summary

❖ The account has many security parameters, but they're straightforward and easy to manage.

❖ Learn multiple group selection and use template accounts. They're great time savers.

❖ Give considerable thought to your site's password technique and, most importantly, teach your users whatever you decide.

❖ For the best security, disable the Guest account.

Quick Check:

✓ If you delete an account then recreate it, have you restored it? For example, does the new account own the old account's files? [125]

✓ What is a password's "space?" Why is a password's strength related to its space, the locking threshold, and reset period?

> **Deleting a Primary group**: Add one of your practice accounts to the global group you created earlier. Make this group the account's Primary group. Now try to delete this group from User Manager's main window. (Select the group and try *User→ Delete*.) You can't.

The Rights Policy

Windows NT has a set of user attributes called Rights. On each workstation, the administrator allocates each Right to accounts or groups allowed on that workstation. When the account is active on the workstation, either by primary or secondary logon, it gets the special capabilities of each Right it has been granted, but only with respect to its actions on that workstation.

☞ Rights are not inherent in an account. For example, Rights associated with a domain account on the domain controller have no effect for that account when used on a workstation in that domain controller. Instead, the Rights policy on that workstation apply to the account's activities on the workstation.

Most Rights bestow administrative capabilities. Some are benign and others quite sensitive. Many Rights are used almost exclusively by NT's system software and while you can grant them to users, you seldom should.

During primary or secondary logon, Rights assigned to that account on the workstation can empower all programs in that logon session. All the programs you run inherit your account's Rights, just like they inherit your identity and group memberships. A malicious program may be able to use your Rights behind your back. You manage a workstation's Rights Policy with User Manager, shown on the top of the next page.

> **Exploring Rights**: Call up this window and peruse the Rights. Select the *Show Advanced…* option and peruse the advanced Rights. The only difference between regular and advanced Rights is that the advanced Rights are less frequently assigned. Click the **Help** button then *User Rights*, which describes the more common Rights. Review them.

NT has a standard policy for allocating Rights to certain administrative groups that's set when you install NT. This policy grants Rights to certain administrative or other groups, and Rights distribution is an inherent part of its local/global group strategy.

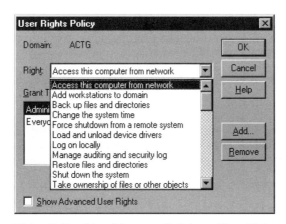

The Rights Policy (User Manager: Policies→ User Rights...)

☞If you want to give an account a certain Right, first consider adding the account to a group that has the Right in NT's standard policy (but be mindful of other Rights this gives the user).

The obvious problem with changing NT's standard policy is that you end up with a unique Rights Policy on each workstation. This is not so bad if it's on only a few servers, but can quickly get out of hand. The following are a few changes you may wish to consider, with NT's standard policy indicated in parentheses.

Bypass Traverse Checking

(Everyone) This Right lets a user enter any directory even when the ACL would seem to preclude access. Because this Right alone doesn't let you read the directory's contents, it's only useful for passing through directories to which you have no access on your way to other directories to which you do. If you give everyone this Right, then closing a directory with an ACL does not "close" its whole tree. If users of the tree carelessly leave ACLs too loose, unintended users can access those portions of the tree.

☞We recommend you disable this Right for all but administrative groups and the system user.

Access This Computer from Network

(Everyone) This Right enables secondary logon, and we know that if you can't secondarily log on to a server, you can't access its services.

Example: A workstation in a tightly protected room is to hold highly sensitive military information. You want a strong assurance that it's inaccessible from elsewhere on the network. You can simply remove all the accounts from this Right on this workstation. (Note that users logged onto this workstation may still be able to access other workstations on the network. Of course if you want to further prevent this you can simply unplug the workstation from the network!) A workstation's Rights Policy is kept on the workstation itself and is therefore administered only from within the room. However if you deny administrators remote access, you must administer the workstation locally, which may or may not be what you want.

Log on Locally

(NT Workstation: Everyone; NT Server: Full administrators and operators.) This Right lets an account primarily log on to the workstation.

Example: A law office has a strong policy that each partner's personal workstation may be logged on to only by that partner and a few administrators. The Rights Policy easily enforces this.

Example: You decide the easy way to determine who can log on to each workstation is to create two local groups named Local Logons and Remote Logons, applying each of our two logon rights Right to the corresponding group.

Normally we avoid changing NT's standard policy because Rights are kept on each workstation and we don't like to maintain lots of tables on different workstations. This example is not so bad because you change it only when you install a workstation. It's easy to change its Rights Policy while you're there.

> Recall that each account can have a list of workstations where it can primarily log on. You can also limit an account's logon to a workstation by removing its local logon Right. Discuss the advantages of each. [126]

☞The Rights to log on locally and from the network fundamentally determine who can use a workstation. Work them into your overall access strategy.

These Rights work hand in hand with the list of allowed workstations in each account. See "Mechanics of Managing Accounts," discussed earlier.

Shut Down the System

(NT Workstation: Everyone; NT Server: Full administrators and operators.) This Right lets a user shut down the workstation. The main danger of shutting down the system is that you interrupt remote users. While it's operationally essential to restrict this on servers, it has little security relevance. You might commonly let everyone shut down workstations that have no significant service responsibilities.

Example: You're in an area where storms cause frequent power outages. You create a global group Shut Downers and grant the shut down Right to this group on each workstation without an uninterruptable power supply.

A Rights Policy is analogous to a local account in that they both name other groups and accounts, and both are allowed only on the workstation on which they are defined.

> The law office wants a few specified users to be able to shut down each workstation, including its primary user and perhaps their secretary or officemate. How should they do this? [127]
>
> You set up a template account with which you associate certain Rights. When you create new accounts from this template, do they get those Rights? [128]

☞ Except as we noted earlier, don't change NT's initial Rights Policy unless you know what you're doing. You can upset some apple carts. If you do make changes, try to limit the granting of Rights to groups (preferably NT's built-in groups) rather than accounts.

Administrative Access

We've talked about administration in bits 'n pieces. NT has a simple strategy for how it subdivides, controls, and distributes administrative capabilities across the network. While you can customize NT's conventions, it's best to change them little or not at all until you feel comfortable with the system. In this section we show you its baseline policy and suggest a few ways to extend it.

In the NT metaphor, the system is not administered through generic account names, but rather through personal accounts that hold administrative capabilities. An account gains administrative powers on a particular workstation, typically through membership in certain local groups. These groups gain some of their power by their identity and the rest by having certain Rights. Stated otherwise, some of NT's administrative programs require you to be in a certain group, regardless of your Rights, while others require you to have a certain Right, which you usually gain through your group memberships.

Full Administrators

Members of the local Administrators group, which we call "full administrators," are all powerful on that workstation. NT has a simple scheme for these administrators:

❖ The **Domain Admins** global group holds the accounts of full administrators for the domain.

❖ Each workstation in the domain, including its domain controllers, includes the Domain Admins group in its local **Administrators** group.

❖ Each workstation (including controllers) grants members of the Administrators group full administrative power on that workstation, partly by assigning it many Rights and partly by its identity.

(This is the same scheme we illustrated earlier for Domain Users and local Users groups.) The end result is that you give an account complete administrative control throughout a domain by placing it in the Domain Admins global group, and control over a single workstation by placing it in the local Administrators group on the workstation.

Each workstation has a local account named Administrator that's a member of the Administrators local group. You can't delete this account or remove it from this group. Hence, it's always a full administrator. As always, if you give its password to more than one person, you loose accountability. You have three basic choices as to how you set full administrative accounts.

Small, Single-Administrator Site

Small sites might make do with a single administrator for all workstations and domains. This is the only person who knows the password to the Administrator account. You might want to rename the account to something that reflects the user's name, like JJones-Admin, or perhaps just rely on the full name in the account to be "J. J. Jones, full admin."

> **Example**: A small, six-person accounting office has only one administrator with complete control over all systems. They keep the single Administrator account with full name to match that administrator. A few senior partners are told the password in the rare event this administrator is not available.

If your site has a few administrators, they could all use this single account, but in this case it's better to go on to personal administrative accounts, as follows.

Larger, Multiadministrator Sites

For sites with more than one full administrator, it's better to give each administrator a personal administrative account with a name that reflects the user's name and the fact that they use this account in their role as administrator, for example JJones-Admin. Place this account either in the Domain Admins group or directly in the local Administrators group itself.

You can leave the Administrator account as a generic, all-powerful account used for rare, emergency cases. Only a few administrators could know its password and be trusted to use it only when their own accounts do not suffice. Because every workstation in the network has this account, if you keep its name and password the same on them all, you can use it to administer any workstation from any other, at least to the extent a workstation can be administered remotely.

☞ We recommend writing down the passwords to the Administrator accounts (horror of horrors!) and locking them in a nice, thick safe. Secure in the fact that you can always recover from even forgotten administrative passwords, you'll choose better account passwords and be less prone to write them down.

Example: A domain, DOM-A, of moderate size has yourself and two other full administrators. You give each an administrative account: JJones-Admin, BBrown-Admin, and CClark-Admin. These three comprise the Domain Admins group, which is included in the Administrators local group on each workstation, including the domain controllers. The Administrator account on each workstation has a single password known only by you, the senior of the three administrators, for use in rare circumstances.

Example: You promote a new administrator with domain account DOM-A\KKorn-Admin, but to control only the six workstations in a single office in DOM-A. You could then place KKorn-Admin in the local Administrators group of these workstations.

Suppose you had two such limited administrators for these 6 workstations. Would you set this up differently? [**129**]

Example: There is a second domain, DOM-B, that trusts DOM-A. You and your team of three are to become full administrators on all workstations in both domains. How could you do this? [**130**]

Use full administrative accounts only for bonafide administrative activities. If you perform day-to-day nonadministrative tasks, do them under a separate nonadministrative account.

There are three reasons for this. First, you carry a lot of power as administrator. During your day-to-day activities you are perhaps not concentrating on administration, and as full administrator your accidents can have far-reaching effects. Second, there's always a danger that you might accidentally run a malicious program. This danger is greater during day-to-day nonadministrative activities. This advice is less important for Power Users, but is as strong for Operators as it is for full administrators. Third, objects that members of this group create are owned by the group, which usually is not what you want in your day-to-day activities.

Recall that the local Administrator account is unprotected by Account Lockout, and this is a good reason to give it a long, random password and use it infrequently. Instead, use personalized administrator accounts (like JJones-Admin) that are members of the local Administrators group. (See "The Account Policy" earlier in this chapter.)

You have two domains that trust each other and you want the members of both Domain Admins groups to be administrators for all workstations in both domains. How do you set this up? [131]

How would you let a particular administrative account in another domain that your domain *does not* trust be one of your controller's full administrators? [132]

Consider our three example domains: SALES, ACTG, and MANUF. ACTG trusts SALES and MANUF trusts SALES and ACTG. Where is the best place to define users who are to administer all three domains? [133]

A site has a master domain model where all "subject" domains trust a single master domain named MAST. MAST keeps all the accounts. A few people are to be full administrators in all domains, and selected ones in each of the subject domains. How would you set this up? [134]

Here's a tough one. Consider our two domain controllers in ACTG and MANUF, where MANUF trusts ACTG but not vice versa. The Administrator account on each system has the same password. Neither Administrator account is a member of the other domain's Administrators or Domain Admins groups. The administrator on MANUF uses User Manager to select the ACTG domain and changes some user accounts there. However, NT disallows the administrator on ACTG who attempts similarly to change MANUF accounts. Why? [135]

These exercises show you the value of a master domain that all others trust for central, networkwide administration. All workstations on the network recognize accounts and global groups from this master domain and can easily include them in their local administrative groups.

Operators

There are several kinds of operators for domain controllers. Each has a part of the full administrator's powers that relate to certain server operations. The domain controller grants an operator capabilities by virtue of being in one of the local operator's groups.

Account Operators

These operators create and manage the domain accounts and groups through User Manager and add workstations to their domain. However, they can't alter the capabilities of full administrators or other operators. How does NT enforce this? Simple. It prevents them from changing these local groups! Account Operators also can't change User Manager policies: account, Rights, audit, and trust relationships.

Server Operators

Server Operators have control of the domain controller's day-to-day operations except it's hard-core security. For example, they can create network share directories as well as shut down the server, change the time, and format its disks. They can also do most of what Backup and Print Operators can do.

Backup Operators

Backup Operators do backups and restores. They have no security-relevant duties other than observing commonsense backup procedures. See "Backups and Replication" in Chapter 4, ACLs.

Print Operators

These operators install printers and control access to printers by making them available on the network.

NT Workstation has only the Backup Operators local group. There's no global group for these operators since they work only on domain controllers.

There's a clear separation of duty here. Account Operators are the only ones with significant security duties, but need know nothing about day-to-day server operations, like installing new devices or printers. Hence, you can make someone an Account Operator with only security training. The other operators have little security relevance, but may need a lot of training in routine server operations.

You could argue that since Backup Operators, for example, have access to backup tapes they can expose them and are therefore security risks, and you'd be right. However, they don't really require any security training other than to keep the tapes locked up, and you need trust them only to not peruse or alter the tapes maliciously.

Backup operators can restore to FAT volumes, thereby circumventing ACLs. One handy suggestion that helps prevent this is to give Backup Operators only the right to backup—not to restore. (You might give only selected accounts the right to restore.) Of course, with a fair amount of enterprise one can write special programs to read backup tapes directly. However, this is not easily done. The bottom line is that anyone who possesses backup tapes can read them if they're determined.

From a security perspective, you must trust all these operators to some degree, but they have to be clever and work hard to cause any real security damage. They generally don't have the "Take Ownership" Right and therefore can't alter arbitrary ACLs. Full administrators control each of these operators, and those operators cannot change which users gain which administrative powers.

Full administrators should have special accounts for their administrative duties, like JJones-Admin, and a different account for day-to-day nonadministrative activities. However, this is a little less important for operators, because their security powers are limited. Perhaps it's a good idea for Account and Server Operators.

You can, of course, place an account in several of these groups. Small NT networks may not even use these accounts, since full administrators can do all their tasks. However, they're a powerful subdivision of authority in larger environments.

Do you suppose you can alter the capabilities that NT grants these groups? If so, who can do it? [136]

How would you let a particular administrative domain account in another domain that your domain trusts be one of your controller's Server Operators? [137]

Remembering that Print Operators is a *local* group, how would you let Print Operators in another domain administer the printers on your domain controller? [138]

How would you set up a group of users to be Account Operators on all the controllers in SALES, ACTG, and MANUF? [139]

Account Operator: Log on to an account that's an Account Operator but not a full administrator.

❖ Create then delete a regular account.

❖ Change some other user's password.

❖ Try to change the Administrator account.

❖ Try to make a regular user each type of operator by placing them in the appropriate group. Try the same with your own account.

Power Users

Power Users are implemented only on NT Workstations and NT servers that are not domain controllers as members of the Power Users local group. Mainly they accommodate the principal user of a personal workstation, giving them modest administrative capabilities, like opening network share directories to the network, and creating and managing local accounts. They don't have access to the User Manager's *Policies* menu.

How would you grant a set of domain accounts Power User capabilities on all the workstations of a domain? [**140**]

How would you let members of a Power Users group on a workstation in another domain be a Power User on one of the workstations in your domain? (Remember that the Power Users group exists only on NT Workstation—not domain controllers.) [**141**]

Can a Power User subvert your site's security much more than regular users? [**142**]

Cross-Domain Administration

Some NT security applications let you manage and administer other workstations; for example, Server Manager, User Manager for Domains, and Event Manager. They present browsing windows that make it easy to select a domain. The remote domain need not have any domain trust relationship with yours as long as . . .

☞The account by which you are represented on the remote workstation (determined during secondary logon there) must be an administrative account of sufficient power on that remote workstation.

Recall there are two cases here, one where your client account is allowed and visible on the remote workstation, and the other where it is not and has been matched to one of the same name.

Hint: You can copy NT Server's User Manager for Domains onto an NT Workstation and use it from there to manage domains. There are also tools that let you manage domains from Windows 95 or Windows for Workgroups, but because they are inherently less secure than Windows NT this is not necessarily a good idea.

Summary

NT has a full range of built-in, administrative roles. You can alter the power of some of these, but try not to do so at first and even then only when a need genuinely arises.

❖ Full administrators grant specific accounts administrative capability by including them in local groups like Administrators, Server Operators, and Power Users or, rarely, by directly assigning the account Rights on particular workstations.

❖ These administrative groups gain their power partly by their access to certain ACLs and partly by holding certain Rights.

❖ Full administrators are all powerful. The various operators and Power Users are limited and can't extend their own capabilities, and of these only Account Operators and Power Users have any significant security power.

❖ The key to cross-domain administration is that the account under which you are secondarily logged on to on the remote workstation gains its capabilities from its membership in that workstation's local groups.

Quick Check:

✓ An administrator decides to keep things simple by creating a Local Acct Operators account with membership in the Account Operators group then giving its password to the several local account operators. Is this proper procedure? [143]

✓ Can a Server Operator make one of their friends a Server Operator? Can an Account Operator make one of their friends an Account Operator? [144]

✓ Should you give the Administrator account the same password on all workstations? [145]

Chapter 8

Security Auditing

Auditing is a part of almost all security systems. It can serve to double-check on other features, like access control and logon, and to investigate the extent of system penetrations. Windows NT has a flexible and comprehensive security auditing system fully integrated into its other administrative logs. The extent to which audit protects your site is something only you can decide, and you can expect to develop and hone your strategy for months. Perhaps your greatest concern is the prodigious amount of data full auditing can generate and your ability to separate the significant events from the innocuous.

In This Chapter We Describe

➡ Which "events" NT can audit and how they're grouped into event "categories"

➡ How to tell NT which categories to save in the security log

➡ Setting up the audit controls for individual files and directories

➡ How to scan and manage the security log, and interpret its events

➡ Several practical auditing scenarios

➡ How to save your security logs for posterity

We defer auditing of printers and the Registry to Chapter 10, Subsystems and Other Security Features.

> You can do the on-line exercises on either NT Server or Workstation. Unless we tell you differently, we recommend you do all these exercises as a full administrator.

The Mechanics of Auditing

In this section we introduce the simple mechanics of managing the audit system. Various modules of NT, called **sources**, write the **events** the administrator selects beforehand to an audit trail called the **security log**. An event can describe a high-level occurrence, like someone logging on, or low level, like a program opening a file. Some events are system related, like assigning a "handle" and are of use only to knowledgeable auditors, or, more importantly, are automated audit analysis tools that we hope to see in the future. Some events inherently relate to others. For example, a logoff relates to its session's previous logon. There are seven event **categories** and you specify which are to be saved. Events that record access to files and other objects are additionally subjected to **audit control information** on the object to see if the event should be saved.

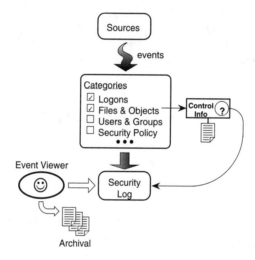

Administrators can view and manage the security log using **Event Viewer**. They can print the security log in a number of different formats, some suitable for import into data analysis programs, like common database programs. They can also save copies for archival purposes. The security log holds only events that occurred on its own workstation.

Events you choose not to save in the audit log are not saved anywhere. *Do Not Audit* disables auditing but does not deselect the categories.

NT and its programs also produce operational events collected into its system and application logs. These are independent of the security log and NT doesn't consider these part of security auditing. We don't cover them.

Categories

User Manager's Audit Policy gives you the basic control of what NT audits.

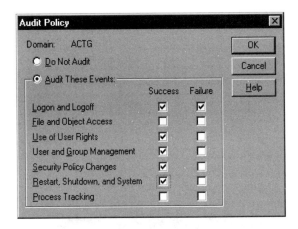

User Manager: Policies→ Audit…

NT groups its security events into seven categories, and characterizes each event as a success or failure. For each category you can choose to audit successes, failures, both, or neither.

Logon and Logoff

This field records both primary and secondary logons and logoffs.

File and Object Access

This field records whenever a program accesses a file, directory, or other objects controlled by ACLs, like printers. (Network share directories have an ACL as a whole. Access through share directories is not audited as such, although access to specific items in the share directories can be audited.) This category is unique because audit control information on each object further determines whether events involving that object are saved. You can think of this category as just enabling or disabling the per-object controls. Disabling does not remove or otherwise alter the controls placed on each object. Hence, you can freely enable and disable without disrupting the per-object controls you carefully construct.

Use of User Rights

This field records when a program attempts some action that requires a Right, like changing the system time.

User and Group Management

This field records adding, changing, or deleting accounts or groups, mainly through the User Manager.

Security Policy Changes

This field records changes in the Auditing and Rights Policies through User Manager's *Policies* menu.

Restart, Shutdown, and System

This includes starting up the workstation and other general events.

Process Tracking

This field records detailed information about programs and other internal attributes NT creates, deletes, and otherwise manages.

Viewing Events

Event Viewer

The Event Viewer lets you view and manage the security log (as well as the system and application logs, which we don't discuss):

Date	Time	Source	Category	Event	User	Computer
8/19/96	2:40:01 PM	Security	Privilege Use	576	Admin	JJONES PC
8/19/96	2:40:01 PM	Security	Logon/Logoff	528	Admin	JJONES PC
8/19/96	2:39:46 PM	Security	Logon/Logoff	538	JJones	JJONES PC
8/19/96	2:39:40 PM	Security	Privilege Use	578	JJones	JJONES PC
8/19/96	2:38:26 PM	Security	Object Access	560	JJones	JJONES PC
8/19/96	2:37:38 PM	Security	Privilege Use	576	JJones	JJONES PC
8/19/96	2:37:38 PM	Security	Logon/Logoff	528	JJones	JJONES PC
8/19/96	2:37:30 PM	Security	Logon/Logoff	538	Admin	JJONES PC
8/19/96	2:37:19 PM	Security	Privilege Use	578	Admin	JJONES PC
8/19/96	2:36:36 PM	Security	Policy Change	612	Admin	JJONES PC

Event Viewer - Security Log on \\JJONES PC — Log View Options Help

Event Viewer Main Window

The "lock" indicates an error or denial, while the "key" indicates a successful event.

Each row represents an event, and each column shows an item common to all events. Most of these columns are self-explanatory or refer to things we've already defined, like "Source" and "Category." The Event (also called the "Event ID") is a number unique to each kind of event. For example, event #529 indicates a failed logon attempt and #528 a successful one. Over time, you may find this the quickest way to identify an event. The "Computer" column is the workstation on which the event occurred. Double-click to expand a particular event.

Events hold a lot of information. The top group of items are those shown on the main Event Viewer window and are common to all events. The *Description* is always present. Although its content varies from event to event, it has many common fields. *Data* is less common and if present holds the data involved in the event.

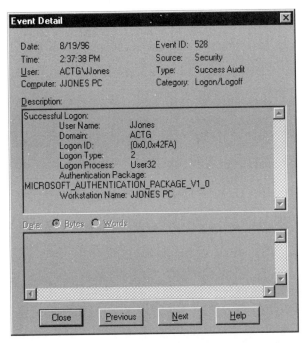

Sample Event for a Successful Logon

☞Use the *View→ Refresh* option (usually the F5 function key) to see events that have happened since you started Event Viewer. You need this frequently during our exercises.

You can instruct Event Manager to show you certain events, called "filtering."

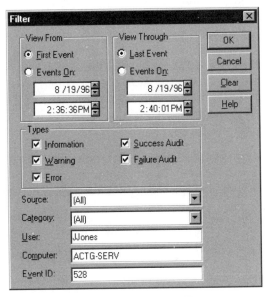

Event Viewer: View→ Filter Events...

(Event Viewer doesn't erase the others, it just hides them.) Each selection criteria corresponds to one of the fields in the top group of the Event Detail window. Each of these except *Type* is also a column in the Event Viewer window. Use *View→ All Events* to disable the filter.

> **Hint**: When you enter fields like *User*, type exactly what appears on the Event Viewer main window. For example, use "JJones" as it appears on the Event Viewer window instead of "ACTG\JJones," which appears on the Event Detail window.

The following exercise introduces you to the viewer options we use during our exercises. We show some advanced options later.

> **Experiment with events**: Use User Manager's *Policies...→ Audit...* options to turn on all categories. Now do some activities to generate audit events: restart the workstation, log on and out (successful and otherwise), make innocuous changes to user accounts, and so forth. Open Event Viewer and peruse the various events. Try several filters. Experiment with all the options on the *View* menu, especially *Find....*

Audit Controls on Objects

Objects that have ACLs also have audit controls that can cause operations on that object to generate security events. These controls are structured like an ACL and some documentation calls them part of the ACL, although we don't because they have nothing to do with access control. We call them **object audit controls**. In this chapter we focus on files and directories, each of which has these controls. An item's Security property sheet lets you set these controls in a manner analogous to setting an ACL.

The following window is for a directory; the window for files is the same except it has no *Replace...* options. You build a list of group and/or account names in the *Name* section of this window. In the *Events to Audit* you denote the operations to be audited for each member of the list. These operations, like "Read," are the Basic Permissions **(RWXDPO)** we discussed in Chapter 4. *Events to Audit* shows only the controls for the member of the list currently selected.

❖ NT puts an event in the log when it finds a match on any one of the accounts or groups in the list, regardless of what any other member of the list might indicate. Specifically, there is no analog to the "No Access" entry in ACLs, which precludes access regardless of the other entries.

❖ Audit controls on files and directories log events only if you enable the *File and Object Access* category.

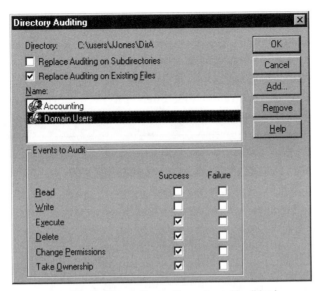

Icon Menu: Properties→ Security→ {Auditing}

❖ NT sets audit controls on a newly created file or directory to those of its parent directory. For other objects, like printers, it initializes the list empty.

❖ CREATOR OWNER works just like in ACLs. Although it does not generate events itself, when an item is created NT adds an entry for the creating account with CREATOR OWNER's audit controls.

❖ Only items on logical disks formatted with NT's native disk format, NTFS, have object audit controls. Even though network share directories have an ACL, there are no audit controls associated with the share itself. In short, you cannot audit disk formats other than NTFS.

❖ Only a full administrator can set the auditing controls on an object.

For a particular object, JJones has "Read" successes and failures, ProjX has "Read and Write" successes, and ProjY has none. JJones is a member of ProjX and ProjY. What audit controls apply to JJones? [146]

Is there any point adding an entry with no RWXDPO events audited? [147]

> **Experimenting with object controls**: Create a directory and experiment with setting up its audit controls. Note especially how the window shows you the **RWXDPO** events for selected *Name* only.
>
> **CREATOR OWNER**: Set up a directory's audit controls for CREATOR OWNER and also your current account, setting different **RWXDPO** events for each. When you create a file in the directory, what audit controls does it get? [148]

Common Auditing Scenarios

In this section we lead you through a series of practical auditing scenarios. For reference, User Manager and the Event Viewer use slightly different names for the categories:

Category Names

In User Manager...	In Event Viewer...
Logon and Logoff	Logon/Logoff
File and Object Access	Object Access
Use of User Rights	Privilege Use
User and Group Management	Account Manager
Security Policy Changes	Policy Change
Process Tracking	Detailed Tracking
Restart, Shutdown, and System	System Event

Note also that the Windows NT Resource Kit (that you can purchase separately) includes an Audit Category Help tool that describes common audit events.

System Startup and Shutdown

Perhaps the most fundamental events you'd like to audit are system startup and shutdown. NT generates System event #512 when it starts up (boots) and #513 when it shuts down.

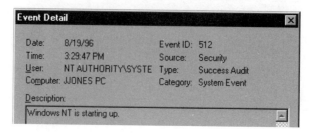

System Startup

> **Auditing system startup**: Clear the security log, set the User Manager's Audit Policy to include only System events, then reboot the system. Examine each event in the security log. Beginning with the system startup (#512), you see the various system services starting.

☞ In case you hadn't noticed, **Privilege** is another name for a "Right."

Summary: Startup and shutdown are important events that you always want to audit.

Logon and Logoff

The category Logon and Logoff includes both primary and secondary logons. Because they are such a fundamental part of NT's security, almost all auditing strategies include logon and logoff, both successful and failed:

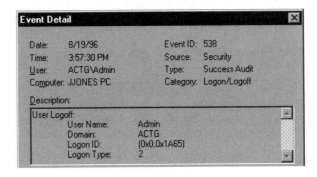

Primary Logon

Primary Logoff

> **Successful logon and logoff**: Clear the security log. Set the Audit Policy to include *only* the Logon category, both success and failure. Log off, log on as a regular user (say, JJones) and immediately log off, and finally log on as administrator. Open the security log.

Locate the logon and logoff events for JJones, #528 and #538, respectively. Their information is straightforward:

❖ The Logon ID is a unique number pair independent of the account but associated with this particular logon session. It's expressed as two hexadecimal numbers like "0x0, 0x2BD9," but you can just think of it as a unique ID. No two logon sessions on a given workstation have the same *Logon ID*—through all time. Use this to pair a logon unambiguously with its corresponding logoff. The *Logon ID* also appears in audit events generated from this logon session so you can associate the event with its user's logon session.

❖ Logon Type 2 is a primary logon. Type 3 is a secondary logon.

❖ The *Domain* is the account's domain or, if it's a local account, the workstation name.

❖ *Authentication Package* is the software module that approved the logon. NT has only one authentication module.

> **Failed logons**: Log off then attempt two unsuccessful logons, one with an undefined account name, and the second with a correct account but incorrect password. Log on as administrator and open the audit log.

This generates two failed logons, #529. These are tagged with the lock icon that denotes failure. The *User* in this case is the logon module, since a valid account was never established. The *User Name* is the incorrect one attempted. Usually, this is an simple spelling error or a correct name not visible from this workstation. As a security precaution, passwords are never displayed, even if incorrect.

> Why is it unwise to show an incorrect password? [149]
>
> The event doesn't tell you whether the failure was a bad account or password. Can you figure it out? [150]
>
> **(OPT) Timed-out logon**: Try a timed-out logon where you use the Trusted Path to log on but don't complete the sequence and NT aborts the procedure. Do you get an audit message? [151]

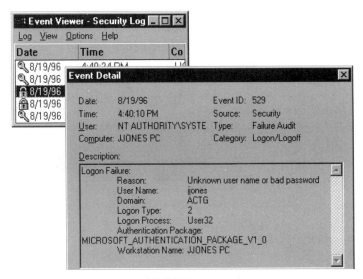

Failed Logon

Now we investigate secondary logon via its most popular use, connecting from another workstation to a network share directory on yours.

Secondary logon: To make this simple, we connect to a network share directory on our own workstation. This triggers the secondary logon as if there were two workstations involved. Clear the security log. Make two new connections to one of your workstation's own share directories. Now close them both and open (or switch back to) the security log. Don't forget to "refresh" the log or you don't see the new events.

Contrary to what you might expect, you see only a single, standard logon event (#528) with Logon Type 3, a secondary logon. This event is generated only on the server. The client generates no events.

Now log off, then log back on and open the security log. You see two logoff events, #528 (see the figure on the top of the next page). The first is a Logon Type 3 and its Logon ID matches the logon event of your first connection. This is the secondary logoff. The second event is a Logon Type 2 and its Logon ID matches the logon event of your primary logon. This is your primary logoff. To summarize:

☞ When you first connect to a server, it establishes a secondary logon session that lasts until you log off your client workstation, which automatically closes the secondary session on the server. The server issues a secondary logon event at the beginning and a log off event at the end of the session, but none for additional connections made during the session. Is it more important to audit successful or failed logons? It depends. Successful logons, and their corresponding logoffs, give you basic useful information about when individuals are working, or remotely accessing a workstation. Successes can also help you spot suspicious individuals using the systems at odd hours or from odd locations. (This might indicate a penetrator using somebody else's account.) Denied logons often show attempts by someone to log on as someone else, although there can be many innocuous denials, like mistyped passwords or denials produced by some networking account-matching scenarios. Unless you find many innocuous denials, we recommend you record both.

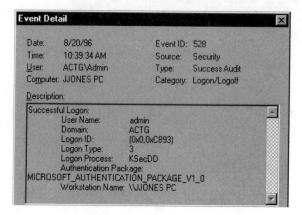

Secondary Logon Event (on Server)

In summary, if you are auditing logons at all, you'll usually want to audit both successful and failed logons. The secret is to learn to match a logon to its logoff, and to match the session's Logon ID to the various other events triggered by the session.

User and Group Management

The events in this subsection comprise the category User and Group Management.

General change to an account: Clear the security log. From User Manager, enable only the User and Group Management category for both success and failure. Make any small change to a user account other than changing its group membership. Exit User Manager and view the security log. Don't forget to refresh.

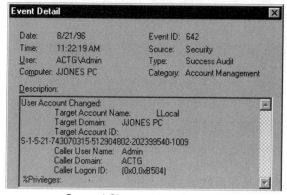

General Change to an Account

The audit record for a general change to an account is #642. This event includes both the account changed (the "target") and the account of the user that made the change (the "caller").

❖ The *Target Account ID* is the unique identity of the account and no two accounts ever have the same Account ID. It's an internal ID that never changes even though the common name for an account, like "JJones," may change. The numbers in this ID don't mean much to most administrators.

❖ The *Caller Logon ID* is the *Logon ID* that NT uniquely associates with your administrative session at logon.

Changing an account's groups: From User Manager, open a test account. Click the **Groups** button. Now add a group to this user's group list. Close the group window. Do this again, only remove the group you just added.

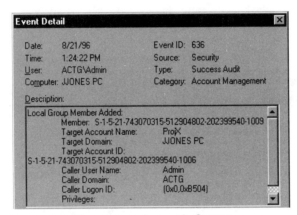

Changing an Account's Groups

NT generates event #636 each time you add an account to a group, and #637 each time you remove it. The *Member* is the *Account ID* of the user added or removed, while the target describes the group itself. The *Target Account ID* (a bit of a misnomer) is a Group ID analogous to an Account ID. You also notice event #642, the generic event for changing a user account that accompanies each of these events.

Changing a group definition: If you're on NT Server, from the main User Manager window, add and remove a user from a *global* group directly from the group list (as opposed to opening an account window).

This interface generates event #632 for adding and #633 for removing a member. The generic event Global Group Changed, #641, accompanies each of these just like #642 does for changes to the account.

> **Changing a local group**: Do the same exercise, but change a local group. What are the event numbers and contents?
> **Creating a group**: Log on as a regular user and create a new local group with a single member. What gets audited? **[152]**

We could continue with variations, but one of our main points is this:

☞ Event IDs are unique not only to an occurrence, like adding a member to a local group, but also to the interface used.

> **Failed change**: Log on as a regular user and try to use User Manager to change an account or group that you can't change. Does NT log an event? **[153]**

As you see, NT doesn't necessarily generate a failure event for each failed attempt to perform some administrative function. Some are so trivially caught, with no damage done, that an event is not warranted.

> **Creating and deleting accounts**: Investigate creating accounts (from a template and otherwise) and deleting them.
> **Account Policy changes**: Make any small change to User Manager's *Policies→ Account* window and observe the event.

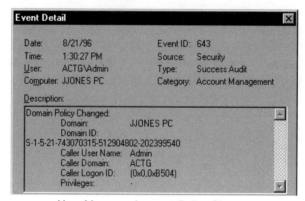

User Manager Account Policy Change

You find the rather bland event #643, Domain Policy Changed, which if you hadn't seen the cause might lead you to surmise a number of other possible sources. Well, not everybody's a poet and not every audit event is precisely stated. All the more reason to study the specific events you intend to audit to understand their nuances. Note also that the "domain" is the workstation name in this case.

When trust relationships or workstation domain members are added (and deleted), NT creates (and deletes) user accounts for those domains whose account names end in "$." These don't appear among listings of regular user accounts. The events are #624 (added) and #630 (deleted). In the following example we allow MANUF to trust our domain:

Changes in Domain Structure

In summary, monitoring the activities of full administrators is not absolute because they can manage the security log. However, Account Operators manage accounts and can't change the security log, so auditing makes a nice double-check on their activities.

Power Users can add accounts to their own workstations and probably should be monitored. A malicious Power User who wants to give system access to someone who shouldn't have it can just lend them the Power User's password or make an account that looks like it's for the Power User's own use. Auditing doesn't help much here. However, auditing can help you detect when Power Users are just using bad judgment.

Finally, regular users can create and manage their own groups. However, creating a group is not particularly security relevant because the creation itself does not give its members access to anything. Adding a member to a group is more important because it may then give the new members access to files they couldn't access before.

The bottom line is that the User and Group Management events are fairly rare and reasonably important.

Audit and Rights Policy Changes

The User Manager's Audit and Rights Policies (*Policies→ Audit ...* and *Policies→ User Rights...*) are important changes to the system and happen rarely in practice. This makes them eminently auditable. Audit these by setting the category Security Policy Changes.

> **Changing the Audit Policy**: From User Manager change the Audit Policy to any distinctive categories you'll remember, but include successful Security Policy Changes. The event that captures this change to the Audit Policy is #612 and shows the new policy.

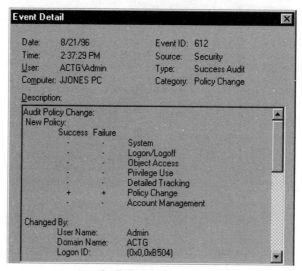

Audit Policy Change

> Why is this a particularly useful event to audit? What are the consequences of turning it off? [154]

Although turning auditing on is audited by event #612, turning it off ("Do Not Audit" in User Manager's Audit Policy window) is not audited. However, if you're auditing as a matter of practice, you don't turn it off.

> **Changing the Rights Policy**: Open User Manager and change the Rights Policy to something innocuous. For example, add our local group ProjX to the Right to change the system time.

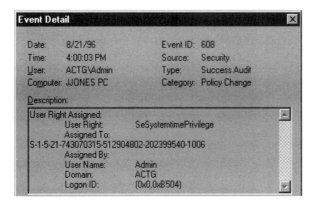

Rights Policy Change

Events #608 and #609 show additions and deletions to the Rights Policy, respectively. The field *Assigned To* is the ID of the user or group added to the Right.

Summary: Audit this category. Changes to the Rights Policy are rare and important, and without Audit Policy changes you can never be sure which events have been saved in the log.

Use of Rights

When you log on, certain Rights may be assigned to your session that give all the programs you run the capabilities associated with those Rights. The Use of Rights category audits whenever a program uses one of these Rights.

Privileges installed during logon: Set the Audit Policy to record only the Use of Rights. Clear the log, log off, log back in, and open the log.

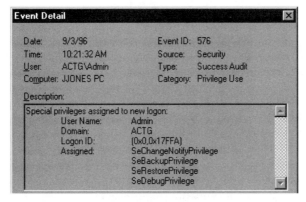

Rights Installed at Logon

Event #576 shows the Rights assigned to a logon session. This doesn't mean they've ever been used, just that they are available for use in the session. This event is likely of little interest. First, you can usually audit when some user actually exercises a Right. (Assigning them to the logon session doesn't mean that user will ever use them.) Second, the Rights assigned to users seldom change and you can audit the change to the Rights Policy. You probably don't care to see them installed at each logon.

> **Use of other Rights**: Now use *Day/Time* on the control panel to change the time. (Change it by only a few seconds.) Examine its event in the security log.

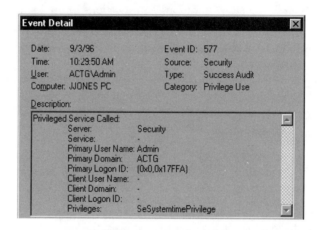

Using the Right to Set the System Time

Event #577 records your use of the "SeSystemtimePrivilege," from which you can infer the system time was changed.

☞ Note the separate sets of primary and client identities. If they're both present, then the client represents the actual user account that initiated the event, and primary is the internal NT module, usually of little interest. If only the primary is present, then it's the actual user account.

Recall from our earlier discussions that shutting down the system is audited via the use of its Right. Use of some of the more benign privileges, like the ability to log on locally or from the network, is not recorded since other events amply record the occurrence. Although NT does record use of the "Take Ownership" Right, you can do this on a per-object basis instead.

In summary, some Rights have potent capabilities. You might like to audit these unless this category produces many innocuous events. Remember that auditing Security Policy Changes shows you when users are assigned new Rights. Perhaps this will suffice in lieu of their actual use.

File and Directory Objects

We saved the most interesting and challenging category until last. When an administrator sets the audit criteria for a directory, it propagates automatically to all newly created items in its tree and can be propagated to existing items, so it's proper to talk about auditing "trees." If the ACLs are set up properly, the items in a tree are fully protected and you may not care to audit them. If the ACLs are not proper, well, audit is a poor substitute for sloppy ACLs. So from this perspective, per-item auditing may seem of little use. However, there are cases where you simply want to record when legitimate users modify an item. It's particularly useful to audit changes to ACLs and ownership. Remember that if you let a user create an item in a particular tree, they can change its ACL and may give inappropriate access to others. What makes this case useful is that it's relatively infrequent.

> Taking ownership does not change the ACL, so it may not be necessary to audit "Take ownership" in addition to changing the ACL. What's your opinion? [155]

> **Setting up**: In the following exercises you need to work as both administrator and a regular user, say, JJones. This means you need to do a lot of logging out then back in. Do everything as administrator unless we instruct you to do it as JJones.
>
> **Auditing changes to the ACL**: Set the Audit Policy to record successful and failed *File and Object Access*. Create a test file and set its auditing to record successful permission changes by Everyone. As JJones, change its ACL.

The security log gains a pair of distinctive events. The important event is #560, the workhorse for changes to files and directories. Its window is shown at the top of the next page.

Examine this event carefully. Note the full name of the file, and that the client fields portray the user. Also note the all-important *Accesses* field, which names WRITE_DAC. DAC stands for Discretionary Access Control and in this case you can think of DAC as another name for an ACL and the audit control information together. This is the same event that denotes when the object's audit control information has changed. The *Operation ID* is a unique code assigned to this operation and has little meaning to most.

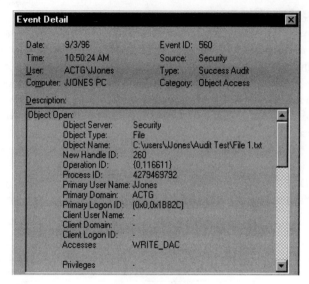

Changing an ACL

Changes to the audit control information: Clear the log if you like, then change the audit control information for a test file. Check the log. (Don't forget to refresh.)

Viewing an ACL: Clear the log if you like, then observe an ACL on your test file without changing it. Use the **OK** button to close the ACL window. Is anything recorded? [156]

Taking ownership: Clear the log if you like. As JJones, take ownership of the file. Check the log. What do you see? [157]

Opening a directory: Create a test directory and set its audit controls to record only successful reads by Everyone. As JJones, expand and contract the directory. Back as administrator, check the security log.

Again #560 logs the opening of the directory and lists "SYNCHRONIZE ReadData (or ListDirectory)" in Accesses.

Successful write: Reset your test directory to no auditing. Create a working text file in the directory and set its auditing to writes by Everyone, both successful and failed. Write to the file, for example, using the MS-DOS "echo xx >> FILE1.TXT" command.

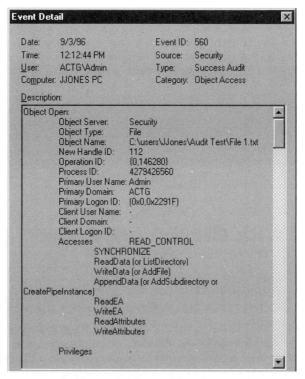

Event Detail   [X]

Date: 9/3/96   Event ID: 560
Time: 12:12:44 PM   Source: Security
User: ACTG\Admin   Type: Success Audit
Computer: JJONES PC   Category: Object Access

Description:

Object Open:
          Object Server: Security
          Object Type: File
          Object Name: C:\users\JJones\Audit Test\File 1.txt
          New Handle ID: 112
          Operation ID: {0,146280}
          Process ID: 4279426560
          Primary User Name: Admin
          Primary Domain: ACTG
          Primary Logon ID: (0x0,0x2291F)
          Client User Name: -
          Client Domain: -
          Client Logon ID: -
          Accesses   READ_CONTROL
                               SYNCHRONIZE
                               ReadData (or ListDirectory)
                               WriteData (or AddFile)
                               AppendData (or AddSubdirectory or
CreatePipeInstance)
                               ReadEA
                               WriteEA
                               ReadAttributes
                               WriteAttributes

          Privileges   -

Writing a File

As before, the important event is #560. *Accesses* shows for what kind of access the program opened the file. However, it doesn't tell you what the program really did to the file. Some programs open a file with more access then they actually need or use. The three key accesses are ReadData, WriteData, and AppendData. Note that the primary information fields describe the user.

Write failure: Set the ACL on your file to allow no access to anyone. As JJones, try to write to the file as before, and of course you fail. Observe the audit event.

Running a program: Suppose you want a record each time someone runs a program. Copy some executable program, like C:\WINDOWS\CLOCK.EXE, into your test directory and make it auditable only for successful execution by anyone. Now run the program from MS-DOS and examine the audit log. Cancel the program and run it again, this time from the desktop.   *(continued)*

> **Side effects**: Set up your test file's ACL to give Everyone "Full Control," and audit successful taking of ownership, only. From the file's property sheet, select the *Security* page and click the **Ownership** button. This produces a Take Ownership audit event even though you didn't try to take ownership. This shows that audit events can be produced by programs without any intent to access by the users themselves.

In summary, in addition to the "side effect" events we just illustrated, you may notice that simple events can produce more events than you expect. Indeed, object auditing can easily get out of hand. Develop your strategy one step at a time.

Working with the Security Log

In this section we present a few strategies for managing the security logs day to day.

Logs on Other Workstations

Event Viewer's *Log→ Select Computer…* lets you manage the security log on any other NT Workstation on which you have full administrative capabilities. Since User Manager for Domains (on NT Server) and an item's Security property sheet let you manage the Audit Policy and per-object audit controls on other workstations as well (at least on NT Servers), you can manage most auditing remotely.

Saving the Log

When you start Event Viewer it shows you the active security log. Use *Log→ Save As…* to save a copy of the active log. You have two basic format choices:

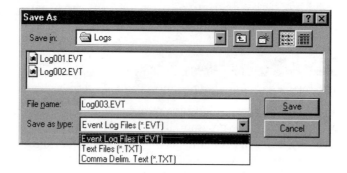

Event log files are files that you can later open from Event Viewer's *Log→ Open* option. Suffix these files with ".EVT." Text Files are files in which the Event Viewer "prints" the security log into a simple text file that you can edit with any text editor. There are two options: one plain and one where the fields are separated by commas.

The latter facilitates reading these files into certain applications for processing, like data base programs.

> **Save the event log**: Save a copy in each of these formats. Now peruse each. Use Notepad to view the text files.

Typically, you save a copy of the log in the appropriate format then clear events from the active log. The copy you saved becomes your permanent record. You can transport it to a central collecting workstation, archive it to tape, and so forth. We recommend you name the file after its workstation and date, for example:

```
ACTG\JJONES PC 95-01-28
```

If you arrange the name carefully like we have, alphabetically sorted file listings are quite handy. Because Event Viewer lets you manage the security log on any workstation, you can collect all the logs from a single workstation, although it's a bit tedious for a large network.

In most cases, event log files save the internal, numeric IDs for accounts and groups, not the actual names. When Event Viewer shows events, it fetches the current name for the IDs. For example, if you rename an account you see the latest name—not the older one. Of course, logs saved as text files don't "adjust" in this manner.

When you use Event Viewer's *Log→ Open* option to view an event log file created on another workstation, it can't show you names of users or groups not visible on your current workstation, like local accounts and groups on the original workstation. Instead, it shows the internal ID.

> **(OPT) Unnamed users**: Create a log file on a workstation under one of its local accounts. For example, audit a simple logon and logoff. From Event Viewer, save a copy in *.EVT format onto another workstation. From that other workstation, open this copied file. Note in place of the user name on the main Event Viewer window you see the internal ID. However, you see the actual name in *Description*, which is saved as text.

The decision is whether to save permanent copies as text or event files. Text files preserve the names no matter where the files get copied, but don't adjust to name changes. Event log files adjust to renaming, but you may not be able to see the names when viewed from other workstations.

Planning Disk Use

The current security log consumes space on your workstation's hard disk. You can limit the space it consumes with the Log Settings window:

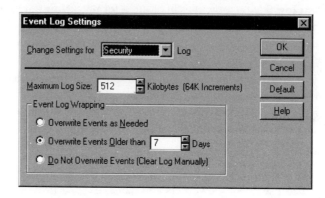

You can set the maximum size of the active log, instruct NT to erase events older than a certain number of days, or, when the log fills, have NT overwrite older events with new ones. Note that the system continues to run normally, just that events are not being recorded in the log.

☞ We recommend you choose *Overwrite Events as Needed*. This means the older events get discarded, rather than new ones. Of course, you'd like never to lose events, so you should be punctual about saving the log.

You can cause the system to shut down if it tries to post an audit event to the log when it's full. Because users are rudely cast off the system, we don't recommend this extreme remedy. However, you can do so by creating a new entry in the Registry. Create a value named CrashOnAuditFail (it really does "crash") to the Registry key:

```
HKEY_LOCAL_MACHINE:
    SYSTEM\CurrentControlSet\Control\Lsa
```

and give it the REG_WORD value of 1. (A value of 0 or deleting it turns off this option.) You need to restart the system for this parameter to take effect. To recover from a crash, restart the system, log on as a full administrator, and clear the log. CrashOnAuditFail is turned off when a crash occurs, so you probably want to turn it on again.

NT keeps the active security log on the same logical drive as the WINNT directory, and it's this logical drive that may fill up. Other system activities may consume space on this logical disk and compete with the security log. Plan accordingly. One option is to keep user trees on other logical disks, reserving the system disk for system use, that has space requirements that grow slowly if at all. In this way you have a relatively predictable space available for auditing. (Each logical disk has a fixed capacity.)

You can change the location of the security log using the Registry Editor. (See Chapter 10, Subsystems and Other Security Features). Open the key:

```
HKEY_LOCAL_MACHINE:
        SYSTEM\CurrentControlSet\Services\Eventlog\Security
```

The File value holds the path name of the event log. You can change this to a new path and it takes effect when you reboot the system. Protect these files so only the Administrators and SYSTEM groups can access the file.

Processing the Security Logs

If you save a security log in one of its text formats (particularly comma delimited) you can program a number of general database programs to read and process the logs. What you can make them do is limited only by the program's capabilities, and your effort and imagination. Database programs with sophisticated programming languages are particularly useful. Or, if you're really ambitious, you can write some programs in your favorite programming language, but this is not for the casual administrator.

Deciding What to Audit

As we've seen, Windows NT can generate a prodigious amount of information. So much so that your main auditing strategy is to decide carefully what your site needs to save and, more to the point, what it doesn't. What you choose to record in the security log is not a simple question, and one that you must ultimately decide taking into account your particular environment. In this section we include some of the criteria you'll want to consider.

Direct Your Auditing at Threats

Base your audit selection criteria on the perceived threats to your system. We cannot overemphasize this point. First do a threat analysis, then try to construct auditing strategies to counter them. Note especially threats that can be controlled only by auditing. Throughout this text we present potential threats.

Example: Suppose you're concerned about Trojan Horse programs (arguably the largest threat to general systems like NT). You could record every program executed on the system by certain user groups, looking for programs you've not seen before. While an active NT system can execute a lot of programs, the events in this particular example could easily be processed by audit analyzers.

Save the Wheat—Not the Chaff

"wheat versus chaff"

Suppose one sign that someone is trying to break into your system is an event that is frequent, common, and innocuous an overwhelming majority of the time. If one or two events that might alert you to skullduggery are surrounded by hoards of legitimate ones, you'll not likely notice them. There's too much chaff surrounding the wheat. In short, the best audit event is one that frequently indicates real skullduggery.

> **Example**: You're worried about the general problem of users seeing data they shouldn't see. You decide to record every time a file is opened for reading. The few kernels of wheat are lost in a mountain of chaff!

How Big Is Your Hard Disk?

The size of the log is a major underlying issue. While you may have plenty of disk space and may therefore want to save everything, even simple tasks like browsing can easily swamp the log. As we've seen, even though Event Viewer has a lot of features that help you peruse a large log, like Filter and Find, you can still lose the wheat in the chaff.

Success versus Failure

Do you care more about recording successful operations or failed attempts? Saving successes helps you reconstruct scenarios. On the other hand, all successful accesses have properly passed NT's access controls. Saving failures lets you know when someone was trying to do something they couldn't. On the other hand, NT caught the attempts and nothing dastardly happened.

Users versus Administrators

You may be more interested in one of these than the other, but which one depends on your own security strategy. Administrators can make many sweeping changes on the system. The advantage of auditing them is that it lets you monitor sensitive activities and track down cases where administrators have made a mess of things. The disadvantage is that administrators are trusted and, as such, who cares what they do? (Full administrators can alter the security log anyway, so auditing is little protection against a malicious administrator.) While regular users are the ones most likely to be malicious, they have little power.

File System Layout

If you use object auditing, your audit strategy will likely influence the way you structure and share your directory trees. Because the object controls tend to propagate through entire trees, you may find them being applied to items that have an audit that has little value. To curb this, place items of high audit value in their own tree.

Time and Date Changes

Because time and date is an important item in an audit event record, you may want to remove the Right to change system time from Power Users. Of course, the security log can audit changes to time, but it's probably better not to let users change it in the first place.

Reviewing the Log

Some sites regularly review their security logs in a timely manner. Others store them until suspicions are aroused in some other manner.

Keep It Secret?

Should you tell regular users the system is auditing them? The value of auditing as a deterrent works only when users think they may be audited, so you should tell them. On the other hand, maybe you want to "spy" on them, so you shouldn't tell them. The choice is yours, but we favor the former.

As a matter of practice you shouldn't tell users which events you audit. If they knew, they could avoid them. But don't consider this a strong security practice. There are many ways people might find out or guess what you're recording. Keeping the precise events a secret is an example of "security by obscurity" that we mentioned in Chapter 1.

Our final, most important advice is:

> Investigate every scenario you decide to audit. Learn the event IDs, their content, and the circumstances under which they're generated. Useful auditing takes careful planning.

Recommended Categories

Not all sites choose to audit, but if you do, consider which categories suit yours best.

- ✓ **Logon and Logoff** All sites should audit these because they are the most fundamental framework of people's use of the system.

- ✓ **Startup, Shutdown, and System** All sites should audit these unless you find the System events overwhelming.

- ✓ **Security Policy Changes (Audit and Rights)** All sites should audit this category. Without the Audit Policy changes, you can never be sure which events have been saved in the log. Changes to the Rights Policy are rare and important, and also an example where auditing can prevent future transgressions rather than just record those of the past.

✓ **User and Group Management**   Of interest to sites with medium security concerns. Some of these events portray legitimate administrators and as such may or may not be of interest, depending on whether you need to audit your administrators.

Example: Your site has several full administrators and Server Operators. While you trust them, you're concerned that a simple lack of coordination in managing the accounts may cause some security holes. Audit this category.

Some events portray the actions of Power Users, who often have the lowest trust among administrative users and you might, therefore, want to monitor their activities.

Example: You give most users Power User capabilities on their own workstation, but want to know for whom they create new accounts. Audit this category.

Other events portray regular users' creation and maintenance of groups. Although creating groups does not in itself give anybody any new access, adding people to existing groups does.

Example: You realize that groups don't enable regular users to open their files to anyone they choose. However, you're concerned that users are confusing other members of their working environment by placing members of groups that others might not expect. For example, someone adds a customer to a group traditionally used for project members only. Audit this category.

✓ **Use of User Rights**   Use of Rights is often of security interest, but it also generates a lot of data that may be of little interest. Our recommendation is that sites with high security concerns try to audit use of Rights unless it produces too much chaff.

✓ **File and Object Access**   Auditing operations on files, directories, and other objects can be of major or minor importance, depending on your assessment of your environment. Your decision depends in part on how thoroughly you police ACLs. Despite its obvious appeal and value, the downside of object auditing is the prodigious amount of events it can generate. If you audit objects, expect to tune your detailed strategy for months.

Example: The focus of a particular directory tree might be your company's highly confidential personnel files. You may want to record each and every read and write of these files. On the other hand, recording this level of detail for general-purpose trees will quickly overwhelm you.

✓ **Process Tracking**   Process tracking is detailed and consumes a lot of disk space. For this reason most auditing strategies won't include it. It can be of some use to an experienced auditor trying to unwind a subtle or complicated sequence of oc-currences, but even in these cases the sheer bookkeeping can be overwhelming. You may also find it necessary for audit analysis programs you might acquire, but they should tell you what they expect to be saved in the log.

Example: You decide that today you have no use for process tracking, but decide to save it anyway in case at some time in the future you might advance to the stage where you can use it. Do you really want to save gigabytes of audit data "just in case"?

Events from Applications

You might acquire applications specifically designed to issue NT audit events. You typically see these on the application log, a companion to the security log that works analogously. But applications may also make entries in the security log formatted by the application itself as it deems appropriate. For example, a database program may have its own protection and administration controls independent of Windows NT. Al-though it may even have its own security log, it could choose to place events in the NT security log under the theory that administrators only need to deal with one security log. Application events can be quite informative because the application has a broad view of its operation. For example, a database could include the precise change that a user made to the database, perhaps even including the new and overwritten data. We can't say much about these events except that their documentation should explain how you interpret the fields in their events. (If they don't explain, ask for a refund.)

Summary

Auditing is the science of planning, determining not only what you need to see but also what you don't. Few sites can save everything. This not only consumes a lot of storage, but also produces a lot of "chaff" (innocuous events) that tends to obscure the "wheat" (genuinely valuable events). You should even consider whether you need to audit at all. As valuable as auditing is, it's a bit like closing the barn door after the horses have bolted.

❖ NT can record a huge number of security-relevant events. Each workstation records its events in its local security log. Event Viewer lets you examine and manage the log on any workstation on the network, and User Manager and an item's Security property sheet control which events are saved. Only full adminis-trators can control auditing, and it's optional.

❖ Event types are grouped into the following categories, and you can tell NT which categories you want to include in the log:
   ❏ Logon and Logoff
   ❏ File and Object Access

- ❑ Use of User Rights
- ❑ User and Group Management
- ❑ Security Policy Changes
- ❑ Restart, Shutdown, and System
- ❑ Process Tracking

❖ File and Object Access is further controlled by audit information on each file and directory, as well as other objects like printers. These let you audit the object based on the account and group, the kind of access (like read or write), and whether the action was a success or failure.

❖ All the other categories except Process Tracking (which is quite detailed) and Use of User Rights are useful, relatively rare, and therefore commonly audited.

❖ There are many considerations as to what to audit. The most important is to target specific threats to your system, especially those you can control only by auditing. You also need to consider whether you're more interested in success or failures, and the activities of users or administrators.

❖ And, of course, you may need to archive the security logs periodically.

There are many more events logged than we've shown. Decide which events you need to monitor and, for each, how to capture the event and what it looks like.

Quick Check:

✓ Summarize the way audit controls on a directory apply to its newly created files and subdirectories. [158]

✓ Cite the account and group "name versus ID" issue between logs saved as *.EVT and *.TXT formats. [159]

✓ What's the distinction between the primary and client IDs in a record? [160]

Auditing a new event: We strongly recommend you thoroughly explore each new event you add to those you monitor. In this spirit, suppose you decide to start auditing when someone changes a password. Explore this event. Remember that people can change another account's password, and can do it from another workstation. [161]

(OPT) Setup up a prototype: Do this exercise with a partner. Set up auditing to capture a broad selection of events from the different categories. Now list on a sheet of paper a series of events for your partner to perform that triggers most or all of your events. Set up an account for your partner that lets them generate all these events except for the ones you want to fail. Outside your view, have your partner log on and perform this list in random order. Have them note the order on a second sheet that you don't see until the end. When they're done, examine the security log and determine the order they used. Check it against their notes.

Chapter *9*

The Internet and
Intranets

Windows NT finds itself squarely in the center of the Internet and intranet explosion. Its strong security, ease of use, and server attributes make it an excellent server platform in this arena. Windows NT is aggressively pursuing networking security through industrywide technologies and partnerships. These are relatively new and will continue to develop for years to come.

What is an intranet? It's a buzzword that means different things to different people. A practical definition is that an intranet is a wide area network, modeled on the worldwide Internet, that contains many exciting communication metaphors, like the World Wide Web and its browsers. More and more corporations are basing their internal corporate networks on Internet technology, thereby creating "corporate intranets."

A wide area intranet usually consists of many connected local area networks. Some of these LANs may know little about each other, and components of an intranet might be downright malicious. Intranets are much more prone to attack than LANs, and when you connect your workstation or your LAN to an intranet you expose it to greater threats.

Intranet technology opens many doors for widespread communication, but also introduces new opportunities for attack. Fortunately a large part of modern intranet technology addresses common network security issues. Many of those issues are discussed in this chapter.

In This Chapter We Describe

➡ An overview of the Windows NT strategy for the Internet and intranets

➡ An description of the cryptographic technology that will pervade NT's networking security

➡ The security aspects of Windows NT Internet Information Server

➡ Other networking topics, including RAS and isolating NT from the intranet

Our approach in this chapter is a little bit different than the rest of this book in that we attempt to equip you with some of the basics of this sometimes-bewildering technology so you can better track it as it emerges.

Windows NT and Intranets

Windows NT and its related products are aggressively targeting Internet and intranet security. A few of the major efforts under way are discussed here.

IIS and the Internet Explorer

Windows NT now includes an Internet server that supports WWW, File Transfer Protocol (FTP), and Gopher services, as well as Microsoft's WWW browser, the Internet Explorer. Both of these integrate fully into the NT domain security environment and employ the latest Internet security standards like SSL. Like NT, they are designed for security "from the ground up."

SSL and Secure Electronic Transaction (SET)

The Secure Sockets Layer is a cryptographic protocol that has emerged as a standard for Internet WWW traffic and as the basis for monetary transactions on the Internet. IIS and the Internet Explorer will fully implement SSL. We give an overview of SSL and what it means to you later in this chapter.

The SET protocol is the emerging standard for securing credit card transactions on the Internet using underlying technologies like SSL. Microsoft is a key partner in the SET effort and this is yet another example of Windows NT's immersion in Internet security.

Cryptographic Application Programming Interface (CAPI)

Windows NT now provides a simple, standard method for third parties to provide cryptographic services and ciphers for Windows NT through the Microsoft CAPI. CAPI allows a third-party application to use cryptographic features without implementing, knowing, or depending on specific cryptographic ciphers. The ciphers are instead provided by yet other third parties, called service providers, designed to serve such applications. CAPI is the glue that binds them.

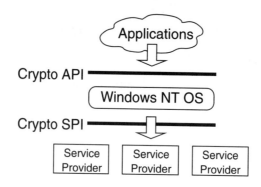

The Crypto API is the interface that applications use, while the Crypto SPI is the service provider interface. While CAPI itself gives NT no networking security features, it's the framework that encourages third parties to make more extensive use of cryptography, and to provide new, stronger, and standard ciphers. It also means that applications that use encryption can instantly implement new or specialized (even restricted) cryptographic techniques of like properties.

Code Signing

While public bulletin boards have long been a source of freeware and shareware, it's becoming popular to distribute commercial software across the Internet. One of the most effective ways to infiltrate your system is to introduce Trojan Horses into such software either by modifying it en route or by selling you modified copies. There are ample opportunities on the Internet's paths for both these schemes!

Fortunately, relatively simple encryption technologies let you determine not only if the software has been modified from the vendor's official release copy, but also the real identity of the original vendor. (Later, we see this is a straightforward application of cryptographic "integrity.") Microsoft has already announced code signature checking in its Internet Explorer.

Unified Authentication

Many Windows NT authentication principles are being integrated into the networking environment. For example, NT never passes unencrypted passwords across a network. It lets you log on only once and then gain access based on that identity to a wide range of remote services (called "single logon"). Most of these efforts are beyond your view, addressed by companies that produce NT software, but you can be assured that the basic, simple Windows NT authentication will integrate nicely and simply into intranet environments.

The "User Wallet"

You need to keep a number of cryptographic parameters when working in a secure networking environment, mostly encryption keys and items called "certificates." The "user wallet" binds together your personal set of these parameters and makes it easy for you to carry them around with you, for example, transporting it between work and home or to your portable computer. As you would expect, your wallet is protected from access by other users.

You need not concern yourself with the evolution of these technologies. They will appear in various forms in the releases of Windows NT and its applications. In the remainder of this chapter we help you understand some underlying concepts and give you practical advice on the security of Windows NT today.

Cryptography

Networking security means protecting information in transit from one network location to another or identifying who it is with which you are really communicating. There are three practical ways to do this: cryptography, cryptography, and cryptography. The heart of cryptographic technology is its "ciphers," mysterious mathematical algorithms fully understood by relatively few. Ciphers are as old as secrets and have long held a mysterious presence in communications security. Their importance to national security has led them to be embroiled in a number of political controversies. Like any deep technology, cryptographs have spawned a plethora of acronyms and misunderstandings. Fortunately, the Internet arena in which Windows NT finds itself is governed by a relatively small number of basic concepts, and it's these that we seek to explain in this section. Armed with this understanding, you can better adapt your systems to the world of networking security.

The Threats

There are many different ways to classify malicious threats in a networking environment, but all center around the following basic threats and their cryptographic solution.

Unauthorized Exposure

This is where "passive taps" on a network capture information you intend to remain private. Packets of information can pass through many hosts and across many communication lines in transition from one host on an intranet to another. Communications lines can be "tapped" and hosts can be compromised or maintained by unscrupulous individuals. Ciphers can "scramble" the information so that only the intended recipients, who know a special "key," can unscramble it. Malicious elements can still see the packets, but they can't understand its content. Using ciphers to prevent exposure is often called ensuring communication privacy or confidentiality. The verb "encrypt" is often used for the process of applying a cipher for privacy, and we use it in this manner. Windows NT has some built-in privacy features. For example, it can encrypt all RAS traffic.

Undetected Modification

Malicious elements along the network may be able to modify your communications. For example, Mallet might like to change a message in transit that says "Pay Mallet $1,000" to "Pay Mallet $10,000." Cryptography lets the sender attach a "seal" to each message so that the receiver can determine if the message is changed in transit. This is usually called ensuring communication integrity. Most modern sealing techniques also uniquely identify the sender.

Replay

A malicious networking element may record your transactions, let them pass unchanged, then later replay them to a remote server in hopes of some gain. For example, you issue an integrity-protected and perhaps encrypted transmission to your bank to pay Mallet a sum of money. Mallet monitors your transmission and, while they can't change the amount, they can later retransmit it to the bank hoping to be paid more than once! This is perhaps the most neglected networking threat even though there are relatively simple technologies that prevent it.

Masquerading

Masquerading is when a malicious party pretends to be someone else. Authentication solves this problem, but one must implement it with care. For example, while passwords are common and effective, they should never be passed across the network unscrambled. An authentication should use a technique to ensure that the subsequent session with the authenticated peer cannot be tampered with. (Knowing that I'm really talking to my bank does little good if someone can insert "pay to" orders during the session.) Windows NT pays particular attention to strong authentication techniques, and SSL fully addresses both server and client cryptographic authentication.

Nonrepudiation

While not really a threat in the classic sense, cryptography provides a way that a recipient of a document (like an electronic credit card order) can "prove" to a trusted third party (like a court of law) that the message must surely have been sent by a particular individual. Unfortunately, there are limits to the provability. Generally, you can show that it is technically infeasible for the message to have been sent by anyone who did not possess a secret key or physical token held by the sender. But of course the sender can always claim they told someone else their secret or lent their key. Nonrepudiation comes as a free, added benefit of many "public key" cryptographic schemes.

Traffic Analysis

The frequency with which you send messages to certain parties is itself information. For example, in a military scenario an inordinate number of command messages sent to a naval fleet might alert an adversary of an impending action by the fleet. Disguising traffic is rarely done in networks because you almost always pay a heavy performance penalty. One exception is when two subnets on the intranet establish a "bridge" between them, an encrypted communications channel through which many communication between entities on the two subnets pass. Eavesdroppers can only assess the aggregate traffic over the bridge—not the details of specific hosts.

Denial of Service

Denial of service is where a malicious element destroys, makes unusable, or delays your communication. Cryptography offers little help. Good network traffic control techniques are the usual solution. Many don't consider denial of service a security issue, although it's important operationally. Windows NT has its fair share of network controls to help prevent denial of service.

Cipher Keys and their Distribution

Keys are secret values held by communicating parties that let them cryptographically protect their communications. Keys are bound to certain ciphers and must be carefully selected. **Private keys** can be used to penetrate the encryption protections and must be kept secret to one or several communicants. **Public keys** (used in conjunction with private keys) cannot be used in this manner and can be freely distributed. Keys used to encrypt user's data are often called **data keys** (or **session keys**).

Key distribution is an important part of cryptographic systems. It is axiomatic in popular cryptographic systems that before two parties can use a particular method to secure their communications, they must receive initial keys through some other secure distribution medium. Their final method is only as secure as the initial distribution medium, since a penetrator may be able to see or change these initial keys on which all subsequent security rests. Keys used to distribute other keys securely are often called **key distribution keys**. General doctrine is that data keys should not be used as key distribution keys, and vice versa.

The classic key distribution technique is to distribute manually key distribution keys to the communicating parties. After that, either the parties themselves or a trusted third party periodically distributes data keys protected by the key distribution keys. Generally, the more data you encrypt with a given key, the greater the chance that it will be broken, so data keys are changed frequently. However, key distribution keys are used for relatively little traffic and can last a long time before they need to be changed. Key distribution is indeed a science unto itself, but one that's usually invisible to system administrators.

Breaking Ciphers

People who attempt to break ciphers are called cryptanalysts and they deserve to be paid well. (And usually are, in one way or another.) They use a diverse collection of techniques but we'll mention only a few that might help you in your administrative decisions.

A cipher may have certain weaknesses generally unknown except to the penetrator. Mathematicians have never been able to "prove" that a cipher has no weaknesses. The best indication that it has none is when a large community of cryptanalysts armed with the cipher's algorithm have tried mightily to break the cipher with little success.

☞The first rule of choosing a strong cipher is to never believe its inventor's claims of invincibility. The second rule is to give great credence to time-tested ciphers with fully published algorithms.

Cryptographic doctrine is that a cipher should never depend on its algorithms being kept a secret for its security. Publicizing its algorithm aids cryptanalysts in trying to break the cipher. When they don't, it lends credibility to the cipher's inherent strength. Anyway, secret cipher algorithms seldom stay that way for long.

Unencrytped data is called **plaintext** (often called "cleartext") and encrypted data is called **ciphertext**. Sometimes, but not always, knowing the data that's been encrypted can aid a cryptanalyst. This is called a "plaintext attack." Sometimes, but not always, being able to choose the plaintext aids the cryptanalyst. This is called a "chosen plaintext attack," but it can be logistically difficult.

The simplest attack attempts to try all possible keys until one works, called the **brute force** attack. Brute force attacks have a calculable chance of success. If a cipher key is 40 bits long there are about 10^{12} unique key values. One hundred computers each attempting one million decryptions per second would have about a 50 percent chance of finding the key by brute force in less than two hours. Increase this to 56 bits and one thousand computers, and it takes a little over one year. Increase the key size to 112 bits and it would take more hours than atoms in the universe. (Well, figuratively speaking.) Most experts feel that breaking 56-bit keys is on the verge of economic feasibility for items of considerable value. (Remember that there's no point stealing something if it's worth is less than the cost to steal it.)

Why are 40-bit keys so popular when they are not very secure? The U.S. government forbids the export of products with privacy ciphers with keys that are more than 40 bits. They don't want the bad guys to use ciphers the government can't break. In our modern Internet world the cipher algorithms are long gone from the United States, but U.S. vendors are reluctant to deliver products that need a special, restricted version for export. It's expensive. The battle continues to be fought and will likely continue for a while.

Of course, a brute force attack depends on the attacker knowing when a key successfully decrypts the data. Hence, they have to be able to recognize plaintext data. If the plaintext data is random, one could not reliably recognize it and probably could never break the cipher. Most user data is not random, however, and clever cryptanalysts can readily recognize even things like binary program code. Data keys are essentially random data and this makes the process of encrypting them with key encrypting keys a little more difficult to break (assuming that only the data keys are encrypted—not accompanying control information).

Many cryptographic systems rely on the generation of random numbers, and a common weakness is when the systems do a poor job of doing so. For example, if cryptanalysts can determine that a random number is within a certain range, even a wide one, it can greatly aid their attack.

> **Example:** A popular WWW browser generated a random number from the microsecond time of day and the "process number" of the browser. However, process numbers are not kept secret and one can narrow the time of generation to about a second or so. These considerably narrow a brute force search.

Symmetric Ciphers and Privacy

A cipher that uses the same key to encrypt and decrypt is called a **symmetric cipher**. These are the traditional ciphers of cryptography. Most modern symmetric ciphers are quite fast and can be readily implemented in hardware. Many of these cipers work on a **block** of data at a time, where blocks are typically eight to sixteen characters long. The classic means to ensure privacy is for the sender to simply encrypt the data with a symmetric cipher and the receiver to decrypt it using the same key. (Of course, one has to provide secure key distribution of the key.) As an NT administrator, you'll likely come across the following symmetric ciphers.

Data Encryption Standard (DES)

The DES is a popular, long-standing symmetric cipher that uses 56-bit keys on 64-bit blocks. (Rumor has always been that the U.S. government persuaded its developer,

IBM, to use 56- rather than 64-bit keys because the U.S. intelligence agencies could break the former but not the latter.) While rumors have always abounded of weaknesses in DES, it has withstood perhaps more cryptanalytic attacks than any other cipher in history. The general consensus (with only minor caveats) is that brute force is the only practical attack.

At 56-bits, DES is on the verge of being outdated. However, a technique called "triple DES" uses two 56-bit keys and three DES encryption operations. Unless there really is some back door into DES, this is effectively unbreakable, albeit half as fast as simple DES.

International Data Encryption Algorithm (IDEA)

The IDEA is another popular cipher often used on the Internet. Its algorithm is public and it's been the subject of a moderate amount of cryptanalytic attack, so far with no real success. Its 128-bit keys make brute force unthinkable. Its only drawback is that it's relatively new and most would like a little more confidence that it has no undiscovered weaknesses.

RC4

RC4 is a proprietary cipher from RSA, Inc. It's much faster than DES, uses a variable key size, and is considered a strong cipher by most. RC4 is often implemented with 40-bit key sizes for export purposes. Windows NT currently uses RC4 to encrypt RAS traffic.

Cipher modes are the techniques for applying a cipher to a stream of data. They can be applied to almost any cipher, symmetric or otherwise. The simplest technique is to encrypt each fixed block of data independently, often called the electronic codebook (ECB) technique. Although simple, the same plaintext block always encrypts to the same ciphertext block. This can aid traffic analysis or even break the cipher. It also makes it easy for an attacker to replace one block in your message maliciously with another undetected.

Other techniques use aspects of the previous ciphertext as well as the key to encrypt the current block. Hence, each block changes all successive blocks against what they would be in ECB. The primary advantage is that two plaintext blocks encrypt to unpredictably different ciphertext blocks, and the performance penalty is small. This also makes it difficult for an attacker to replace one block with another. **Cipher block chaining** (CBC) is a popular feedback technique. Each block of output is logically (bitwise) "or'd" with the next block of input before the latter is encrypted. The first block is "or'd" with an **initialization vector**, a randomly chosen block known to both sender and receiver. While they should be kept confidential, exposing the initialization vector seldom significantly compromises an encryption method. The net effect is that feedback techniques like CBC are generally much more secure than others like ECB.

Public Key Ciphers

Public/private key (PPK) ciphers are relatively new and have revolutionized cryptography. They were invented in the late 1970s and today the RSA cipher from RSA, Inc., dominates all others. A PPK cipher uses two matched keys. One, the **private** key, is

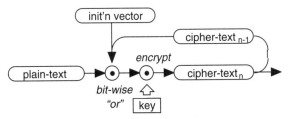

held secret by its owner and the second, the **public** key, is fully publicized, even to the bad guys. PPK ciphers have a deceptively simple but incredibly useful property: Data *encrypted* by the public key can only be *decrypted* by the private key. Conversely, data *encrypted* by the private key can only be *decrypted* by the public key. (Reread this a few times and let it sink in.)

You need to work through a few examples to understand the importance of this property. Consider the simple example of key distribution:

> **Example:** Alice needs a private communication with Bob. They can agree on a simple symmetric cipher but need to share a data key. Simple. Alice carefully selects a new, random data key, encrypts it with Bob's public key then ships it to Bob. Bob is the only one who can successfully decrypt the data key and hence the only one (besides Alice) who can decrypt Alice's forthcoming messages.

PPK ciphers are typically much slower than symmetric ciphers. Hence, the usual practice is to use a symmetric cipher to encrypt the data and use PPK to distribute the symmetric data key, just as Bob and Alice have done. Message integrity (discussed in the next section) is another common example that you'll see frequently in the world of Windows NT and the modern Internet.

The RSA cipher dominates the rush to securing the Internet. It uses variable-size keys, and the longer the key the more difficult for a brute force attack. RSA is a published algorithm that has been scrutinized for almost a decade and there have been no public successes on the larger key sizes. There was much ballyhoo over one compromise of RSA, but the "modulus" size in this attack was 116 digits—well below commonly recommended sizes. (The modulus size is a measure of key size in RSA.) Ultimately the strength of RSA depends on the ability to factor large numbers; a long-standing, unsolved mathematical problem. Given a large enough key size, there is great public confidence in its strength. One 1992 security workshop judged that a 300-digit modulus would be "sufficiently strong" until 2002.

Integrity

You may be concerned with attacks that attempt to change your data, its integrity, even when you aren't concerned with its privacy. Data integrity techniques use ciphers to derive a "seal" for each message. The sender computes and attaches the seal using a cipher and some key; the receiver recomputes the seal using some key (which may or may not be the same as the sender, depending on the technique used). If this newly computed seal is different from the one sent, the message has been tampered with. Security depends on the fact that an attacker cannot change the message and apply a new, accurate seal without knowing a secret key held by the receiver, sender, or both (illustrated below).

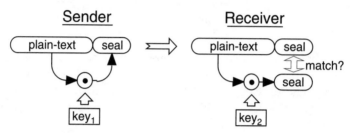

Consider the following simple technique for computing the seal.

The sender encrypts the entire message with their private key and sends the result with the message as the seal. The receiver decrypts the seal using the sender's public key and ensures the result matches the message exactly. Without knowing the sender's private key, an attacker could not have computed an accurate seal for an altered message.

The seal is often called a **digital signature** (or message authentication code, [MAC]) and the act of applying the seal is therefore called "signing" a message. While secure, this technique is cumbersome because PPK is slow and payload size almost doubles. Enter the **one-way hash functions**, a key element of modern cryptography. A one-way hash function takes as input an arbitrarily long message and produces as output a fixed-size number, typically 16 bytes long and called the "hash." Hash functions have two important properties:

❖ Given only the hash, one should not be able to determine anything about the original message.

❖ It must be computationally infeasible to construct a message that produces a given hash.

Modern hash functions are considerably faster than PPK. Consider how we can now redesign our integrity scheme:

Integrity with Hashing: The sender submits the message to a one-way hash function then signs the hash by encrypting the hash with their private key and attaching the result as the seal. The receiver submits the plaintext message to the hash, decrypts the seal with the sender's public key, and compares the two results. If they are different, the message or its seal have been changed!

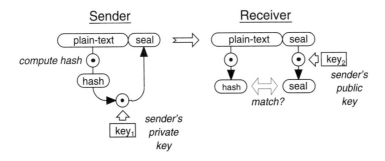

Suppose the sender encrypts the hash with the receiver's public key and the receiver decrypts it with their private key. Does this provide integrity? [162]
Does this integrity scheme provide nonrepudiation? [163]

The great majority of integrity schemes you'll encounter in Windows NT and the Internet use a variant of this simple scheme. MD5 from RSA, Inc., is the most popular one-way hash function in the Internet community. ("MD" stands for "message digest," an alternative name for one-way hash functions.)

The U.S. government also designed an integrity method called the Digital Signature Standard (DSS) similar to the one we just described. It uses a unique PPK and hash function. DSS cannot be used to encrypt data for privacy, so it is not subject to the 40-bit key restriction of the U.S. government. Although popular within the U.S. defense community, it receives little attention in the general Internet community.

Note again that one can use integrity and encryption alone or together. They are essentially independent. You could, for example, encrypt each block then seal the result, or vice versa.

You and a friend share a secret "phrase." How might a security protocol ensure the integrity of your communication using only this phrase and a hash function? [164]

Challenge/Response

Windows NT frequently uses a classic cryptographic technique called "challenge/response" where one party sends a random, nonsense message (often called a "nonce") to the other, who then performs some cryptographic operation on the challenge and returns a response. The first party has a means to determine if that response could only have been performed by the legitimate, other party. This proves to the first party that the other party is legitimate, at least with respect to this simple operation. The parties typically weave other parameters into the interaction. It's usually important that an attacker not be able to predict the value of a given challenge.

235

Example: A server and client engage in a simple logon scenario where the client must present a user name and password. The server begins by passing a challenge to the client. The client then concatenates the user name onto the challenge, encrypts the result under some agreed-upon cipher using the user's password as the encryption key, then returns the result and the plaintext user name to the server. The server can verify the logon by performing the same encryption of the user name and challenge using the server's local copy of the password. Only a client that knew the same password could have produced the same ciphertext.

> Is this scheme prone to replay? [165]
> Could you do the same thing using a hash function instead of a cipher? Justify that your method is secure. [166]

Windows NT servers must authenticate the client user before performing any services and often uses a classic challenge/response scheme. We present this figure as a simplified version of its logon algorithm as an example of challenge/response[1].

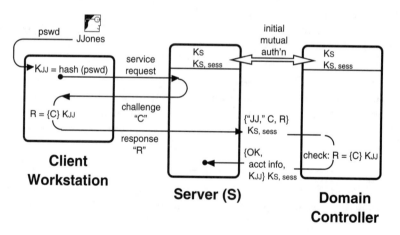

Windows NT Internal Authentication Scheme

This scenario has three computers: a client workstation, a server that is not a domain controller, and the domain controller. When the user JJones logs on, the client computes a hash on the user's password (K_{JJ}) then discards the password. The domain controller stores this same hash of JJ's password. When a client requests a service, the server sends a challenge ("C") to the client. The client encrypts the challenge using the user's password hash (K_{JJ}) as the encryption key and forwards the response to the

---

1. As described in Kaufman, et. al. *Network Security: PRIVATE Communication in a PUBLIC World.* (Englewood Cliffs, New Jersey: Prentice-Hall, 1995).

server. (The notation "{C}K" denotes a message C encrypted using the key K.) The server forwards this information, encrypted with the server's session key, $K_{S, sess}$ (currently using RC4), to the domain controller, which holds the user's hash as well as a set of account information for the user. (The domain controller uses this key for all such communication with that server.) The controller verifies the user by also encrypting the challenge with the user's password hash (K_{JJ}) and ensuring that the result is the same as the response computed by the client (R). If so, the controller returns success to the server along with the account information, all encrypted with the server's session key.

The controller and server share a long-term secret key (K_S) used for initial, mutual authentication and the establishment of the server session key ($K_{S, sess}$). Each generates this session key by adding the two challenges used during their mutual authentication and encrypting the result with K_S. Messages between the controller and server ensure sequencing but not, in general, integrity, and only selected fields are cryptographically hidden.

Subsequent requests from the client to the server reference a session number that reflects the original logon. An eavesdropping attacker can record this session number then send its own requests to the server identified by the same session number and the server would honor the request. Windows NT does not ensure the integrity or prevent replay on these in-session requests. This is left to specific services, like RAS and SSL, or to NT add-ins from third-party vendors.

> What are the strengths of this scheme? [167]

Certificates

Certificates are perhaps the most visible part of the Windows NT/Internet encryption technologies and the one on which you'll likely spend most of your time. Most PPK schemes depend on at least one party knowing the other's true public key. Consider the way in which an attacker in the middle, named "Mallet," can thwart our key distribution example:

Example: Alice needs Bob's public key to encrypt the data key. She might obtain it across the network from Bob, from a mutual friend, or from a public key server. Suppose Mallet can intercept the transmission. Mallet can generate a false PPK key pair then send the public part masquerading as what is supposed to be (and what Alice takes to be) Bob's public key. When Mallet intercepts the encrypted data key, he can decrypt it, encrypt it with Bob's real public key, and forward the result to Bob. Mallet now has the data key with Alice and Bob none the wiser.

Can Mallet foil the integrity scheme we discussed above? [168]

Simply stated, a certificate is a message that holds the name and public key of a person or entity, that's signed by a certification authority using a technique much like our integrity scheme above. If you know the public key of the CA and trust the CA to have properly identified the person before signing the certificate, you can verify that the public key in the certificate is the true key for that person. A lot of "ifs."

How do you know the CA's public key? Perhaps they came to your office, introduced by your security officer, and entered their public key into your computer. Or perhaps the CA is of national scope and publishes their public key, in every major daily newspaper. You can gather an assortment of papers from different sources (very hard for an attacker to falsify) and compare them. If the same, you install the key in your software as reliable.

Or perhaps you can fetch the CA's, who we'll call CA_1, certificate from some convenient key server. It will be signed by some other CA, say CA_2, whose key you have already verified by some independent technique, like the two we just described. If not, you can fetch the certificate for CA_2, which will be signed by CA_3, and so forth until you find a CA whose key you already reliably know. This is called a "certificate chain" and you can now unwind it: Use the CA you already know to verify CA_n's certificate, use CA_n's now-reliable public key to verify CA_{n-1}'s certificate, and so forth until you finally verify CA_1 and the original person. Of course all this would be done within your software and you would see little of it.

Note that you never believe a certificate unless it checks against a CA chain with a root you already know. Bogus certificates always fail your software's tests. This means that a public key server does not strictly need to be secured. If an attacker changes its certificates, your software will detect it.

How you manage certificates varies widely among applications. One simple scheme is to allow you to import CA certificates into the program designating them as trusted. The application then searches this list for a CA for all certificates it processes. It may also chase down certificate hierarchies. More complicate schemes automatically query public certificate servers and chase down hierarchical chains, although they still typically let you designate certain certificates as trusted CAs.

The most common format for certificates is X.509, named after the standards body that defines it. Its major fields are described here.

Subject Name This field is a common, recognizable name for the person or entity whose public key the certificate holds. This could be a common name like "Chris P. Public" or perhaps an e-mail address like "CPPublic@TrustedSystems.com." However, most modern usage advocates an X.500 style name that uniquely identifies the individual in a large community, for example:

```
C=US/ S=Illinous/ L=Urbana/ O=TrustedSystems Inc/
OU=Marketing/ CN=Chris P. Public
```

identifies Chris P. Public from the marketing department of Trusted Systems, Inc., in Urbana, Illinois, USA. Network servers need their own certificate and the marketing server at Trusted Systems might have the same except for the common name (CN):

```
.../ CN=WWW.TrustedSystems.com
```

Subject Public Key   This field is the entity's public key of a type and format specified elsewhere in the certificate.

Validity   This field is the two dates between which the certificate is valid.

Issuer Name   This field is the name of the CA. This is the subject name in the CA's own certificate, presumably signed by the next higher level CA.

Signature   This field is the CA's seal on the entire certificate, analogous to the seal in our previous integrity example.

Serial Number   This number must be unique among all certificates that this CA issues. In a given usage community, CA names should also be unique, which means the CA name and serial number uniquely identify a certificate in that community.

Other fields hold various control information, like the type of public key and sealing cipher. The latest X.509 format allows a number of extensions that can be defined by various communities for their own use.

Subject Alternate Name   This field modifies and further serves to identify the subject the certificate represents, providing either more detail or alternative descriptions (for example, an e-mail address [when *Subject Name* is not an e-mail address] or postal address).

Key Usage Restrictions   This field constrains how the public key can be used. For example, it might prevent the key from being used to encrypt other encryption keys and could therefore only be used as a data key.

While the format and intent of its fields are clear, there will always be some flexibility over the conventions of how certain fields are represented. As administrator you will probably apply for certificates for your servers and perhaps users. It's important to understand the conventions for the subject names you request. It's the responsibility of the CA that signs your certificates to ensure that they are not misleading or downright mischievous, but many of the fields (like *Organization Unit*) are at your discretion and you should be accurate and consistent.

Although you don't see much of them (and don't need to), complete certificate management systems circulate "certificate revocation lists" of certificates that have been invalidated by their CAs before their normal expiration date.

The security of the certificate mechanism itself rests on two more fundamental principles. First, you must believe that the CA that signs a particular certificate can be legitimately trusted to ensure the identity of the holder of that certificate. For example, suppose you obtained the certificate for "B. Clinton, President, USA" signed by a low-level CA in a small country considerably removed from and not too friendly to the USA. Could you believe this certificate?

Second, you must believe the name in the certificate represents the individual that you intend to authenticate. Suppose you want to communicate with a long-lost business associate named B. Bell, who you know used to work for a particular company. You find a certificate on a local certificate server with this name and company. The certificate is signed by a CA you trust, but are you sure it's your associate?

> Suppose this same B. Bell sends you an integrity-protected e-mail message and includes their own certificate signed by a CA you trust? Is the message legitimate? [**169**]

Code signing, where you are assured that software you've received has not been tampered with, uses a simple integrity scheme like the one we presented here. Consider how a CA hierarchy might be established:

Example: A worldwide, umbrella organization establishes its own certificate and publishes it widely. Vendors "hard code" this certification into the software that distributes and receives software. This organization then certifies a small number of software CA organizations who establish their own certificate signed by the umbrella organization. The CAs then issue and sign certificates to individual software vendors and distributors. These certificates might be marked with a "Key Usage Restriction" that restricts them to validating delivered software.

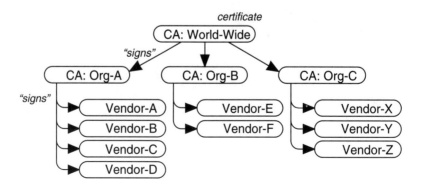

When you receive software, it includes the certificate of the distributing organization, which your software verifies with respect to the CA certificate, which it in turn verifies with respect to the umbrella certificate.

CAs in this scheme are duty bound to provide some level of assurance that distributors are reputable. In this scheme, your major point of concern is that the distributor guards their own secret key. (CAs are highly trusted entities and you can safely assume they guard their private keys.)

SSL

All the encryption technology we've presented so far culminates in SSL, one of the most important encryption schemes on the Internet today. It's implemented in almost all WWW servers and browsers, most notably IIS and the Internet Explorer, and is central to most of the cash and credit card transactions over the net. You can almost think of SSL as an encapsulation of modern network encryption technology. The details of SSL are public and it has received considerable security review. While there have been problems with some implementations, by most accounts it is solidly secure.

SSL is not a cipher. Instead it's a protocol used by a client and server to secure their communications cryptographically. It can use a number of popular ciphers as long as they are understood by both client and server. Basic SSL provides three basic security protections.

Server Authentication This assures the client that the server is really who its name indicates. Basically, the server passes its certificate to the client in a way that cannot be tampered with by a middleman and the client then validates the server's certificate. In many simple implementations, the server certificate must be signed by a CA whose certificate is hard coded into the client software. This means the server's administrators must obtain the certificate from a particular source. While it's not exactly in the interest of free market economics, it's simple and effective.

Privacy SSL can encrypt all communication between client and server. It generates new data keys that last for a "session," which might typically be a few minutes or a few hours, although the communicants can usually update the key if an inordinate amount of data is passed.

Integrity SSL can ensure the integrity of data between the communicants.

Both client and server control which ciphers SSL uses and whether they are used at all, although client users may or may not be given many options. RSA PPK ciphers are popular for integrity and certificate verification, the MD5 hash function for integrity, and the DES, triple DES, or IDEA ciphers for privacy.

Client authentication is optional in SSL and requires the client to have a certificate validated by a CA that the server can validate. This is left as an option because it's unrealistic to expect public client users to obtain a certificate. (They cost money.) Servers can require client authentication although few that deal with the public do so.

WWW clients and servers are the first to make widespread use of SSL. However, it is a general cryptographic scheme that could apply to almost any network communications. There are several proposed modifications to SSL, but they only deal in the details and have little effect on your Windows NT security decisions.

Summary

Have these ciphers secured the Internet? In theory, yes. While no one can be certain, the ciphers seem plenty strong and keys can be made plenty long. While one will find implementation errors from time to time, the days when an active or passive Internet tap can see data it shouldn't see or change data it shouldn't change are effectively eliminated by these ciphers and the protocols that use them.

Internet Information Server

Internet
Service
Manager

Windows NT Server includes the Microsoft IIS, a "Web" server that serves WWW, FTP, and Gopher clients on the Internet or across any TCP/IP[1] network. All three of its services share the same basic security features that we present.

From a security perspective, IIS services are analogous to NT file sharing. A server advertises certain directory trees on the network under certain names, protecting access to each tree as a whole, analogous to the "share-level" ACL for file sharing. If those trees are on NTFS volumes (a clear choice for security), the individual files and directories are additionally and individually protected by ACLs. Remote clients access these trees and can, in general, Read and Write their information (although Gopher is Read-Only).

NT associates an account with the actions of each remote client, and supports explicit accounts that require the client's user to enter a name and password, or "anonymous" accounts available to anyone (and whose users are therefore unknown). Like file sharing, clients cannot access (or even name!) files outside the advertised directories.

The most significant difference from NT file sharing is that WWW services can include running server-side programs that can accept data from and send data to the clients. These programs may be able to access data outside the advertised directory trees and must be carefully scrutinized. (More later.)

Authentication

You can manage any IIS server on your network using the Internet Service Manager. The working window in "report view" is shown on the top of the next page.

There are other views that show you other computers running IIS grouped by service or computer. It even has a menu that searches for computers hosting IIS. You normally run the Service Manager from a full administrative account or as a Server Operator.

---

1. The Internet—and many intranets—are based on the TCP/IP protocol pair, although technically only the Internet protocol (IP) forms this basis. Almost all major operating systems support TCP/IP networking.

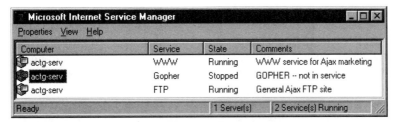

Internet Service Manager

All services can support anonymous users. This is an account associated with re-mote users that does not require a password. Hence, its users are anonymous. This is analogous to the Guest account in NT. Although we normally advise against the Guest account, you can accept anonymous IIS access because you often intend the services it provides to be publicly accessible.

WWW Property Sheet

The Service property sheet configures the basic authentication (logon) parameters for the server. If you intend to allow anonymous access, enter the anonymous account name here along with its password. (You need to define the account's password from the User Manager program. The password you enter here is the one IIS uses to access the account and must, of course, match the account's password.) When you install IIS it creates and configures an anonymous account with the name IUSR_ followed by the name of the computer. It's perfectly fine to accept this default, and we talk more about it more later.

The basic security property you set up from this sheet is the authentication (logon) mode, Password Authentication. You must select at least one of these on the following list and you can use all combinations.

Allow Anonymous   This allows anonymous logons. In this mode, IIS first tries to open all HTTP files as the anonymous user. If this does not succeed (for example, if the ACL doesn't allow it) and if one of the other two authentication techniques are enabled, IIS then requires client-side authentication. Except for these cases, WWW client users do not log on when anonymous is allowed. In FTP, users can use the special user name "anonymous" during their normal, required FTP logon. By convention, they also enter their e-mail address as the password, but IIS does not enforce this.

Basic   This enables a Basic user name and password authentication that works with client programs from many vendors. (It's sometimes called "UUencode password encoding" from its UNIX origins.) IIS presents the client user with a short window in which they enter an account name and password. IIS fetches these back to the server to be checked against the domain accounts. If you do not allow anonymous access, each user must authenticate at the beginning of their session, but need do so only once. IIS reauthenticates them if they attempt to access a file and fail (for example, if the ACL precludes access), and they can then try another name and password.

☞ The danger of this mode is that the name and password pass across the network as plaintext (unencrypted) and can easily be captured by any eavesdropper.

Windows NT Challenge/Response   This method is similar to *Basic* but it uses an algorithm that does not transport the password as plaintext across the network. Microsoft WWW clients (the Internet Explorer) will support this mode but it's not clear which others might.

The interaction between anonymous and the other modes can be a bit confusing. If you enable anonymous, IIS always tries first to access objects with the anonymous account. If that fails, it then tries the most recent successful authentication (if there is one). If this fails, it prompts the user to reauthenticate.

IIS can authenticate domain (global) accounts—not local ones—and these can be accounts from other, trusted domains. The Basic and Windows NT methods apply only to WWW services. The standard FTP logon passes the name and password unprotected. For this reason, many sites will allow only public, anonymous FTP access.

Accounts intended to access IIS need the Right to Log on Locally, which is by default granted only to administrative users on Windows NT Server. The downside, of course, is that these users can now log on directly to the server, but since it's a server you should physically restrict access anyway.

In short, Basic authentication is a significant security risk. Anonymous use is fine for "public" access. Remember that anonymous users don't necessarily get access to all your documents, only those to which the anonymous account has Read access.

Directories and Access Control

IIS provides client access to the directory trees you list in the Directories property sheet:

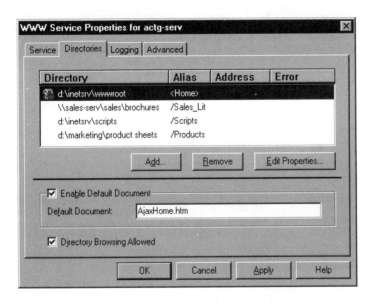

IIS can service requests directed to IP addresses in addition to its own (called "Virtual Servers"), although we show only the simpler case. You must include a single home directory with a URL that consists of only the host. In our example for Ajax Corporation, "http://Ajax.com/" refers to the directory WWWROOT. You can name other directories whose URL is the "alias" you specify; for example, "http://Trusted-Systems.com/Products" maps to the BROCHURES directory. The *Virtual Server* field applies only if this directory is to service IP addresses other than the IIS host's. Define these directories using the Directory Properties window, shown at the top of the next page.

You can name network share directories (for example, "\\sales-serv\...") and if so you must name an account and its password on the sharing host. All access to the share directory is under this account regardless of whether the client is working under the anonymous or an authenticated account. The three Access fields are important.

Read   This field lets clients read the contents of the directory tree.

Execute (WWW Only)   This field lets clients execute "agents" within the directory tree. (An agent is a small program that runs on your system loaded from a remote Web page you are viewing.)

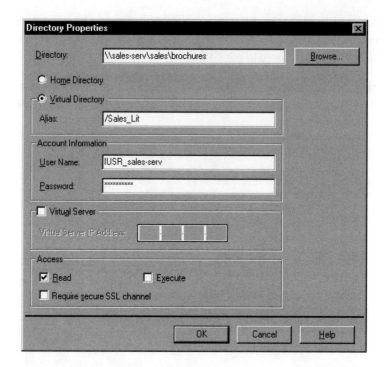

Require Secure SSL Channel (WWW Only) If you select this, IIS serves only "HTTPS://" queries that use SSL. Before you can service HTTPS:// requests, you need to obtain a certificate for your server from an approved CA. Check your system documentation for the procedures.

Write (FTP Only) This field lets clients add files and directories within the directory tree.

Like share ACLs, these IIS access restrictions are in addition to protection afforded by share and file ACLs. Carefully consider how you configure these directories:

❖ The simplest and best advice is to plan your directories carefully based on both operational and security requirements. Use IIS directories set to Read alone whenever you can. Carefully and tightly coordinate the ACLs on the IIS directories with their use and IIS access controls.

❖ Users on your local network typically need to update the files in these directories using file sharing. Use share and file ACLs to accommodate them.

❖ Install agents in directories with IIS and ACL "Execute" permission, but with ACLs that preclude writing or adding new files by other than the appropriate administrators. This helps prevent the small chance that clients can insert new agents onto your system or modify existing ones.

❖ In practice, IIS directories that are network shares from other computers can only be used for public access because access is always under the account you specify. (In our example we just used the anonymous IUSR account on the remote server.) You can use this account to prevent local users from modifying these shares, but any IIS client can access these directories. This is of course subject to the IIS access controls on the directory, and share and file ACLs on the share for that account. You can use the account in the share's ACL to control portions of the share. If you intend only Read access to the share, set the IIS control to Read, the network share ACL for its account to Read-Only, and the ACLs within the directory to Read-Only, for that account. If you are careful, you can securely use network shares. However, opening up your network to IIS clients leaves one a bit uneasy.

Anonymous and Special Accounts

The anonymous account ("IUSR_*computername*" by default) governs access to all users who aren't authenticated in the sense that they must supply a password for the account.

✓ This must be a domain (as opposed to a local) account. In User Manager, give this account a complicated password that no one knows and also enter this password in IIS as the account's password. Since no one knows its password, no one can directly log on to the account and IIS will be the only entity that uses the account.

✓ You can rename this account if you like or direct IIS to use another account, but you don't have to. Make sure you type the accurate account name and its current password in the Service property sheet.

✓ Make sure the only User Right this account has is the ability to Log on Locally. Also ensure that each of the groups in which this account is a member (including Everyone) has only this Right. (Some other benign Rights may be okay, but it generally doesn't need any others.)

✓ Make sure users can't change the anonymous password and that the password never expires.

✓ IIS may install this account in the Guests group. We recommend you remove it unless your security strategy dictates otherwise. Your best bet is to create a group for anonymous access that would hold the IIS account, and others as appropriate. Name the group something obvious so that your users don't access it accidentally. Remove the IIS account from all other groups.

✓ If you have several IIS servers, they can share the same anonymous account, rather than the default one per computer. Having one account per IIS server limits that account's scope. Having a shared account is a little simpler. Choose whatever is appropriate.

A few special techniques that you should consider about this and other accounts:

✓ When your accounts are accessible across a dispersed network, like the Internet, it is particularly important that you activate the Account Lockout feature. Choose a generous threshold, perhaps a dozen attempts.

✓ We recommend you exclude the anonymous account from Users and Domain Users, then use these groups rather than Everyone to grant "general access" to your non-IIS file trees, like the Windows SYSTEM folder. (This is the approach we advise in Appendix A, Secure Installation.) IIS performs its service actions under the client user's account, but this seldom requires access to files outside IIS's advertised directory trees.

✓ You can create other accounts for general access to IIS services, either ones without a password or those with a password that you distribute by other means. While not quite secure, they can add a degree of protection. However, IIS treats only one account as its special "anonymous" account.

✓ You can set the Registry entry:

```
HKEY_LOCAL_MACHINE\SYSTEM\CurrentControlSet
    \Services\W3SVC\AllowGuestAccess
```

to 0 to prevent the Guest account from using WWW. The theory is that the Guest account is commonly not well regulated (certainly no longer the case on *your* system!) and a danger when accessed remotely. You should only allow Guest to use WWW if you have a good reason to do so.

IIS and NT Gateways

The NT Server hosting IIS must be on the intranet and is usually also on your local network (LAN). It's a good idea to uncouple these two networks as much as practical. This reduces the opportunity that malicious remote computers can directly access those on your local network. The most common technique is to let your NT IIS Server stand between the LAN and the intranet with a separate hardware interface for each, but not function as an IP gateway, which would make the LAN a part of the intranet.

This can be easy if NT's "interface" functionality is limited to IIS and special **proxies** that you can install on the NT Server, like a WWW proxy. Proxies are special programs that let your LAN computers access certain intranet services through the proxies on the server without giving them direct access to the intranet and without Windows NT having to act as a full IP gateway. The disadvantage is that the NT Server (or some other gateway) must now function as a gateway between the two networks if workstations on your local network need to access the intranet. The following figure illustrates a common configuration of an IIS server on NT acting in this capacity.

Windows NT
(not an IP gateway)

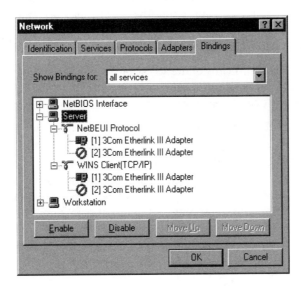

You can also use various firewalls, including some that run on Windows NT, and routers to uncouple the networks logically and protect the LAN.

Windows NT has several system services that serve your local network, most notably file and printer sharing (the "Server" service). You can configure these services to serve the intranet by binding them to the intranet hardware interface. However, this is *truly dangerous* because it offers many opportunities for malicious intranet computers to invade your system. Use the Network control panel to unbind NT LAN services (most notably the Server, Workstation, and the NetBIOS Interface) from the intranet interface adapter.

In the figure above IIS serves both the intranet and the LAN. NT system service programs are bound only to the internal network hardware and therefore serve only the internal network. The Network control panel bindings for NT services illustrates this setup.

The first adapter, [1], is to the LAN and the second, [2], to the intranet. (The other two services look the same.) You can install various proxy servers on this gateway that let internal hosts access certain intranet services, like FTP or WWW. IIS and these proxies use the TCP/IP protocol to communicate with both the LAN and intranet through both interfaces. With this configuration computers on your network can still access shared directories on the gateway and would typically do so to update the files offered to the intranet.

This is not the only configuration with strong security, but others involve networking techniques far beyond our current scope. However, see "Isolating NT Services from an Intranet" later in this chapter for a similar scenario.

Agents: Common Gateway Interface (CGI) and Internet Server Application Interface (ISAPI)

FTP transfers files in both directions (access control permitting) and Gopher transfers only from server to client. WWW can transfer information in both directions, but its "programmable" services require special security consideration.

WWW pages can direct user input to special programs on the server for processing, which we simply call "agents." The most common case is when the client user fills out an HTTP form. The form's information is passed back to the server and given one of these agents. The two common protocols for passing the form information to the agents are the CGI, popular throughout the Internet community, and Microsoft's ISAPI. These are sometimes called "scripts," although this term is not accurate for ISAPI.

Agents are simply programs that someone creates to perform some service. They commonly use a form's input to search a database and return the database items in a WWW page. By default agents run under the client user's account (which of course could be the anonymous account). Your cautions with respect to agents is the same as other programs on your system:

❖ IIS can store its agents in any of the accessible directories that have "Execute" permission. Set the ACL on this directory and its contents so that only administrators can add or modify the contents.

❖ Agents are usually scripts that must be run by some application indicated by the suffix in the URL. For example, a client may submit a request to the URL:

```
/Scripts/FindPhone.BAT?Name=JJones
```

which is processed by the application that processes the ".BAT" suffix, in this case the DOS CMD.EXE program. This is called "file name extension mapping." You need to define the extensions and path names for the applications that process them in the Registry. Check your IIS documentation for details. From a security perspective, it's better to store these applications outside the WWW directories. In all cases, protect them carefully from change.

❖ Carefully scrutinize agents for malicious or unsecure practices. Even though agents run under the user's account, they can have access to files outside IIS's advertised directory trees unbound by the access constraints IIS globally places on those trees. You must protect all local files and all network resources from agents.

❖ The Registry entry:

```
HKEY_LOCAL_MACHINE\SYSTEM\CurrentControlSet
   \Services\W3SVC\AllowGuestAccess
```

lets agents run under the all-powerful SYSTEM account. These agents are fully a part of the TCB and must be thoroughly trusted. Do not run in this mode unless your agents are duly trusted!

IP Filtering

IIS can control which remote hosts can access its services based on the host's network (IP) address. Use the Advanced property sheet:

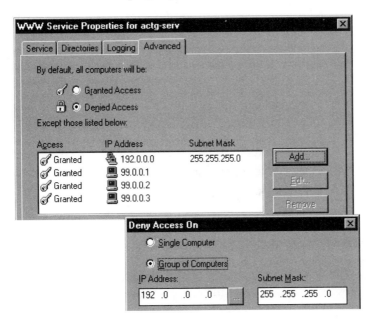

Add IP addresses to this list and select whether the ones on the list are the only ones granted access, or the only ones denied access. You can add either an individual computer or an entire subnetwork to the list. In this example, we allow access only to hosts on the network 192.0.0.0 and three hosts on the network 99.0.0.0.

A brief note about "subnet masks." Each IP address has a network portion that refers to the computer's network and is held by all computers on its local network. (The Internet is actually a network of subnetworks.) The IP address has four numbers, each ranging from 0 to 255. Depending on the size of the first (leftmost) number, the address' network portion is either its first number (when the first number is 1–126, called

Class A), first two numbers (first is 128–191, Class B), or first three numbers (first is 192–223, Class C). For example, for the IP address 192.0.0.3, the "192.0.0" portion is the network portion. If you want to exclude or include an entire subnet, you must supply the network portion in a subnet mask that has "255" for each number in the network portion of the IP address. For example, the mask for network hosting the IP address 192.0.0.3 is 255.255.255.0.

The problem with IP filtering is that malicious, remote hosts can insert any IP address in packets they send to your system and therefore masquerade as other hosts to pass your IP screening. This is called "IP spoofing." Even though your system returns its replies to the legitimate host, the penetrator may be able to intercept or at least view these replies. While IP filtering is a useful protection against nuisance or casual hackers, it's not a strong security protection against a determined penetrator. Use it wherever you can, but don't depend on it heavily.

Note that SSL does not protect against IP spoofing by clients unless you require client authentication. If you require SSL client authentication, while the malicious host can falsify the IP address it cannot impersonate client authentication without the client's private key. However, IIS does not currently implement client authentication.

Security Logs

New IIS authentications appear in NT's security log, as do accesses to individual files and directories. IIS also maintains a Spartan transaction log that you control with the Logging property sheet. This log can help you track down suspected transgressions and it's a good idea to save it. Check your IIS documentation.

Other Networking Topics

The following miscellaneous but nonetheless important topics round out our presentation of intranet topics.

RAS and PPTP

The Windows NT Remote Access Service lets a workstation running remote RAS client dial into an NT Workstation running the RAS service. This effectively connects the remote workstation into the server's network as if it were directly connected to the network, although the server can limit access to its own shared services as opposed to other workstations on the network. There are RAS clients for a number of operating systems, including, of course, Windows NT and Windows 95. The Point-to-Point Tunneling Protocol is an extension to RAS that lets the client dial in to an intranet service provider, then connect across the intranet to the RAS server.

RAS services on Windows NT use its standard security techniques. For example, the RAS client must furnish an account name and password, and passwords need not be passed as plaintext. Installing these services is straightforward, and we make only a few observations about configuring them securely.

You can specify the accounts that can logon to a RAS server. (See "General Security Controls" in Chapter 7, Managing Groups and Accounts.) For each account that can log on, you can set a dialback option where the server closes a newly authenticated connection then dials back to the client, all transparent to the user. Dialback can be to a number supplied by the client, used mainly for economy, or to a number you specify for the account, a significant security feature. Alternately, you can specify user permissions from the *Permissions...* menu option on the Remote Access Admin program (an administrative tool installed with RAS). The parameters on the bottom apply to the selected user.

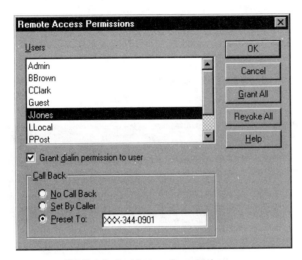

RAS Admin: User→ Permissions...

Servers can give remote clients network access through the TCP/IP, NetBEUI, and/or IPX[1] protocols. Use the Network control panel, shown on the next page, to call up the properties of the Remote Access Service, then select the **Network** button.

You can prohibit protocols for security reasons, since it effectively prevents the client from gaining services on the ones not permitted. For example, if you permit only NetBEUI, remote clients to the LAN cannot directly access the Internet through the LAN (assuming the LAN is on the network), because Internet access is available only through TCP/IP protocol.

RAS can use more than one authentication method and negotiates with the particular client as to which it uses. You can restrict the methods the server accepts. "Clear text" logons pass the password as plaintext with the obvious insecurity. "Encrypted authentication" schemes are industry-standard ones that don't pass the encrypted password. You can consider these safe as far as not exposing the password. Microsoft encrypted

---

1. NetBEUI and IPX are networking protocols frequently used on Windows and Windows NT networks. You can enable any combination of TCP/IP, NetBEIU, and IPX on Windows NT, depending on which ones are being used by other workstations that you want to communicate with. NT's various networking services can be "bound to"—or set up to be used with—any of these.

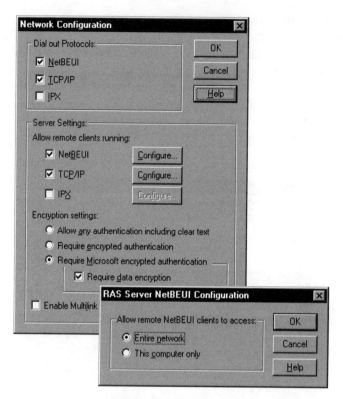

communication is the most secure and is used by RAS clients on NT, Windows 95, and Windows for Workgroups. It not only does not pass plaintext passwords, but lets you encrypt your communications using a fast, 40-bit key cipher. Use Microsoft authentication and its encryption option for maximum security. The Microsoft RAS client has similar options.

You can also specify whether each protocol should have access to the RAS server's entire LAN or the server itself. Use your own judgment here, but never give more access than necessary. The biggest danger is that a malicious remote attack might guess an administrator's password, but your site policies should be set up to counter this threat.

You can configure a remote workstation as a member of a LAN domain or in a workgroup. The section "Using the Remote Access Service" in Chapter 5, Special Situations, describes the operational differences. Neither scenario is significantly more secure than the other, although putting the workstation in a domain makes better use of NT's domain-based philosophy of central account control and as such is probably the better choice. It largely depends on how often the workstation connects. If seldom, the workgroup may be better; if frequently, the domain membership is better.

One basic security issue is users "caching" (saving) passwords on the client. This stores a password for a network account on a remote client whose physical security may be beyond your control. However, if the password is not cached, the user must type their password to the RAS client, which is not on the Trusted Path and is therefore exposed. The threat in any case is that of malicious software on the client, and it's probably better to save the passwords. This makes it a little harder for such programs to capture a password, although the unwary user can still be easily "spoofed."

Isolating NT Services from an Intranet

By some estimates, one computer on the Internet is broken into every 20 seconds.
—The *London Financial Times*, April 15, 1996

How do remote sources attack a workstation? They could induce you to download a Trojan Horse program, perhaps one modified in transit by the attacker. The following attacks are more to the point of this chapter.

Data Eavesdropping and Spoofing

Attackers may be able to eavesdrop on messages sent across the intranet. (Note that your local LAN gateways generally ensure that messages between two workstations on the same LAN are not placed on the intranet.) Attackers may also be able to place messages on the LAN that appear to be from a remote workstation either initiating or currently engaged in a legitimate dialogue. The only practical protection against these attacks are the cryptographic solutions we presented earlier.

Local Service Attack

Attackers can make requests of the workstation's active networking services, whether those supplied by Windows NT or by third parties. It's important that you control and limit the networking services of each workstation accessible from the intranet. While we've talked about the security of many of Windows NT's own services, you should understand how services from other vendor's ensure security. Such services should always require authentication from the remote source, like a password, but should not allow plaintext passwords. Allowing service based only on the IP address of the other party is dangerous, because attackers can often insert the IP address of a legitimate remote host into the message they send to the LAN (called "IP spoofing," see above).

NT Support Service Attack

This is a special case of a local service attack where remote hosts attack the common servers on an NT network, like the Server service that controls file and printer sharing. While NT includes many protections in these services, attackers can be quite clever and who's to say where they may find a foothold. In the text that follows, we present ways to isolate critical services from an intranet.

Trojan Horses

Malicious programs or malicious scripts run by otherwise trustworthy programs are the primary technique for invading a networking client system. Unfortunately, there are more and more opportunities for these to find their way onto your systems. Much of your defense is to counsel users about such programs. The rest is to make sure users with sensitive capabilities (administrators) never run untrusted programs. (See Chapter 11.)

There are two general ways to attach a Windows NT LAN to an intranet like the Internet. The first technique inserts a firewall between the LAN and the intranet, forcing all traffic between the two through the firewall. Firewalls differ greatly in detail, but their basic purpose is to restrict the kinds of communication between the LAN and the intranet by providing both proxy services with lots of security controls and packet-filtering services that work much like IIS's IP address filtering. There are many excellent books on this topic and we defer to them for details.

If your NT LAN is on or directly accessible from the intranet, you can use NT's protocol bindings to isolate NT's own critical services, like the Server service that handles file sharing. Many intranets like the Internet support only TCP/IP, which forces attacks from outside your LAN to use TCP/IP. Many native NT services like Server use NetBIOS, which can run over either TCP/IP or another protocol, like NetBEUI. If you configure them to run only over NetBEUI (and not TCP/IP) external attacks, which must use TCP/IP, are isolated from the services. Configuring is simply a matter of setting the right protocol bindings in the Network control panel. You should particularly unbind Server, Workstation, and NetBIOS from TCP/IP, leaving them bound only to NetBEUI. Do this for all computers on your LAN (or at least those that have direct access to the intranet). This figure shows the *Bindings* page of the Network control panel after you uncouple these services from TCP/IP:

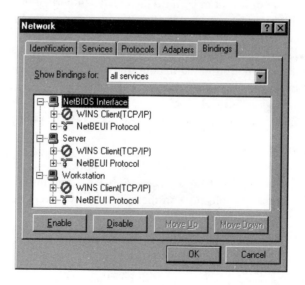

Even if these services use NetBIOS over TCP/IP (often because you've selected TCP/IP for your LAN for performance reasons), you can isolate these services from the network using filtering routers. NetBEUI over TCP/IP uses special ports on the router. If you instruct your router to disable UDP[1] and TCP ports 137–139, you sever these NT services from the external intranet. (Note that you may want your router to block other TCP or UDP ports for services that systems on your LAN should not be providing, like FTP, Telnet, NFS[2], and so forth.)

Of course, these solutions prevent services like Server from servicing legitimate requests from across the intranet. Unless you find special cryptographic protection for these services, this is quite dangerous. Ultimately, you have to make the trade-offs and we hope we've given you a little appreciation of the problems involved.

---

1. UDP is a networking protocol similar to TCP. Unlike TCP, UDP does not establish a persistent communication channel, but instead uses discrete, separate, independent datagrams for communication.
2. NFS is a client-server file sharing protocol popular on UNIX systems. It's not a part of native Windows NT although you can purchase third party NFS software that runs on NT systems.

Chapter 10

Subsystems and Other Security Features

The basic features we've discussed so far pervade the NT environment. If you've mastered these basics, you have nothing to fear from the many other places they are used. This chapter closes our operational presentation with a few final topics that include the more common of these other uses.

In This Chapter We Describe

➥ Setting the ACLs on printers and auditing their use

➥ Customizing the logon scenario by adding a logon banner

➥ How to administer Windows 95 and Windows for Workgroups

NT Registry

The NT Registry is a single, logical database kept on each NT Workstation that holds many parameters that control the system, including all security parameters. Many administrative programs both read and write entries in the Registry, and you can manage the Registry "manually" through the REGEDT32 program. REGEDT32 works like the Explorer and your view of the Registry is analogous to your view of your file system:

REGEDT32

❖ Just like your file system might have four logical drives, the Registry is divided into four major divisions.

❖ NT presents each of these four divisions as a tree structure with elements called **keys** (which organize the tree and are analogous to directories in the file system) and **values** (which hold data and are analogous to files). Keys can contain other keys (often called **subkeys** with respect to their parent key) and/or values.

❖ Similar to directories, keys have an owner, an ACL, and audit control information. However, items don't have ACLs but are instead protected by their parent key's ACL.

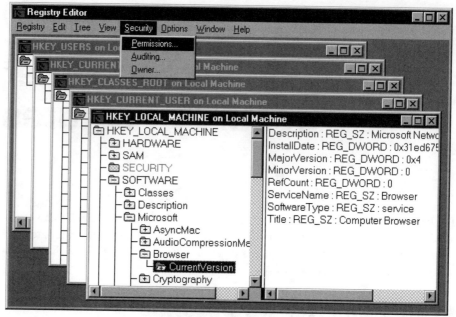

REGEDT32 and the Registry

This window shows REGEDT32 with the four major Registry divisions, each in its own subwindow. The left panel of the front window shows the tree structure of this division (called HKEY_LOCAL_MACHINE). REGEDT32 shows keys as little folder icons like Explorer shows directories. The panel on the right shows the eight values of the "CurrentVersion" key. Each value has a name, a type, and a value.

☞ Before you venture too far into Registry editing, it's a good idea to read your system documentation. However, we mention a few simple changes in other parts of this book that you can safely make.

The *Security* menu is the one of interest to us. ACLs on keys are like ACLs on files:

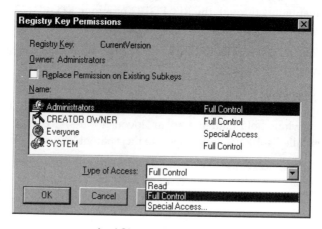

An ACL on a Registry Key

There are only two standard sets of permissions: "Read" and "Full Control." Just like for files, Special Access lets you set combinations of the Basic Permissions for keys, but this is seldom necessary. You can also take ownership of keys. NT newly installed properly protects its Registry entries and does not require you to maintain its ACLs.

You can also audit accesses to a key and its values analogous to auditing access to items in the file system. The audit category File and Object Access enables these events. However, given that the Registry is properly protected and seldom changed manually, we expect that few administrators will find auditing necessary.

View special access permissions: Run REGEDT32 from an MS-DOS window. On the "HKEY_LOCAL..." window, expand the editor's path. Choose "Special Access" and study the Basic Permissions. There are many more than files!

View audit controls: Select a key and use the *Security→ Audit...* option. Inspect the audit controls. (**OPT**) If you are ambitious.

In summary, most administrators need not manage ACLs in the Registry or audit it, but if you do, you'll find these features work analogously to the ones for file and directories.

System Policy Editor

The Policy Editor sets various parameters that control the user's logon environment, many of which are security relevant. These parameters are all kept in the NT Registry and could be edited using the Registry Editor, although the Policy Editor is considerably more friendly. NT can automatically apply "policy files" you create using the Policy Editor to user logons throughout your domain environment.

Policy
Editor

The Policy Editor can edit the Registry directly (seldom the case) or store its parameters in a "(system) policy file." A policy file has two kinds of entries: one that applies to a user or user group, and another that applies to a computer. You typically define a default entry for each. You can also define a policy file entry for specific users, NT user groups, or specific NT Workstations. Policy files use the ".POL" suffix.

When a user logs into NT Server or Workstation, NT can use a policy file to govern that logon session. There are two modes under which NT locates this policy file on the network.

In **manual mode** you can place the policy file anywhere on the network where it is share accessible, for example:

```
\\ACTG-SERV\NETLOGON\NTCUSTOM.POL
```

stores the policy file NTCUSTOM.POL on the primary domain controller in the share named NETLOGON.

In **automatic mode** you must name the file "NTCONFIG.POL" and place it in the share directory the domain controller exports under the name "NETLOGON." (Check your domain controller to determine the location of the directory with this share name.) In our example, this would be stored in:

```
\\ACTG-SERV\NETLOGON\NTCONFIG.POL
```

Windows NT uses the mode defined in the policy (which we describe later).

```
Local Computer\Network\System policies update\Remote Update
```

Simply set this entry on an NT Workstation (and nondomain controller NT Server) to the appropriate mode to activate the workstation's use of the policy files.

Of course you might ask, how can it check in the policy where to find a policy before it finds it? The answer is that it uses its current Registry setting to find the location, which as we see later could have been set by another policy file. When you first install Windows NT Server or Workstation, you at least need to set this parameter for the mode you select. By default, NT installs with "automatic" selected. Note also that you would normally specify this mode in your policy files.

☞ Make sure you install the policy file so that its ACL is public readable but writeable by administrators only.

What happens if NT can't find the file on the network? It logs the user on anyway using parameters from the previous logon session, which may not be appropriate for the new user! One of the automatic/manual policy parameters instructs NT to issue an error message in this case and you should advise users to come see you when this happens.

One advantage of automatic mode is that you can also set a "load-balance" parameter that searches not only the primary domain controller but also backup controllers and Windows NT Server installed as simple servers. However, you must place the policy in the NETLOGON share on all backup controllers manually. Setting this is a good practice when you are using backup controllers. You can use the Replicator service to synchronize the various copies of the policy files.

Your general strategy is to define the automatic file, NTCONFIG.POL, that applies to as many NT users and workstations as possible. You can handle specific exceptions by giving those workstations and users named entries in NTCONFIG.POL, but this increases your workload. If you have a large group of exceptions to NTCON-FIG.POL, it may be easier to load them from an manual mode policy, although you lose load-balancing capabilities.

Managing the Policy File

Setting up the shared policy file is relatively simple.

1. Log in using an account that can modify files in the share directory where you're going to place the policy file, usually a full NT domain administrator.

2. Start the Policy Editor. Use the *New File* option on the *File* menu, then the *Add User...* and *Add Group...* options from the *Edit* menu to create your entries (note that you can browse for user and group names). Besides the defaults, this figure shows one specific computer, one user, and two groups:

3. Use *Save As...* to store the file into its network share directory on the domain controller. From now on, use *Open* from the *File* menu to edit this policy file.

4. Now your job is to set the various parameters in these entries according to your site policy. We discuss these parameters and suggest some options later. This figure shows a typical editing session. Some parameters (wallpaper in this case) have several settings that appear the bottom of the window when you select that parameter.

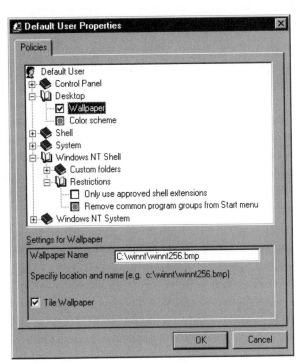

Note that when you select a parameter, you can set it "on" (checked), "off" (not checked, clear box), or "undefined" (gray box). (The figure on the previous page shows all three cases.) Both on and off parameters overwrite their locations in the Registry, but undefined parameters leave the preexisting Registry parameter unchanged. (The only effect of a policy file is to overwrite specific locations in the Registry when a user logs on.) You can use this and your knowledge of the order in which entries are loaded to set up your policy scheme. A few examples:

❖ You might decide to define some parameters on each workstation, excluding their definition from the policy file. For example, whether or not you allow remote logon to a workstation could be defined on each workstation then left undefined ("grayed" out) in the common policy file.

❖ Group policies typically impart extra, administrative-type parameters to certain users. All other group parameters are left undefined.

☞ It's a common mistake to turn a policy off (clear box) when you really intended to disable it (gray box). Be careful.

After a user successfully logs on to Windows NT, the system fetches the policy file from its remote location. It uses the defined parameters that apply to this user to overwrite the local Registry. When the user logs off, these remain in the Registry but are usually overwritten by the next logon.

If a computer entry is defined for this workstation (the one onto which the user is logging), the system loads it into the local Registry. Otherwise, it loads the default computer entry.

If a user entry is defined for this user, the system loads it into the local Registry. Otherwise, it loads the default user entry and also loads the parameters for each group entry in which the user is a member (if any) in a priority order, starting with the lowest priority first. (Use *Group Priority...* on the Policy Editor's *Options* menu to set this order.) The effect is that defined parameters in each group loaded overwrite the corresponding parameters for entries previously loaded. Your usual strategy is to give groups with the most capabilities the highest priority so they are loaded last. Note that the system does not load groups for users who have specific user entries.

Deciding what to leave undefined is a challenge and you need to plan your strategy carefully. Consider the following exercise:

> You set a policy parameter to a specific value for one user entry but leave it undefined for another. The first logs in before the second. What value of the parameter does the second user get? [170]

Following are some final points on managing your policy files:

❖ When you create a new entry, Policy Manager copies its initial values from the corresponding default entry.

❖ You usually create a group by first graying out everything, then setting the added capabilities on, since each group just adds to any others. This is not the strategy with new users or computers because they do not add to other entries; they are stand alone. Leave these entries undefined only when they should always revert to the logon workstation.

❖ You frequently want to give added capabilities to the administrative groups, including Operators and Power Users.

❖ User policy parameters overwrite corresponding ones in a user's personal profile file. Hence, although users may be able to change some aspects of their environment during their logon session, at next logon these revert to the policy values defined in the policy.

❖ Both user and computer policies are taken from the domain controller that holds the user's account—not the domain controller for the workstation onto which they are logging. If an account from domain A is used on a workstation on domain B, then A's computer policy applies. This may cause problems if domain B does not implement a shared computer policy. Once the workstation's Registry has been overwritten by the computer policy entry from A, it remains as such for subsequent users from domain B (it's own domain) and it is likely different than its original configuration in B. In effect, A's logon may change the workstation's policy for an indefinite number of logons.

☞ If you add computer entries or define any entries in the default computer entry in NTCON-FIG.POL for one of your domains, you should define the same parameters in the entries for all domains that trust it.

❖ The parameters that the Policy Editor shows you are the Registry entries defined in one or more template files with names that, by convention, end in ".ADM." You can see the editor's current templates by selecting *Policy Template...* under the *Options* menu. Templates are just text files with a prescribed format. If you can obtain the definition of this format (or figure it out from examples) you can modify existing templates or create your own.

> How do you switch a workstation that's been using automatic mode to manual mode? [171]

Using policy files still allows Windows NT to save each user's personal environment (like their desktop configuration, color scheme, and automatic connections at logon). However, the policy overwrites settings that are specified as other than default in the policy file.

Note the *Open Registry* option on the *File* menu that lets you view and modify the current Registry, although you seldom need to. You can also edit the Registry on another NT system using *Connect…* on the *File* menu.

User Policies

In this and the next section we list the policy parameters that especially bear on security and suggest how they be set. (We omit ones that have little security relevance.) Windows 95 also incorporates the Policy Editor and although its policies intersect with those for NT, they also differ. Therefore:

Legend	✔Set this ON.
	✘ Set this OFF.
	? Set this depending on your site's requirements.

☞In the list that follows, parameters that apply only to NT are marked as "(NT)" and those that apply only to Windows 95 are marked as "(95)." Ignore the "(95)s" until you read "Administering Windows 95" in this chapter.

Control Panel

Most of these parameters control which pages of certain control panels are shown to the user or whether the user can access the control panel at all. The first parameter for each control panel disables the entire applet, which you should do whenever you disable all its pages.

Display
- ? Restrict "Display" Control Panel
  - ? Hide Background Page
    Not security relevant except for the following case. Some sites create a custom background page that labels the information content of the workstation. For example, a military site might create a background that displays "Secret." Hiding the background helps prevent users from changing the background.
  - ? Hide Screen Saver Page
    You can help enforce password-protected screen saving by setting it up for a given user then hiding this page so they can't undo it. If you do so, hide this screen saver page.

Network (95)
- ✔ Restrict Network Control Panel
  - ✔ Disable Network control panel
    The Network control panel contains several sensitive parameters. We recommend hiding the entire applet.

Passwords (95)

✔ Restrict Passwords Control Panel
All but the *Change Passwords* page are sensitive and should be disabled. Disable the entire applet if you don't want users to change their own passwords.

  ? Disable Passwords Control Panel

  ✔ Hide Change Passwords Page

  ✔ Hide Remote Administration Page

  ✔ Hide User Profiles Page

Printers (95)

✔ Restrict Printer Settings
Some sites consider the control of printers security relevant. If so, you may wish to hide or disable the following, giving these capabilities only to an administrative group.

  ✔ Hide General and Details Pages

  ✔ Disable Deletion of Printers

  ✔ Disable Addition of Printers
  These last two disable the deletion and addition of printers using the properties of printer icons.

System (95)

✔ Restrict System Control Panel
While none of these have any strong security relevance, it's not a sound operational decision to let regular users change such fundamental configuration parameters of a workstation. Most sites will therefore select all these restrictions.

Desktop

As we just discussed, some sites create security-relevant wallpaper or color schemes. If so, they should restrict the *Background* page of the Display control panel and specify the wallpaper and color scheme here.

  ? Wallpaper
  Lets the user name the wallpaper and whether it's tiled.

  ? Color Scheme
  Lets the user name the color scheme.

Network (95)

Sharing
These prevent users from sharing directories and printers on the network, and this policy varies from site to site. Note that even users that can share directories can nonetheless import and export great quantities of data from remote shares. Windows NT Workstation restricts these operations to its Power Users, so you might also limit them to an administrative group, like an Admins 95 group.

  ? Disable File-Sharing Controls

  ? Disable Print-Sharing Controls

Shell

The "shell" refers to the desktop elements, like the **Start** button and the rest of the tool bar.

Custom Folders (95)
We don't regard any of these as security relevant in our context.

Restrictions

? Remove Run Command

In Chapter 11 we discuss the importance of preventing users from running malicious programs. Disabling *Run* menus like this help to accomplish this goal, although it's often fruitless because there are so many inherent ways to run program files, including through common applications with *Run* options.

? Disable Shutdown Command

Shutting down personal workstations is typically not restricted to administrators, but some sites may want to disable the shutdown command anyway.

Windows NT Shell (NT)

The same scope as "Shell" but for NT only.

Custom Folders
We don't regard any of these as security relevant in our context.

Restrictions

✔ Use Only Approved Shell Extensions

Sound advice unless you have a good reason to do otherwise. You should "trust" such extensions with the same rigor you trust applications you install on the system.

System

Restrictions

✔ Disable Registry Editing Tools

Standard tools that edit the Registry refuse to do so if you select this option. However, other programs can in general still edit the Registry. Nonetheless, you should limit this capability to full administrators.

✔ Run Only Allowed Windows Applications

If you select this option, you can create a list of allowed command names. (Use a simple program name, like "WINWORD.EXE." You don't need the full path name.) Windows then refuses to run commands not on the list, even from a DOS window. This does not restrict control panel applets.

☞ However, *be forewarned*. This is easily gotten 'round. Users can simply rename a prohibited command to an allowed name and run it.

One cannot call such easily compromised features "security" features. However, if you are trying to restrict programs users run on the system setting up this list does no harm, except that you have to type them all! If you restrict general users, make sure your policy for administrators turns off these restrictions.

✔ Disable MS-DOS Prompt (95)

If your policy disables Run commands, you should also disable the MS-DOS prompt.

✔ Disable Single-mode MS-DOS Applications (95)
A good security precaution if you disable Run commands.

Windows NT System (NT)

? Parse Autoexec.bat
If properly set up and protected by an ACL so that only administrators can modify it, AUTOEXEC.BAT does not pose any security risk.

Computer Policies

The following computer policy parameters are of particular security relevance:

Network

Access Control (95)

✔ User-level Access Control
Required for our domain scenario. This selects user-level as opposed to share-level access to network shares, and allows Windows 95 to participate more fully in NT domains. Enter the domain name as the authenticator name and choose *Windows NT Domain* as the *Authenticator Type*.

Logon (95)

✔ Logon Banner
This is the logon banner and we recommend it. See the "Windows NT System" parameter for more on logon banners.

✔ Require Validation by Network for Windows Access
Required for our domain scenario. Does not allow Windows 95 logon unless the name and password are authenticated by the primary network logon authority, like Windows NT or Novell Netware. (Select this authority on the *Configuration* page of the Network control panel.)

Microsoft Client for Windows Networks (95)

✔ Log on to Windows NT
Required for our domain scenario. Settings for Windows NT when designated as the primary network logon authority in the Network control panel. (Note that there are no policy parameters that designate the primary logon authority. This can only be set from the Network control panel.) Enter the domain name.

✗ Display Domain Logon Confirmation
This serves little security purpose and is a minor irritant to users.

✔ Disable Caching Of Domain Password
Windows 95 may try to include your domain password in its password cache that is unlocked by your Windows 95 password. There's relatively little harm as long as they're the same password. However, we recommend you not cache this password unless you later find it necessary.

✔ Workgroup
Required for our domain scenario. Enter the NT domain name. Among other things, this makes the Windows 95 computer appear to be a member of the domain in browser lists.

✗ Alternate Workgroup
Not generally needed in the NT domain environment.

Passwords (95)

✔ Hide Share Passwords with Asterisks
It is sound security practice to never echo passwords to the screen.

✔ Disable Password Caching
Password caching is little used under our user-level security, but you should disable it anyway.

✘ Require Alphanumeric Windows Password
Because you want the NT and Windows 95 password to be the same, you may have some conflicts if you select this because NT has no similar restriction.

✔ Minimum Windows Password Length
Make this the same value as on the NT domain controller.

Dial-up Networking (95)

? Disable Dial-in
Disables dial-ins to this computer. Whether you allow dial-in depends on your site policy. Generally you should not allow it unless you intend to use it. One option is to allow it in the Registry of workstations where it's allowed, and then not define it in the policy file.

Sharing (95)
Whether you allow this computer to advertise shares is a site policy. (Does not restrict accessing other computers.) This restriction overrides a user policy that allows users to share files and printers.

? Disable File Sharing

? Disable Print Sharing

(System Policies) Update

✔ Remote Update
Required for our domain scenario. Instructs the client logon system to download the policy file from a server. Select *Automatic* or *Manual* mode. (See "Managing the Policy File" discussed earlier.)

✔ Display error messages
Instructs Windows 95 to issue an error message if it can't open the remote policy file.

✔ Load balance
If off, Windows 95 fetches the automatic policy file only from the domain controller. If on, it fetches it from the primary controller, any backup controller, or any NT Server configured as simply a server. See "The Policy File," above.

System

✔ Enable User Profiles (95)
Required for our Windows 95 domain scenario.

Windows NT Networking (NT)

Sharing
These entries create "hidden" shares used by many system servers. They are protected with an ACL that allows only administrative access, which can't be changed, so you can consider these safe. While there's little security reason to disable them, if you know they're not needed, it is prudent to disable them.

Windows NT System (NT)

Logon

✔ Logon Banner
Instructs NT to insert a logon banner between the entry of the Trusted Path and the logon window, for example:

This serves an important notice to all users and you can use it in a few ways. Some sites feel their legal remedies against discovered intruders are strengthened if intruders are explicitly warned that they are not allowed to use the system. The window above contains such a warning. Alternately (or in addition), you might use this as a security warning to legitimate users, perhaps a restriction on how the workstation is to be used, for example, "Do not enter company-classified data on this workstation." You can specify both the title of this window (the "caption") and its contents (the "text").

✔ Automatic Logon
While it's obviously not secure, you can dispense with the logon scenario altogether by giving the workstation a default logon account and password. In this case, the system automatically logs on using this account and password. You don't use the Trusted Path and don't see the logon window, although you do see the logon banner. The password is kept in the Registry and may be visible to general users. Because you're allowing everyone access to the workstation anyway exposing the password does no harm—unless you intend to enforce the password for this account on some other workstation.
> **Example**: You set up a workstation in the lobby of your company for use by all your visitors. You carefully ensure it runs only a few company product information programs. You set up an account with as few capabilities as possible and use the automatic logon to that account. Whenever the workstation is turned on, it starts up logged on to this account.

✘ Enable Shutdown from Authentication Dialog Box
Determines whether the **Shutdown** button appears on the logon window. If it does, anybody can use it to shut down the system without logging on.
Should you enable this button? Certainly not on a major server. On an individual workstation it does little harm, since it can be used only when no one is logged on. Someone passing can usually cut the power anyway, which is far more disruptive than using this button.

✘ Do Not Display Last Logged on User Name
Removes the last logged on user from the logon dialog window. While there may be some rare scenario in which this could be considered a security risk, it seems to obscure to counterbalance the convenience on computers regularly used by the same person.

271

Windows NT Remote Access (NT)

✔ **Max Number of Authentication Retries**
If initial authentication fails, RAS holds the connection open and queries the user for retries. This parameter limits the number of retries (not counting the initial failure) after which the server hangs up the line. Set this to some reasonable limit, like five. The net effect is to slow down guesses on the account, since the attacker must reestablish the connection, which takes a little time. If you are concerned about this attack you should set accounts to lock also.

✔ **Max Time Limit for Authentication**
The server hangs up the line if the user does not complete a successful retry within this time. The small danger is that a remote user may have left their computer unattended in the midst of their logon. Set this to some reasonable value, say twenty seconds.

✔ **Auto Disconnect**
Directs the server to hang up the line if there is no communication over the RAS connection for this time period. Many services on the remote client use the connection even when the workstation is unattended, and these can keep the connection alive. This disconnect is more for the case where the remote workstation has frozen or crashed without closing the RAS connection.

Working with the Policy Editor: Create an automatic policy (NTCONFIG.POL) on the domain controller's NETLOGON share.

❖ First, change the logon banner for the default computer to say something distinctive. Log out then back on twice to see if you see the new banner the second time. (The new parameters don't get loaded until after a successful logon so you don't see it during the first logon.)

❖ Make an entry for a user and change something distinctive, like restricting parts of the Display control panel. Log on as that user to see if they take effect.

❖ Experiment with setting up some group entries. Note the group priority order. Give different values to the same parameter in two different groups and see if the higher priority group supersedes the other.

Now that you're done with the exercise, suppose you'd like to undo all the changes you made and return to the way it was before. Can you just delete the NTCONFIG.POL file? [172]

Printers

The Printers folder in My Computer lets administrators create printers and make them accessible both locally and from remote workstations. As administrator, you can manage a number of parameters that control and audit who uses each printer. Mostly you use these for operational reasons to keep people outside your department from tying up your printers, or to keep others from running unnecessary jobs on your new eight-dollar-per-page color laser. However, there are some security considerations.

Printers

ACLs and Other Security Controls

Each printer has an ACL that controls who can print on and manage the printer. Set the ACL from the printer's property sheet:

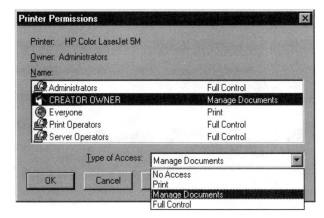

Setting a Printer's ACL via Icon Menu: Properties→ Security→ {Permissions}

The ACL applies to the printer's jobs as a whole—each job does not have its own ACL. Printer ACLs are straightforward and easy to use. There are four permissions. **Print** lets users submit jobs. **Manage Documents** lets them delete or change parameters for a print job. **No Access** and **Full Control** are self-explanatory.

This window shows your customary ACL on NT Server. Everyone can send jobs to this printer. They become the owner and pick up "Manage Documents" permission through CREATOR OWNER. Full administrators and certain operators can fully manage this printer and all its jobs. On an NT Workstation, you might want to include the Power Users group with "Full Control." Earlier, we mentioned that certain groups can manage printers. This ACL gives them those capabilities and if you change the ACL you remove those capabilities. The accounts and groups you see in a printer ACL are the same as you see in file ACLs on that workstation.

You can print to printers on other workstations if they're shared on the network and if their ACLs permit. The accounts and groups you see in a printer ACL are the same as you see in file ACLs on that workstation.

You can share a printer with remote workstations using the *Sharing* page of the property sheet:

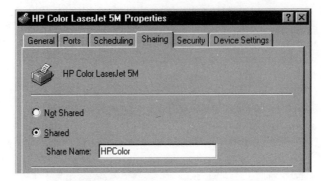

Icon Menu: Properties→ Sharing

There is no separate ACL for the share itself, rather the printer's ACL controls both local and remote access. The *Scheduling* page lets you set the times when the printer is available:

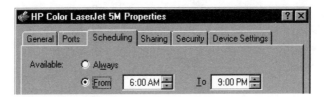

Icon Menu: Properties→ Scheduling

Available From lets you set the hours during which jobs can be submitted. Its use is straightforward. The *General* page also lets you set a *Separator File* that is printed at the beginning of each job. It's a text file written in printing language like PostScript and you need a specialist to create one. NT supplies a few defaults and their names have the ".SEP" suffix. You may use the *Separator* page to identify the security relevance of the job, and we give an example later.

> **Testing the Printer ACL:** Try some simple access tests on one of your printers. For example, remove permissions for CREATOR OWNER and see if the user who submits a job can cancel it.

Auditing

A printer's Security property sheet lets you audit the actions on a printer:

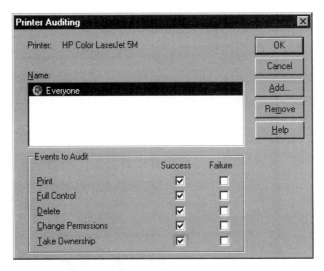

Icon Menu: Properties→ Security→ {Auditing}

Its events and use are straightforward once you've learned NT's file and directory auditing. The File and Object Access category in User Manager's Audit Policy window enables these events. The print event is the workhorse for object access, our old friend #560:

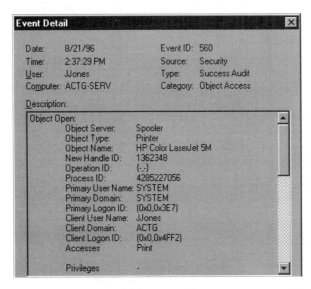

Typical Printer Audit Record

> **Printer auditing**: Clear the security log. Set up the Audit Policy for successful File and Object Access. Set your printer's ACL to audit successful printing for Everyone, nothing else. Print a job, for example using Notepad, then open the security log. (Don't forget to refresh the log.)

Protecting Printers

Now that we know how to protect printers, we turn to the question of when. As we mentioned earlier, operational reasons determine most of your printer policy. However, there are a few cases where access control is important:

Example: A printer is loaded with a stack of signed checks that are to be mechanically stuffed and mailed. You obviously want to ensure that only certain users can print to it.

Example: You have a printer in a relatively unprotected area of your building. You know that some of your groups, like the sales department, regularly handle sensitive information that you'd like not printed in such loosely protected sites. Exclude those groups.

If you share printers on the network, the INTERACTIVE and NETWORK groups can be quite handy:

Example: You want to allow all local users to print, but only members of the ACTG\Accounting group to print from remote locations. Its ACL is as follows (not showing the administrative entries):

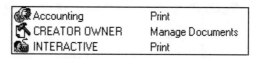

You can use the *Separator* pages creatively:

Example: You've set up several printers in an area accessible by print operators only. They remove completed jobs and hand them to users at a "printer services window." You'd like to control printouts from certain sensitive departments, like personnel, by making the user sign a log when they receive their printout. You can do this by setting up logical printers for groups in certain departments with a distinctive banner page that screams "Signature Required" to the print operators.

Example: You want all printouts from the research department to have a distinctive banner page that says something like, "Sensitive Material." You then set up a logical printer for use by the research department with this banner page. Of course, you must rely on the users themselves to keep the banner with the material and to handle the documents accordingly, but you at least give them a banner page that helps.

Print jobs are kept in NT's "spooling" area until they are completely printed, usually the directory:

```
WINNT\SYSTEM32\SPOOL\PRINTERS
```

Anyone with Read access to this directory and its contents can read those jobs using any text editor like the Notepad. It doesn't look pretty, but they can see the basic text of what you're printing. Protect this directory's ACL as tightly as you can unless it impacts printing functionality.

> **Protecting the spool directory**: Check the ACL on the PRINTERS directory. Is it tight enough? If not, how would you improve it? [**173**]

Administering Windows 95

We talked about using Windows 95 in the Windows NT domain environment in Chapter 5. We now turn to administering its security in the domain environment. Windows 95 interfaces to the security features of several networking environments, including Windows 95 itself, Windows for Workgroups, Novell Netware, and Windows NT. We show you how to fully integrate Windows 95 into the NT domain environment, which it does quite nicely.

You can set up each Windows 95 workstation to act much like "member" of a Windows NT domain. While this is not quite membership in the sense that NT Workstations are members of a domain, it is close. The great majority of your job is setting various parameters in the Windows 95 Registry, some through common programs like the Network and Password control panels, and others through the **System Policy Editor** (or simply "Policy Editor") that we discussed earlier. The Windows 95 System Policy Editor lets you edit certain parameters in the Registry, many of which are security relevant. Like NT, rather than set these on each Windows 95 workstation, you set up a central policy file on the Windows NT domain controller that each Windows 95 workstation uses.

Some of your administration of Windows 95 will be from a Windows 95 workstation. The rest will be from Windows NT. While you can use an NT administrative account to log on to Windows 95, it's a bit dangerous because Windows 95 cannot protect passwords as well as NT. We suggest you create a global group on the NT domain controller for use in these situations, then give this group whatever capabilities it needs to administer Windows 95. The main capability is to modify the CONFIG.POL file, and you can set this up in the file's ACL and its share directory. Add the accounts that are to administer Windows 95 to this group.

Basic Domain Installation

You must first set up a Windows 95 computer in a Windows NT domain using what we call a "basic domain installation":

1. On the *Configuration* page of the Network control panel make sure the basic networking protocols, adapters, and the "Client for Microsoft Networks" are installed. Set the primary network logon to "Client for Microsoft Networks."

2. Also on this page, call up the properties for the "Client for Microsoft Networks." Check *Log on to Windows domain* and enter the domain name. Choose whichever of the *Network Logon Options* is appropriate for your site.

3. On its *Identification* page, type the domain name in the *Workgroup* field. Enter any description you like.

4. On its *Access Control* page select *User-level access control* and enter the NT domain name.

5. On the *User Profile* page of the Passwords control panel, select *User can customize....* Set the User Profile Settings (which are not security relevant) to whatever is appropriate for your site.

6. Install GROUPPOL.DLL in the Windows System directory, usually in C:\WINDOWS\SYSTEM.

We assume you've chosen to use automatic policy mode, which is the case in a default install. However, if this becomes disabled or you want to use manual mode, edit the workstation's Registry with the Policy Editor (having either loaded it on the computer or set up the computer for remote editing). For automatic mode choose the *automatic* update mode. For manual, choose *manual* update mode and fill in the network share location of the policy file.

Although you don't have to, it's a good idea to enable each Windows 95 workstation so that its Registry can be edited remotely by Policy Editor:

1. Install the Remote Administration service on each Windows 95 workstation that you wish to participate in remote Registry editing. Follow the installation instructions in the Resource Kit.

2. Enable remote administration from the *Remote Administration* page of the Passwords control panel. Select the administrative groups that may remotely edit this workstation's Registry. You would typically select the special Windows 95 administration group we discussed earlier.

We recommend you enable remote administration because you can lock yourself out of a workstation where the only way to extricate yourself is to change its Registry remotely. For example, if you disable the network but require domain authentication to logon, you can't log on to enable the network. However, you can fix this by remotely relaxing the network log on requirement in the Registry.

Using the Windows 95 Policy Editor

Your major task is to define a policy file, place it on a central server (usually the NT domain controller), and then set up all the Windows 95 workstations in that domain to reference that file. This procedure is much like we described for NT.

Policy Editor

Note: Current releases of Windows 95 include the System Policy Editor as an administrative tool in the Windows 95 Resource Kit. The help files in the kit tell you how to install and use this utility. The kit also has a Remote Administration server that lets you use edit policies on other Windows 95 workstations.

The Policy Editor for Windows 95 is the same as Windows NT, although its policies differ a bit. A few notes about using the Windows 95 version:

❖ Use the Policy Editor from a Windows 95 workstation. Log in using a domain account that can modify files in the share directory where you're going to place the policy file, like an account in our Windows 95 administrative group.

❖ Windows 95 uses the default automatic policy file named CONFIG.POL instead of NT's NTCONFIG.POL, but for automatic updates it's stored in the same domain controller share directory (NETLOGON).

❖ Like NT, Windows 95 installs with automatic mode selected by default. But the Policy Editor path is a little different:

```
Local Computer\Network\Update\Remote Update
```

❖ You can also use manual mode to load the policy file from an arbitrary network share location.

❖ Install GROUPPOL.DLL on each Windows 95 workstation. If you don't, NT ignores group policies.

❖ If you set up the Remote Administration service on both systems (above), you can edit the Registry on another Windows 95 workstation using *Connect...* on the *File* menu.

See "System Policy Editor" earlier in the chapter for a description of the Windows 95 policy parameters. You should synchronize your Windows 95 policies with those for the Windows NT systems. This can be a bit of work and all the more reason for planning this beforehand.

You may want to create a few NT global groups to use for those who generally administer the Windows 95 workstations. For example, you might create one called Operators 95 to allow modest administrative duties, and a second called Admin 95 to grant full administrative capabilities. Define these groups beforehand as global groups on the NT domain controller and populate them appropriately.

The procedures we discuss here create the Windows 95 user environment that we described in Chapter 5, which you may want to review. Check the documentation in the Resource Kit if you have any problems with the Policy Editor.

Synchronizing Computer Entries

A Windows 95 user can log on using an account from any domain by simply typing the name, password, and domain in the logon window. This is different than Windows NT Workstation where a user can only log on to accounts in the workstation's domain or one of the domains its domain trusts.

Recall that the domain controller automatic computer policy file that's applied to the local Registry at logon is the one from the user's logon domain. This means a user can apply a computer entry from any domain in which they know a logon. Users from different domains using the same Windows 95 workstation create the same effect.

Consider an example. There are two domains A and B, and a Windows 95 workstation named CRYSTAL. Both A and B have CONFIG.POL files that include a Default Computer with all parameters defined (no gray boxes). When a user on CRYSTAL logs onto a domain A account, A's computer policy is applied to CRYSTAL, but when another user logs into a domain B account, B's policy is applied.

Even though these computer policies could be quite different they are applied to the same computer. Several computer policies are based on the computer itself instead of its users (user entries hold lots of nice user-specific controls) and as such they should not change with different users. There can also be some troublesome side effects. For example, suppose A's and B's policies each use their own name as the source of users and groups that are applied to share ACLs. While our A user can apply names from domain A but not B, our B user is just the opposite. Also, these name sources don't switch unless the system is rebooted anyway! There are several solutions that can help you avoid confusion:

❖ The solution we recommend it to ensure that Default Computer entries in your automatic update policy files do not define parameters that should be specific to each computer. Parameters that are the same across the entire breadth of your network should be defined, but think carefully about others. Especially consider the fields in the left-hand figure below:

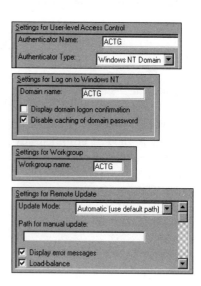

The right-hand figure shows the basic parameters of how Windows 95 participates in the domain environment. The parameters are usually specific to the computer itself, regardless of its current user. Define these appropriately on each Windows 95 computer and leave them undefined (gray box) in your network-based policy files.

❖ You can use manual updates, since they are always loaded from the same source. The major disadvantage is that you often want user policies loaded from the domain controller that holds the user's account and for this you need automatic updating.

❖ You can define a specific computer policy for each Windows 95 computer and distribute it to all domains, although changing them is a headache.

❖ You can fully set up the local Registry on each Windows 95 computer and delete the Default Computer in your domains' policy files. In this manner the local Registry is never changed. The disadvantage is that you have to set up the entire Registry on each computer.

User policy entries don't have these issues because in automatic mode they are always taken from the same domain controller as the user's account, whether the default or a specific user entry. Windows 95 places user policy restrictions on an account regardless of the computer from which its user is working, which is normally what you want. Note also that this issue is not quite so pronounced on Windows NT Workstations because NT confines their logons to their own domains.

A Windows 95 computer is set up always to load its ACL user and group names from a particular domain, just as we recommend. A user logs on using an account from another domain. Can they add their account to network shares? [174]

How Secure is Windows 95?

In the world of Windows NT-class security, it's not very. The major problem is that Windows 95 has no ACLs so its Registry and its system and user files cannot be protected from malicious users or programs. It does have a number of well-designed, commonsense security protections, like the Windows 95 logon that unlocks the encrypted password list for share-level security or, as we've seen, its Registry has many parameters that aid in maintaining a "secure" system. And of course it protects its network share directories and printers with share ACLs. However, without file and directory ACLs in its basic file system there's no protected security base within the system.

Note especially that in the Windows NT environment Windows 95 processes the user's domain password. Even though it encrypts the password when on the network, the password is exposed on Windows 95 and can easily be grabbed by a malicious program. This then compromises the security of the entire NT network.

For this reason, you should avoid using the domain's administrative accounts on Windows 95.

If these threats to Windows 95 security concern you, we have an easy and pleasant solution: use Windows NT instead!

Administering WFW

ADMINCFG

We talked about using Windows for Workgroups to access Windows NT in Chapter 5. We now turn to administering its security as it relates to working in a Windows NT network. Use the ADMINCFG program to set up a WFW security control file, usually named "WFWSYS.CFG" and kept in the WINDOWS directory. This file is encrypted for security.

Note: WFW version 3.11 documents ADMINCFG.EXE only in its Resource Kit, although it has on-line help information. You must install this command manually from your delivery media using the command "expand admincfg.ex_" to copy and expand it into a convenient command directory on your hard disk, for example C:\WINDOWS. Add it to Program Manager if you like.

You can and should assign a password to ADMINCFG that you must enter each time you start it up. (It comes without a password. We see how to give it a password later.)

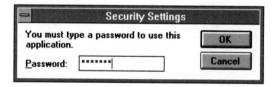

ADMINCFG Startup Password

ADMINCFG then asks you for the security configuration file and you can accept the defaults. Next it presents its main window:

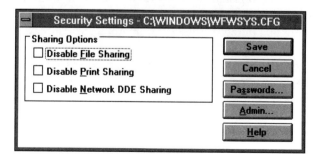

ADMINCFG Main Window

Sharing Options let you disable this workstation's ability to make its resources available to the network, although they don't affect the workstation's ability to connect to the resources of other workstations. The **Admin**... button produces a simple window that lets you change the password that guards ADMINCFG and define the title on the WFW's logon window, called its "banner." The window pertinent to our NT discussion comes from the **Passwords**... button:

```
┌────────────────────────────────────────────────────┐
│ ▬            Password Settings                      │
├────────────────────────────────────────────────────┤
│ ┌─ Password Options ──────────────┐   ┌──────────┐  │
│ │ ☒ Disable Password Caching      │   │    OK    │  │
│ │ ☐ Show Share Passwords in       │   └──────────┘  │
│ │   Sharing Dialogs               │   ┌──────────┐  │
│ │ ☒ Logon Password Expiration     │   │  Cancel  │  │
│ │   ┌────┐                        │   └──────────┘  │
│ │   │ 60 │▲ days                  │   ┌──────────┐  │
│ │   └────┘▼                       │   │   Help   │  │
│ │ ☒ Minimum Password Length       │   └──────────┘  │
│ │   ┌────┐                        │                 │
│ │   │ 3  │▲ characters            │                 │
│ │   └────┘▼                       │                 │
│ │ ☐ Force Alphanumeric Passwords  │                 │
│ │ ☒ Require Validated Logon to    │                 │
│ │   Windows NT or LAN Manager     │                 │
│ │   Domain                        │                 │
│ │ ☐ Allow Caching of User-Level   │                 │
│ │   Passwords                     │                 │
│ └─────────────────────────────────┘                 │
└────────────────────────────────────────────────────┘
```

Disable Password Caching

This completely disallows the "caching" of passwords, where WFW stores your domain password to use for later domain authentication. If disabled, WFW does not present the option to cache passwords in the Domain Logon window users must enter the domain password each time WFW authenticates them into a domain. The security issue is whether you consider WFW's local storage of the cached passwords to be exposed. On the one hand, WFW has no ACLs to protect locally stored passwords (although they're encrypted), so you may want to disable caching. On the other hand, WFW also has no Trusted Path so it's easier for "spoofing" programs to coerce users into typing their domain password, so perhaps it's safer to allow caching to minimize their entry. This is a difficult trade-off that you must assess for yourself.

Logon Password Expiration, Minimum Password Length, and Force Alphanumeric Passwords

These help control the strength of local passwords. They are particularly important because the local password alone protects the domain account when you enable password caching. Each WFW account has a list of passwords its user presents to access remote WFW resources, which are individually password protected. The list is protected by the WFW password and you need to consider this also when you set these password controls.

Require Validated Logon to Windows NT or...

This has the same affect as the *Logon to Windows NT...* option on the Startup Settings window in the Network control panel. If either one of these is selected, WFW does not allow a local logon unless it can concurrently perform a successful domain logon. This serves an important security purpose. It requires WFW users, who are not authenticated because they can freely create new accounts, to have a valid domain account before they can access the network at all. This account can be either a domain or local account on the domain controller.

If you disable password caching and require domain logon, then WFW no longer requires you to log on locally to WFW. Instead it asks only for the domain logon.

For maximum WFW security:

✓ Give ADMINCFG a suitably strong access password.

✓ Use *Require Validated Logon to Windows NT...*

✓ Decide if you need to disable domain password caching. If you leave it enabled, enforce appropriately strong WFW passwords.

The other fields on this window are not particularly relevant to NT access and we leave their description to the WFW documentation.

Recall that a WFW user can access any NT Workstation participating on workgroups or any NT Server visible on the network without domain authentication if their WFW account name matches an account on that workstation. There's nothing inherently unsecure about this, but it's more secure to require a domain logon before they can even attempt to access the network.

The ADMINCFG event log is a sort of audit trail, but it can be changed by anyone. For this reason it's not a strong security audit log like NT's audit log. You may find it handy for operational reasons or for "soft" security.

Other Topics

Viewing Current Activities and Alerts

Server Manager lets you view current resource use on any workstation to which your account has administrative capabilities. Its features are more operational than security related. While you can forcibly log users off the system or disconnect remote users, these are seldom used for security, since few sites have their administrators constantly monitor system activity at this level.

NT's Performance Manager can send alerts to certain workstations when a certain threshold of occurrences have happened. Some of the "server" alerts are security related. Check your NT documentation.

Performance
Monitor

What's Not Security Relevant

As we've mentioned a number of times, Windows NT has many important operational features either not directly related to our definition of security or that bear no special security discussion. For example:

❖ Desktop environments

❖ Disk mirroring and stripping

❖ Networking protocols

❖ Directory replication

❖ Emergency repairs and "last-known-good" configurations

❖ Backup domain controllers

❖ Daily backups

While we mentioned a few aspects of these, for example how some of them interact with ACLs, we don't consider them mainstream security topics. Note that none of the standard networking protocols have any particular security advantage over the others.

We don't mean to imply that these topics are not important, and if you consider some of them security issues your points may be well taken. It's mostly that these topics are of importance even to sites who have little need or interest in security as we have defined it.

Chapter 11

The TCB

Security features are to no avail unless the base on which they rest and the software that enforces them is rock solid and impenetrable. While NT affords this stability, it's up to you to protect and maintain its basic strength. The **Trusted Computing Base** is the sum total of security-critical software and hardware that makes up a network system. It includes any module capable of subverting security and is therefore responsible for maintaining security. We call these modules "trusted." In a well-managed system, the TCB controls the non-TCB and prevents the latter from violating the basic security rules of the system, called its "security policies." For example, the TCB prevents programs from accessing files unless they pass the ACL, users from logging on unless they present the correct password, and regular programs from directly placing messages on the network. But who protects the protector, the TCB? You do. This chapter shows you how.

In This Chapter We Describe

➡ The importance of and what constitutes the TCB

➡ Some ideas for how to protect it

We introduced the topics of TCB and threats in Chapter 1 and we don't repeat it here. You may want to review it now.

☞ Appendix A, Secure Installation, gives detailed specifications for protecting the TCB and other elements of the as-installed system.

What Constitutes the TCB?

Broadly, you must consider any running program with the ability to subvert one of the system's security policies a part of the TCB, and you must trust it to act responsibly. Further, any data files that such a program relies on for its security decisions must also be a part of the TCB. While you can certainly consider administrator's themselves as part of the TCB, we don't take this tack because our goal is to show you how to protect the TCB, and you can't "protect" administrators in this sense. In this section, we're not so concerned with the delivered Windows NT software that's part of the TCB, but rather the third-party programs you might add to the system.

When we speak of a "program" in the TCB, we are talking about its algorithms, as captured in any form: from source code through binary modules to the contents of the final executable file. We protect a program by protecting all these files from unauthorized change. The following programs are included in the TCB.

Programs Run by Users with Administrative Capabilities

As we've said before, a user's capabilities are inherited by all the programs they directly execute. Trusted programs must be trusted not to abuse these capabilities. Capabilities include the account identity, which allows inclusion in administrative groups and Rights. The difficulty is that there's no "tag" on a program that declares it trustworthy. Instead, you must trust users with sensitive capabilities to avoid programs you deem not trustworthy. Later we show you some techniques to limit the programs they use to the ones you trust. Although malicious users can circumvent some of these limits, you can prevent careless accidents. We also see that window execution environments, like your desktop, are usually safer that the MS-DOS command environment.

Programs Installed by the System (Servers)

Programs that function as servers don't directly inherit the capabilities of the requesting users, although they may receive reliable information about those users. Servers must instead obtain their basic power from the entity that started them, usually the system itself. We presume the system is properly configured to start only programs properly trusted and protected.

Programs on Which TCB Programs Rely

Any program on which a trusted program implicitly or explicitly relies in enforcing security is also part of the TCB. You need not worry about NT's own programs, only the ones you add to the system. Suppose a trusted program relies on a program to sort a file of security data. While the sort program may not have any capabilities itself, it could certainly torpedo security by making a few strategic changes in addition to sorting.

There are many files and directories in the TCB, most in the WINNT directory:

Files with Security Information

These are files containing information a trusted program relies to make security decisions. Most of these are in the NT Registry.

Files Holding Trusted Programs

These are any files that hold a trusted program. After all, if someone could change the file, they could change the program and make it no longer secure. Your focus is on the executable files—the issues of source and binary code are in the domain of the application programmers.

Device and Library Files

You should consider the plethora of device driver files a part of the TCB (*.DRV and *.SYS). Treat dynamically linked library files (*.DLL) as part of the TCB because they hold code that trusted programs might use.

Common Commands

Although commands in the command directories, like C:\DOS and C:\WINDOWS, need not necessarily be part of the TCB, you should protect them as if they were. Administrators frequently use them and even regular users expect system commands on a secure system to be above reproach.

Protecting the TCB

ACLs protect the TCB files and your freshly installed system is reasonably protected. In this section we talk about keeping it that way. To reiterate an earlier statement:

> Malicious programs are the biggest threat to the TCB. They are usually introduced as Trojan Horses, seemingly innocent programs with a hidden, malicious agenda. If they're run by users with sensitive capabilities (most notably administrators) your TCB becomes their playground.

Sometimes these programs are content to do damage themselves, but they can be insidious and attempt to change other programs on the system, thus propagating their nefarious schemes to other seemingly innocent programs. This technique is called a "virus" and is much in vogue. A virus that propagates from one workstation to another is sometimes called a "worm." But these vermin are all just aspects of "malicious code." Of course, you assume that programs you "trust" are not malicious. Otherwise, you wouldn't trust them. But you must protect them from being changed by viral infection. Ditto for all TCB files.

> What are the advantages of infecting other programs to do the dastardly deeds? [175]

✔ **Use tight ACLs for the TCB.**
Wherever practical, protect TCB files by keeping them owned by full administrators (the Administrators local group) with ACLs that grant at most "Read" and "Execute" access. While it's safe to give SYSTEM "Full Access," only give administrators more if necessary.

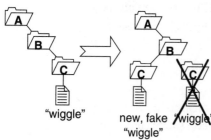

"wiggle"

new, fake "wiggle"

✔ **Beware the "delete-and-replace" scheme.**

If a malicious program has "Full Control" of a directory ("B" in this example), it can remove items, like the directory tree "C," from the directory (even without "Delete" (**D**) access to the individual items) and replace them with new, "false" copies, like our false copy of C and the file "wiggle." For example, a virus might try to infect trustworthy programs by replacing them with copies. Ensure that regular users don't have "Full Control" of directories that are ancestral directories to programs (especially trusted programs) and other TCB files. While you may not need to protect all programs that regular users use, it's a good idea. It's essential to protect all programs that administrators use. Additionally, it's safer to just assign **RWXDPO** rather then "Full Control," except maybe for the SYSTEM user.

✔ **Restrict administrative access to untrusted programs.**

If you don't trust a program and administrator's don't need to use it, preclude "Execute" (**X**) access to administrators, typically the Administrators and Operator groups. You need not restrict SYSTEM. This advice may strike you as backward. After all, administrators are trusted, why shouldn't they be allowed to run any program? We hope that by now you appreciate that while the administrators may be trusted, a program they run may not be. While you can advise them to not run such a program, it helps if the ACL doesn't allow it. Of course, a determined administrator can "Take Ownership" and give themselves "Execute" access, but this technique helps curb careless mistakes. This restriction should not unduly inconvenience administrators. Untrusted programs are seldom used for administration—only nonadministrative tasks. Because administrators should not do non-administrative tasks as administrators, they shouldn't be running untrusted programs anyway. Alternately, you could audit execution of these programs by members of these administrative groups, but it's better to keep them from running untrusted programs in the first place.

✔ **Limit the importing of programs.**

Perhaps easier said than done, but try. Watch for the creation of executable files, either by name or by permissions, although auditing this generates a lot of chaff and you need to look hard for the wheat. The best bet is to impress upon users that they should ask you first.

You could prevent users from adding new applications to their task bar *Start* menu, but they can still run the programs from MS-DOS. You can remove access to the MS-DOS window and various *Run* menu options, but they can still run them from the Trusted Path Security window and Explorer. Vigilance is still your best bet.

If you install programs as common groups, encouraging all users to share the same copy, you can ensure that new programs are properly protected from change.

✔ **Use virus-checking programs.**

Use virus-checking programs liberally. Although they are no panacea and less important on Windows NT than systems like MS-DOS, they're cheap protection that do no harm. Preferably, check all new software on isolated, noncritical workstations before introducing them into your general environment.

> The rule of thumb is to protect everything in the WINNT directory from change unless it interferes with day-to-day operation.

Working in the Command Environment

The command environment is likely the most dangerous for administrators because it offers the greatest chance to run an untrusted program accidentally. A few hints:

✓ Protect AUTOEXEC.BAT, CONFIG.SYS, and similar files by keeping them on an NTFS file system and setting their ACL to prevent writing. This is partly because the path variable is defined in the AUTOEXEC.BAT file, but also because such files contain other important information (although some are no longer used by NT). If you can't put them on an NTFS file system, define the path variable in the logon script to supersede its vulnerable definition in AUTOEXEC.BAT. You can do this for other definitions in this file also.

✓ If you're concerned that aspects of your environment (like the path variable) are vulnerable, write a logon script to check them. While a little involved for most users, MS-DOS experts can easily write such scripts.

✓ For maximum safety, administrators should use only the Security window to run programs and switch between them. The danger is that spoofing programs may present you with windows that look legitimate and steal sensitive information you type. Using the Trusted Path helps eliminate this threat, although it's a bit cumbersome for switching between windows.

✓ From a TCB perspective, treat batch files (*.BAT) like program files. Batch files inherit the capabilities of users who run them. Although you can trust the MS-DOS command interpreter that runs these files, the interpreter performs whatever the batch file instructs without question.

Other Tips

Booting from Floppies

Remember that since most workstations can boot from the floppy drive, users can boot another operating system like MS-DOS and with a little work gain raw access to NT disk partitions. There's not much you can do about this unless your machine has physical controls, like a key lock, boot password, or switches on its CPU card.

Network Threats

You may have workstations on your network that are not Windows NT and that allow their programs direct access to the network, like MS-DOS. On most local area networks, like Ethernet, unless the network is protected with cryptographic techniques, programs on these workstations can snoop on messages between workstations, attempt to masquerade as other workstations, and attempt other schemes. While these attacks involve complex software, someone with a programming flair and determination can write them. While NT uses the network conscientiously, for example it encrypts passwords in transit, it's hard to be sure when you're safe. Beware.

Your best security is an all-Windows NT network.

See the Chapter 9 for tips on securing your network when it's connected to the Internet or other wide area intranets.

Summary

There aren't many features associated with protecting the TCB. Just understand the principles and maintain proper ACLs.

❖ The TCB includes the programs and data files on which the security of the system rests, mostly programs used by administrators or system services.

❖ The toughest issue is that a user's capabilities extend to programs they directly execute, so users with sensitive capabilities and especially administrators must studiously avoid running programs that can't be trusted. This is difficult to ensure.

❖ Working in the MS-DOS command environment is dangerous for administrators because they can sometimes be fooled into running a fake program. Guarding their MS-DOS command search path is the best defense.

❖ Booting alternate operating systems and untrusted workstations on the network can also pose security threats. Fully protecting against these threats are beyond what NT itself can reasonably address.

Checking the TEMP Directory: NT programs commonly use the TEMP directory for temporary files. Check the ACL on TEMP and also create a file in TEMP. Are these ACLs tight enough? If not, how would you change the ACL on TEMP? (See "Applications and ACLs" in Chapter 4.

Perusing WINNT: Peruse the ACLs in the WINNT directory tree, which holds much of the TCB. Do they look sufficiently strong? (Note information presented in Appendix A.)

Restate the "search path" problem. How do you protect against it? [176]

You know that some sensitive service can be provided only by one of NT's trusted servers. Is it immune to Trojan Horse attack? [177]

You receive a new administrative program from some source. How do you know if you can "trust" it? [178]

Cite the "delete-and-replace" threat. You have a directory with items that you don't want untrusted users to delete, so you protect each item with "Read" (**RX**) permission. Is it okay to give everyone "Change" permission (**RWXD**) to the directory itself? How about "Full Control"? [179]

Chapter 12

Summary and Checklist

We now condense our many recommendations into a checklist for both regular users and administrators. This also serves as our general summary and pulls together advice presented in different places throughout the text. Our first section is for regular users; all sections are for administrators. These items don't replace a thorough study of the entire book, but highlight the major cautions we've covered. We suggest you write a Site Security Policy and Procedures document. This checklist should help ensure that its topics are complete.

☞ The phrases in parentheses at the end of some checked items cite the index entry for this topic. Use these to quickly locate the topic. A checked item with no explicit reference uses the same index entry as the previous checked item.

General User Education

General users should understand these points (and administrators should ensure they do).

Passwords

✓ Know how to make up sufficiently strong passwords and know when to change them. *(Passwords: choosing strong)*

✓ Never lend a password, but tell administrators when you are forced by circumstances to do so.

Trusted Path

✓ Windows NT never presents the Security window unless the user keys in the Trusted Path. *(Trusted Path)*

✓ Use the Security window exclusively for changing a password, locking the workstation, and logging off.

✓ Never type a password except through the Trusted Path. One exception is when you connect to a network share resource where your account is matched to a remote account with a different password.

Workstation and Screen Saver Locking

✓ Understand site policy for using the Security window's locking function. (*Locking, workstation*)

✓ Understand site policy for using screen saver password unlocking. (Screen saver locking)

✓ Use only safe, approved screen savers for password unlocking.

Untrusted Programs

✓ Understand that each program you use obtains your full capabilities and can sometimes use them without your knowledge. (*TCB: for general users*)

✓ Protect all personal programs and their data files, allowing no one to change, delete, change permissions, or take ownership (except perhaps administrative groups like Administrators and SYSTEM). (*TCB: protecting*)

✓ For maximum protection, have administrators own your program files with write access to no one. This means other applications you run can't maliciously change the protection on these program files.

Special Groups

✓ Know site policy for the difference between the Users and Everyone groups. (*Groups: special*)

✓ Know site policy for the Guests group.

✓ Understand the meaning of the special groups you can use in ACLs: NETWORK, INTERACTIVE, and SYSTEM.

ACLs

✓ Understand the mechanics of ACLs. At a minimum, know how to set up a typical home directory. (*ACLs: home directory setup*)

✓ When you first inhabit your home directory, set up its ACL securely. When in doubt—disallow.

✓ Put ACLs on directories that by default properly protect their entire, subsequently created directory tree. (*ACLs: protecting trees*)

✓ Understand the site policy that states which administrative groups to include in all your ACLs, typically the Administrators and SYSTEM local groups. (Administrators: Define this policy!) (*ACLs: administrative entries*)

✓ Appreciate that accounts and groups named in an ACL are relative to the workstation and domain where it's located. (*ACLs: entries relative to location*)

✓ Remember that when you copy or move a file its ACL might be either preserved or reprotected, depending on the scenario. When in doubt, check. (*ACLs, preserving and reprotecting*)

Matching Accounts

✓ For remote requests, when the user's current account is not allowed, NT attempts to match it with an account on the remote workstation with the same name and password. (In some cases, NT asks for a password if it finds a matching name but not a matching password.) *(Accounts: matching)*

✓ Matched accounts may have different passwords and capabilities.

✓ Users must maintain matched account passwords independently.

Creating and Managing Groups

✓ Clearly define the criteria for membership. *(Groups: naming)*

✓ Use names and descriptions that intuitively describe the intended membership.

✓ Avoid using a group name already taken—networkwide when practical.

✓ Include the creator's name in the group's description.

Domain Model and Network Administration

Define your domain model early because it's cumbersome to rearrange it after the system is in full use. Your scheme for network administration bears on your model.

Domain Model

✓ The domain structure has several operational criteria but one main security criterion: A domain **A** should not trust a domain **B** if you feel the general population of domain **B** is not trustworthy inside **A**. *(Domains; Domains, planning)*

✓ Accounts not allowed onto a workstation by their domain affiliation can be allowed through matching accounts, typically local accounts. This is a clean way to handle exceptions without unnaturally structuring domains. *(Accounts: matching)*

Administrator Account

Decide your strategy for the built-in Administrator account:

✓ Option #1: Make the Administrator account a global maintenance account-of-last-resort. Keep the "Administrator" name and use the same password on every workstation on the network, including domain controllers. Make its password long and random. (This is especially important if you are depending on account lockout.) *(Administrators: full; Lockout)*

✓ Option #2: As a variation on #1, vary the password; for example, give this account a different password in each domain.

✓ Option #3: Assign the Administrator account to individual users renaming them accordingly. (We recommend this only for small networks.)

✓ Write down Administrator passwords and secure them, especially for #1 and #2.

✓ If you are depending on account lockout, to which the local Administrator account is exempt, you can deny RAS access to this account or even remove its Right to access the computer from the network. But beware that this does not preclude IIS access. (*Lockout*)

Domain and Network Full Administrators

For all but the smallest networks, decide which accounts can act as full administrators:

✓ Building on the global Domain Admins and local Administrators group, decide which accounts are to administer fully which domains. (*Administrators: full*)

✓ Decide if any workstations need extensions or exceptions to this general scheme and adjust their Administrators group accordingly.

Server Operators and Power Users

✓ Assign operator roles to each NT Server, noting that some roles contain the capabilities of others. (*Operators: strategy*)

✓ Decide if you need to create global operator groups that can administer several domains.

✓ Decide whether you need to appoint Power Users, and if so which ones to which NT Workstations. Also decide if you need to create global groups to include in the workstations' Power User groups. (*Power Users: strategy*)

✓ Ensure that Power Users receive sufficient administrative training. (*Power Users; Power Users: strategy*)

Miscellaneous

✓ Create at least two accounts for each administrator: one to use only during their administrative activities and another for other activities. (*Administrators: separate accounts for*)

✓ Name administrative accounts and groups so that it's apparent they are administrative.

✓ Ensure that administrators choose passwords with a strength that is commensurate with their power. (*Passwords: choosing strong; Passwords: policy*)

Groups

Special Groups

✓ Decide your criteria for membership in the local Users group, mainly whether it should include only accounts from the same domain. (*Groups: special*)

✓ Decide your criteria for membership in the Guests group.

Predefined Groups

You may want to predefine obvious groups, although we recommend you be conservative and let your evolving operations guide you.

✓ Understand the criteria for why you create user groups: basic file and directory access, access to network share directories, Rights assignment, resource use (like printers), profiles, and multiple account selection. *(Groups: criteria for)*

Multidomain Groups

✓ Are there local groups that need to include one or more domain global groups of the same intent, analogous to Users and Domain Users? For example, a Domain Managers group in each domain and a Managers local group on each workstation that includes the Domain Managers from some or all visible domains. *(Groups: multidomain global)*

General Access to Workstations

These include basic issues of which regular users can use which workstations.

Rights to Primary and Secondary Logon

✓ Decide which groups you assign the Right for primary logon ("Log on locally") and the Right for secondary logon ("Access this computer from network"). Decide this early since you assign Rights on each workstation. Use global groups if appropriate. *(Rights: logon)*

Allowed Workstations

✓ Decide when you should set each account's list of allowed workstations, although the list has limited length. *(Accounts: workstations allowed to log on to)*

Logon Hours

✓ Decide if the per-account logon hour restrictions are important and, if so, for which accounts. *(Logon: allowed hours)*

✓ Decide whether you want each domain controller to suspend services forcibly to a remotely connected account when the account enters a prohibited time period.

✓ Consider defining groups to simplify the selection of a set of accounts to be restricted identically; for example, Work Hours, Extended Hours, and All Hours. *(Groups: criteria for)*

Shutdown

✓ For each class of workstation, decide to which accounts or groups to assign the Right to "Shut down the system." Consider a special Shutdown group strategy. *(Rights: shutdown)*

✓ Decide whether to allow the shutdown from the logon window. This feature lets unauthenticated users shut down the workstation. *(Shutdown: button)*

Accounts

General Account Setup

✓ Set limited-term accounts to expire after an appropriate time. *(Accounts: expiration)*

✓ Choose a consistent scheme for account names and descriptions that unambiguously identifies the person who uses the account. *(Accounts: naming and describing)*

✓ Avoid accounts to be used regularly by more than one person, even in situations like job sharing. They lack accountability.

✓ Generally, set up a home directory for each new user with a proper ACL. *(Home directory)*

✓ If you have a large installation, create a few account templates. *(Accounts: templates)*

✓ Disable each template account. For good measure, give it a nonsense password that you quickly forget.

Passwords

✓ Define and distribute site policy for the strength of passwords. *(Passwords: policy)*

✓ Decide which users can be trusted to choose responsible passwords and which cannot. Allow the former to change their passwords. Periodically assign passwords to the latter. *(Accounts: general security controls; Accounts: Account Policy; Passwords: policy)*

✓ Set password uniqueness to the maximum allowed and minimum age to a few days.

✓ Set the expiration date based on your site security. We recommend:

Low:	6 months
Medium:	3 months
High:	1 month

✓ Set all account passwords to expire, although you may want to exempt full administrators. (Don't forget to update "fail-safe" administrative passwords you wrote down and stored.)

✓ Set password lockout and minimum length to values appropriate to your site. (Regardless of length, you should always set password lockout even at low-security sites where its values can be liberal.) Recall that lockout parameters and a password's "space" (related to its length) together determine the probability that the password can be guessed in a certain period of time. Based on your site security, we recommend the probability of a guess in one hour at the maximum guessing rate:

Low: 1/1,000
Medium: 1/10,000
High: 1/100,000

Note: Smaller probabilities might seem to increase security, but this demands longer passwords, which are more difficult to remember and therefore are more likely to be written down. Passwords written in unsecured locations pose a much greater threat than modest probabilities.

✓ Decide whether to require the Account Policy that "Users must log on in order to change password." We have no recommendation.

✓ Be vigilant that users with more power have stronger passwords.

✓ Formulate a policy on the passwords for matched accounts. That is, when a user has several accounts on the network of the same name, should the passwords by convention be kept the same? Keeping them the same avoids typing passwords outside the Trusted Path. *(Passwords: in matching accounts)*

✓ We base our advice mostly on the threats that one user could guess another's password and that complicated passwords tend to be written down. However, you may have certain internal threats, like encrypted passwords passed on the network. Factor these risks into your policy. *(Passwords: policy)*

Guest Account

✓ Decide if you wish to enable the Guest account. We recommend against this unless operational reasons require it. *(Guest account)*

✓ If enabled, don't allow the password to be changed. Decide if you want to improve its security by giving it a password.

Security Auditing

We suggest you formulate an auditing policy and practice it over a period of time, perhaps months.

Threats

Appraise the threats to your system and the extent to which you can usefully audit them:

✓ Consider separately the importance of actions by administrators and regular users. *(Auditing: strategy)*

✓ Consider separately the importance of successes and failures.

✓ Is the tracking of printed material a concern to your site?

✓ Decide whether to tell users they are being audited, but keep the events you audit a secret.

Choosing Categories and Objects

✓ Mindful of the "wheat versus chaff" argument, select the categories you choose to audit. *(Auditing: strategy)*

✓ Select the files and directories and the operations on them you wish to audit.

✓ Consider whether you should group similarly audited files and directories into the same tree.

✓ Precisely examine test cases for each occurrence you intend to audit. Judge whether its information is sufficient and whether it generates too many innocuous events.

✓ Decide which printers should you audit, if any. *(Auditing: printers)*

Log Management

✓ Allocate sufficient storage for the security log, mindful that it's the log's logical disk that fills. We recommend you set the log to overwrite the oldest events as necessary. *(Security Log)*

✓ Develop procedures for regularly reviewing the logs, unless your strategy is to use them only after your suspicions are aroused in some other manner.

✓ Develop procedures for securely storing the audit logs, including whether they are stored as events (*.EVT) or text files.

✓ Because time and date is an important item in a audit event record, you may want to remove the Right to change system time from Power Users.

✓ Although extreme, decide whether continuous security auditing is so important to your site that you demand (certain) workstations shut down when their audit log fills.

The TCB

☞ See Appendix A, Secure Installation, for details on many of the items in this section.

Controlling Introduction of Untrusted Software

✓ Develop a site policy under which administrators approve all new software before it's introduced onto the system and, when practical, even personal software. *(TCB: for general users; TCB: for administrators)*

✓ Use virus-checking programs liberally. Preferably check all new software on isolated, noncritical workstations before introducing it into your general environment.

Protect the TCB

✓ List the elements of your TCB. Don't forget third-party administrative software and screen savers with password unlocking. *(TCB: protecting)*

✓ Set ACLs so that only administrators can alter or replace elements of the TCB.

✓ Beware of the delete-and-replace scheme. Protect all ancestral directories of all TCB files, avoiding "Full Control" where possible.

Keep Malicious Programs from Administrators

✓ Administrators must be careful not to execute untrusted programs in the MS-DOS command environment. *(TCB: protecting)*

✓ For maximum safety, use only the Security window to run programs and switch between them.

✓ Administrators' search paths should include only directories protected from change by untrusted programs and nonadministrators.

✓ Use ACLs to protect AUTOEXEC.BAT, CONFIG.SYS, and similar files.

✓ Set untrusted programs of no administrative use to be nonexecutable by administrators.

Hardware and Network Protections

✓ Use every method available to prevent the unauthorized booting of other operating systems, for example BIOS[1] passwords, cabinet locks, and CPU board switches. *(TCB: protecting)*

✓ Where possible, do not allow computers on your network that allow untrusted programs direct, packet-level access to the network. A 100 percent NT network is your best security.

Disk Formats

✓ Use the NTFS disk format wherever possible. *(Formats, disk)*

✓ Floppy disks and perhaps other portable media do not carry ACLs. Formulate site policy for their transport and storage.

---

1. BIOS is the firmware that starts up your computer, independent of the installed operating system. Some computer BIOS programs let you define a password that one must enter to change the various BIOS parameters. One of these parameters often prevents booting the computer from floppy disks; this can be used to circumvent Windows NT. If you set up the BIOS to prevent such booting you should also, if allowed, protect the setting with a password.

General

System Policy Files

✓ While you don't have to establish global policy files to be secure, it makes your job easier by centralizing the definition of key security parameters. We recommend you do so. *(Policy Editor)*

✓ Create the centralized files (in automatic mode if possible) and set up each NT Workstation to reference them.*(Policy Files: setting up workstations; Policy Files: managing; Policy Files: user policy parameters; Policy Files: computer policy parameters)*

✓ For computer policy files, carefully decide which fields to leave undefined (and therefore permanently defined in the Registry of each workstation) and which to define in the policy file. (Recall that user policy files have fewer issues because their parameters are almost always fully defined in the policy file.)*(Policy Files: managing; Policy Files: user policy parameters; Policy Files: computer policy parameters)*

☞Note that considerations for setting many of these parameters are presented elsewhere in this summary and throughout the text.

Program Interactions with ACLs

✓ Recall that programs that don't know about ACLs can have some interesting but not necessarily unsecure side effects. Keep an eye toward how your mainline programs interact with ACLs. Appraise users of any security issues. *(ACLs: applications' use of)*

✓ Properly set the ACLs on temporary directories, like TEMP.

Remove the Traverse Bypass Right

✓ We recommend you remove the Right to "Bypass traverse checking" from all accounts except perhaps administrative accounts. *(Rights: bypass traverse checking)*

Backup

✓ When restoring trees to their original workstations, direct Backup to restore ACLs. *(Backup and Restore)*

✓ When restoring to other workstations, consider whether a significant number of the ACL groups or accounts are not visible on the system. You may then choose to reprotect the restored trees, but ensure that the new ACL protections do not compromise the restored data.

✓ Where practical, choose the backup option to *Restrict access* to backup tapes. This limits who can restore them.

✓ Even if you restrict access in this manner, store backup tapes securely because their data can nonetheless be gleaned by programs that can read the tape in the drive.

Printer Access Policy

✓ Are there any printers with access that must be strictly limited for security reasons, for example ones that print presigned checks? *(Printers)*

✓ Are there printers for which you need to prohibit their use by certain groups because the data those groups typically handle is too sensitive for the physical security of the printer?

✓ Are there printers and/or groups that warrant special security banner pages?

Other Rights Issues

✓ Remove the "Bypass traverse checking" Right from all but SYSTEM and, optionally, full administrative accounts. This ensures that users denied access to a directory cannot pass through the directory into its subtrees. *(Rights: bypass traverse checking)*

Logon Banner

✓ Decide whether you wish to post the logon banner either for legal reasons or as a security note. *(Logon banner)*

Workstation Locking Policy

✓ Formulate site policy for using the Security window's locking function. Appraise users and monitor use. *(Locking, workstation)*

✓ Define site policy for screen saver unlocking. Appraise users and monitor use. Ensure that users use only trusted, approved screen savers for password locking. *(Screen saver locking)*

Pseudoaccount Passwords

You may need to create accounts for internal purposes, as opposed to actual user logon. Protect them appropriately.

✓ Give the Replicator account a strong password. No need to remember it. *(No index entry.)*

Windows 95

✓ Install each Windows 95 workstation in the mode that most fully integrates with the Windows NT domain model. This is Windows 95's most secure mode. *(Windows 95: basic domain installation)*

✓ Install and enable remote administration between Windows 95 workstations. *(Windows 95: Remote Administration service)*

✓ Install a Windows 95 policy file on the domain server. *(Windows 95: policy files, general)*

✓ For computer policy files, carefully decide which fields to leave undefined (and therefore permanently defined in the Registry of each workstation) and which to define in the policy file. (Recall that user policy files have fewer issues because their parameters are almost always fully defined in the policy file.)(*Windows 95: policy file parameters; Windows 95: computer policy files, considerations for*)

WFW

✓ Require domain logon concurrent to WFW logon unless you have a strong reason not to. This ensures that WFW users can't access the network without an account strongly controlled by NT Server. (*Windows for Workgroups (WFW): regular use; Windows for Workgroups (WFW): administration*)

✓ Decide whether to allow password caching, most importantly for the domain password. On the one hand, without ACLs, stored passwords are vulnerable on WFW. On the other hand, with no Trusted Path you'd like to limit the number of times passwords must be entered.

✓ Ensure that each WFW logon password is at least as strong as the password of the domain account to which it is matched during domain authentication.

Day-to-Day Monitoring

While many of our checklist items bear constant vigilance, we point our a few in particular:

✓ Monitor the creation of groups by regular users. Watch for cases where people who use the groups might misunderstand the group membership as maintained by the creator. Be wary of groups not logically connected that have the same name. (*No index entry.*)

✓ Monitor the administrative activities of Power Users, especially the network share directories they create. (*No index entry.*)

✓ Monitor the consistent and proper use of the Trusted Path, and workstation locking (through the Security window), and screen saver password unlocking. (*No index entry.*)

Networking

Internet Information Server

✓ Decide which authentication modes you will allow. Avoid the basic mode because passwords are transported unencrypted. (*Internet Information Server: authentication modes*)

✓ Carefully designate the directories to which IIS allows access. Set their ACLs as tightly as possible. Note especially the anonymous user account. (*Internet Information Server: directories*)

✓ Be especially careful when you set up IIS to allow access to network share directories. Set the share ACL tightly. (Recall that these can only really be used for anonymous access.) *(Internet Information Server: network share directories)*

✓ If you are allowing anonymous access, set up the anonymous account with a strong password that you tell no one and designate the account to IIS. (Check the checklist in "Anonymous and Special Accounts" in Chapter 9.) *(Internet Information Server: anonymous account)*

✓ It is safest to provide IIS services to an intranet from a Windows NT server with separate connections to the intranet and your local net. If possible, disallow direct traffic between the LAN and intranet, perhaps providing proxy services on the server. For safety, set up NT's sharing services to service the LAN only. *(Internet Information Server: on an NT gateway)*

✓ Properly protect your network from "agents." Unfortunately, there is little specific advice we can give, but you should understand the general dangers of various kinds of agents and deal with them appropriately. *(Internet Information Server: agents, CGI and ISAPI)*

✓ If appropriate, set up IP filtering, but remember that there are relatively easy ways for remote elements to get 'round your filters. *(Internet Information Server: IP filtering)*

Remote Access Service

✓ Install RAS if you need it. Don't allow cleartext logons if at all possible. Choose to encrypt RAS traffic. Install PPTP if you want to run RAS across the Internet. *(Remote Access Service)*

✓ Set the RAS policy parameters to reasonable values. Note that a RAS environment may have a more critical need for Account Lockout. *(Remote Access Service: policy parameters; Lockout)*

✓ Decide whether you want your RAS server to allow access to the entire LAN or to only itself. *(Remote Access Service: whole-LAN access)*

✓ Choose the accounts that can use RAS. Make sure they have the Right to log on remotely. For security, use callback to specific phone numbers where possible. *(Accounts: Dial-in permissions; Remote Access Service)*

✓ Decide whether users should use the name and password on their client computer to access the server network remotely and cache passwords on the remote client computers. *(Remote Access Service: caching passwords remotely)*

Isolating NT from an Intranet

✓ Isolate your NT systems from any intranet of which they are a part. Most important, isolate NT's "Server" service from the intranet by unbinding it from the TCP/IP protocol. *(Networking: isolating NT from common threats)*

Educate Your Users

✓ Make sure your users have a general appreciation of the kinds of viruses and threats in an intranet environment. *(Intranet: threats and security)*

✓ Make sure they understand the basics of "SSL-secure" modes in Web browsers. Develop a site policy for the kinds of communications that should only be run in this secure mode.

✓ Be especially wary of applications that automatically run attached programs when opening a document for viewing. Make this a part of your checklist for approving new applications for your site. *(Intranet: viruses)*

✓ Learn the ways of protecting your users from WWW applets ("agents") and make sure users understand the essential precautions. (These depend on the particular browser.) *(Applets, in WWW)*

PART III

Assessment

Chapter 13

NT Security Discussion

Like beauty, security is relative to the beholder. What's secure enough at one site may not be for another. You alone can decide how well NT serves your security needs. Now that you've seen the basic security features, we discuss some issues that help get you started on your assessment. Use them as your point of departure as you see fit.

The TCSEC

One yardstick by which many secure systems are measured today is the U.S. *Trusted Computer Systems Evaluation Criteria* (or "Orange Book") that we introduced in Chapter 1. If you are one of those who must assess the security of computer systems, you'll want to know a little about the TCSEC. It's not so much that the TCSEC is the best document around, it's the only major yardstick. (There is a similar European document called the *Information Technology Security Evaluation Criteria* [ITSEC] but they are similar from our perspective.) While the TCSEC is a superb document in its own right, it's also about ten years old and discussions about its successor are in progress. As we see later, the TCSEC's shortfall is that a simple grade like C2 is just not enough information about how secure a system is. Whether or not you are concerned in military-grade security, the TCSEC is a compendium of modern security practices and serves as a valuable framework for our discussion.

First a few terms. The National Computer Security Center **evaluates** a particular computer system on a particular hardware base in cooperation with that system's vendor. The TCSEC is their guiding light, but it's a *criterion*, not a *specification*, and the NCSC must "interpret" the criteria in the TCSEC against the system. Indeed some of the criteria are rather vague. The TCSEC is like a nation's constitution, a statement of basic intent with details to follow.

☞ It is not our prerogative or intent to evaluate Windows NT against the TCSEC. Only the NCSC can officially do this, at least in part because many of the criteria have "interpretations" understood and appreciated only by the NCSC. But we can present an educated opinion for your careful consideration.

It is not the intent of the NCSC to force anybody to use security. Instead, the purpose of the TCSEC grade is to inform a prospective buyer—a point-of-sale consumer guide. For example, the NCSC does nothing to prevent a buyer of even a highly evaluated system from turning off its security. A particular institution must assess a particular computer system for its own use. This is usually called certification. Certifications are based on a breadth of information, one part of which is often an NCSC evaluation. Your assessment of your own security needs is a certification.

The TCSEC evaluation rates a system on a progressive scale of increased security:

(least secure) C1 → C2 → B1 → B2 → B3 → A1 (most secure)

The rating is based on two kinds of criteria: **Features** are the various security mechanisms built into the system, while **assurances** present evidence that the system's security works reliably as advertised. You can think of assurance as evidence of good software design and the absence of bugs. Assurance is not stringent below B2, but difficult and expensive at B3. To meet a given level, a system must pass both the feature and assurance requirements. Each level includes all the features and assurance of lower levels. Thus you could never say a system is B1 but not C2.

D is complete failure. Systems without a security kernel like traditional MS-DOS can go no further. C1 offers too little security to be of much interest. A1 adds only certain analytic studies over B3. Because of its expense, A1 is seldom discussed anymore. Today's focus is C2 through B3.

C2 requires a protected operating system kernel, logon, security auditing, and a **discretionary access control** like ACLs or even the more primitive UNIX "mode bits." Except for auditing, C2 is an easy target for most modern operating systems and not even a challenge for Windows NT. The features pertinent to our discussion added by each level beyond C2 are:

B1 Mandatory access control based on sensitivity labels, collectively referred to as "MAC." An access control separate and in addition to ACL-like controls, MAC serves to prevent the unauthorized *disclosure* of information based on sensitivity labels like the familiar "Unclassified," "Confidential," and "Secret." MAC prevents people only from seeing what they shouldn't see. It does not prevent them from changing what they shouldn't change. In short, it's a strong "read-protect" but not a "write-protect" control. (See the Glossary for a more complete synopsis of MAC.)

B2 An NT-like Trusted Path but only for logon and logoff, and a separation of operator and administrator roles.

B3 Extensions to the Trusted Path to include other functions but without specifics, a strengthening of the administrator rule to a bonafide "security administrator," and full ACLs like those in NT.

For example, consider the B3 language that describes Trusted Path additions:

"The TCB shall support a trusted communication path between itself and users for use when a positive TCB-to-user connection is required (e.g., login, change subject security level)."

The bold text shows additions to the B2 wording. As you can see, this is a broad mandate and precisely why evaluations can be done only by the NCSC who interpret the intent of these words much like a high court might interpret a country's constitution. Other parts are a little more concrete. There are only a few assurances of interest to us and a discussion of them follows.

B2 Modularity Requirement

At B2 the system is required to be "internally structured into well-defined largely independent modules." This infamous "modularity" requirement largely precludes operating systems with spaghetti-code kernels. Although there's by no means any consensus on this issue, most of today's major, general-purpose operating systems seek modularity as a primary design goal for reasons other than security. Any solid implementation is a solid candidate for B2 modularity.

B2 Least Privilege

The same B2 paragraph also states, "the TCB modules shall be designed such that the principle of least privilege is enforced." (The TCB is the sum total of security-critical software and hardware. This includes any portion of the system capable of subverting security and that must, therefore, be responsible for maintaining security or being "trusted.")

Least privilege states that the system should be capable of giving trusted programs degrees of security power. The system must allow for gradations of security powers between "none" and "all." This doesn't mean that no programs can be all powerful, just that ones that need only modest security capabilities be given only modest power.

Traditionally this translates to a "privilege" mechanism that allows each of several security-relevant privileges to be assigned to specific programs, where "several" ranges from a handful to a few dozen. Historically, at B2 monolithic kernels don't need to be subdivided into modules that are themselves least privileged. Instead, this requirement has been applied only to programs (or, in operating system language, processes).

B3 Architecture

The intent of B3 is that the system be designed from the ground up and from day 1 with a distinctive architecture with security as its primary goal. For example, B3 states, "significant system engineering shall be directed toward minimizing the complexity of the TCB...." At B3, not only must the traditional, monolithic kernels be subdivided, but their subdivisions must be thoroughly least privileged.

The problems with applying B3 architecture to commercial, general-purpose systems are risk and cost. While technically feasible, a system designed so distinctively for security may slight other important requirements, like performance. A B3 development is lengthy and expensive, with the prospects for profit a distant horizon. It's no small wonder that no general-purpose operating system has attempted B3.

The intent of these assurance requirements is largely to reduce the chance for bugs and the damage they can do. While these assurances are nice in theory, the degree to which the more esoteric ones enhance security varies in practice.

Windows NT and the TCSEC

How does NT stack up? Mindful that we are not the NCSC, we can offer some observations:

❖ NT's ACLs are fully B3, beyond question. Historic systems have attained B3 with simpler ACLs.

❖ NT's Trusted Path is fully B2 and at least approaches B3.

❖ The publicly stated intent of the Windows NT design team was to build a "modular" kernel of the sort required at B2, not for evaluation, but because a modular system is easier and cheaper to maintain. While we can't judge the fruits of their efforts, their stated intent seems pure. NT's strongly separated and centralized "security reference monitor," and its uniform treatment of objects ("access tokens" and the "object manager") are certainly key components of B2 modularity.

❖ Administrative roles seem squarely B2. Whether they are B3 is open for debate. It's difficult to argue for B3 as long as the role used for security must be used for day-to-day operations of little security relevance. If you relegate all day-to-day chores to NT operators and reserve the security role for full administrators, you may approach the intent of the B3 requirement.

❖ NT's Rights and their assignment are a B2-style privilege mechanism. Because they apply to all programs run by a particular user session, the major question is whether they can be sufficiently withheld from programs. (All the Rights from an account with a bushel basket of Rights carry through to all programs run during the logon session.) Only the NCSC can judge.

❖ Windows NT has no MAC. More later.

If NT has so many B-level features why is it only C2? The intent of the TCSEC is to inform consumers about the security strength of a product. To the extent that it could be more informative, or that its simple rating system might overstate or understate a system's security, people can claim the TCSEC should be improved. Two basic improvements are frequently discussed.

First, it's legitimate for a user to seek features from the higher levels yet be willing to accept more modest assurances, for example C2, perhaps because they're willing to rely on the reputation and stability of the vendor and product in lieu of the TCSEC architectural requirements. Such a system can be rated only C2, even if it is far more "secure" than a system that is barely C2. You can see how the NCSC's intent to foster the development of secure systems becomes a bit self-defeating. Why should a vendor of the aforementioned system add C2+ features when they don't get credit for them? Why indeed.

The European sister criteria to the TCSEC, the ITSEC, addresses this issue by separating features from assurance. Using a TCSEC analogy, a system could be rated, for example, B2 in features and C2 in assurance. While some might decry that this encourages vendors to build less-secure systems, we submit that it encourages them to build ones that are more secure.

Secondly, consider a system with all the features and assurances of the TCSEC except MAC, a delightfully secure system for a site that doesn't need or want MAC. Unfortunately, systems without MAC can be evaluated no higher than C2 despite their strength. This aspect of the TCSEC comes from its military origins. Its original target was an audience that always required MAC in its more "secure" systems, so moderately secure systems without MAC has never been an issue.

In the late 1980s, the U.S. Congress chartered the National Institute of Standards and Technology to join with the NCSC to make the general evaluation process applicable to the commercial as well as the military sector. Although the TCSEC has not yet been changed, there are a number of proposals under consideration. Both the ITSEC and one of these proposals lets an industry, like the banking industry, define a security "profile" that you can think of as a specific set of security features and assurances that are internally consistent. Vendors could then design systems and have them evaluated according to that profile. For example, a profile with all the TCSEC features except MAC, and B2 assurance might be quite popular and readily built.

We've led you down a long-winded path, but we're ready to make our point. If you were to sketch the ideal commercial, broad-based operating system with tight security, that could be economically produced with little risk, and that's completely compatible with a broad base of commercial applications, you might well reply, "Give me all the TCSEC features (they all have great commercial value) except MAC (great idea, but not ready for prime time), with B2 assurance (modularity is common today anyway)." Windows NT comes very, very close.

Networking

TCSEC evaluations cannot include broad-based, heterogeneous networking. They address only systems like NT in stand-alone mode. Networking must be done under the Trusted Networking Interpretation (or "Red Book"). The TNI is relatively young and precious few vendors are submitting to its evaluation. Don't expect much from any general system soon. However, Windows NT is well designed for a C2 TNI evaluation, and you should keep an eye on developments in this area.

Summary

We've talked a lot about the TCSEC because it's by far the largest yardstick for secure systems. What about "commercial" security? The issue is a bit of a red herring. The commercial world needs—and requests—the features in the TCSEC, from ACLs through least privilege to administrative roles, except MAC, as commonly as any other community. Moreover, the features omitted by the TCSEC, like encryption or mandatory write protection, are equally valuable in all communities. It's not that Windows NT is everything to all audiences, it's more that all computer users need the same basic protections because they face similar threats. Windows NT aims squarely in the middle.

You may also hear that items excluded from Windows NT's C2 evaluation are "not secure" and if you turn them on you're "violating C2 security." These comments usually come from those new to the TCSEC. While it is true that features outside the C2 evaluation have not been scrutinized, this does not make them "unsecure," it just lessens one's confidence a bit. And you cannot "violate" C2 security because it's not an operational mode. It's simply an assurance that the system as shipped has certain features that have been scrutinized by a team of impartial evaluators according to a published criteria. This point-of-sale assurance does not disappear just because you turn off or add new security features.

The final questions: Will the broad NT market require it be evaluated under the TCSEC? Probably not. Does it help to assure these customers that NT is secure as advertised? You bet!

NT Security Feature by Feature

We now take a look at some of NT's security features in a somewhat less-formal light.

Logon and Passwords

NT's logon scheme uses a single password for logon, then presents the authenticated user identity around the network to various access controls. This is common for highly secure systems as opposed to schemes where a different password protects each resource—too may passwords.

NT's password controls are everything you'd expect in a modern commercial or military system. NT does not do "password screening," where the system attempts to prevent simplistic passwords. While such schemes catch overly simplistic passwords, like people's names, determined users can readily get around them. NT also does not generate passwords from which users must select the one they dislike the least. In our humble opinion, the best password schemes are where users conscientiously make up their own. If you force difficult passwords on users, they write them down and this can devastate security. NT allows both the scheme where administrators don't generally know user's passwords and where administrator's alone assign user passwords.

ACLs

ACLs have long been a staple security feature. Multics, a popular TCSEC-like system of the '70s convinced the security world that ACLs are both convenient and valuable. After the '80s, when UNIX replaced ACLs with the simpler but less flexible mode bits, there's been something of a resurgence of ACLs. You see them everywhere today—for good reason.

Windows NT's ACLs are a careful balance between flexibility and ease of use. You see few schemes that are better. One of the keys to an ACL's success is its technique for setting the ACL for a newly created file or directory, usually from the parent directory. The Windows NT scheme seems particularly well designed. And once you've seen it, its special CREATOR OWNER seems impossible to do without.

Trusted Path

This is another time-honored, popular, and valuable feature. It's important that the system never display the Trusted Path unless the user specifically requests it. NT upholds this except for certain secondary logons to local accounts, which can be eliminated by synchronizing passwords. Perhaps the most important function of the Trusted Path is the entering of passwords, which NT universally enforces (with the minor caveat we just mentioned).

Administration and Rights

That full NT administrators are all powerful is not a security issue because the lesser operator roles perform most of the day-to-day administration. NT is careful to prevent operators from expanding their own power, and keeps them fully under the control of full administrators. For example, only full administrators control the security log. NT's Rights Policy is a strong commitment to least privilege.

Consistency, Centralization, and Compartmentalization

Consistent and centralized administration are not really direct security features, but they minimize the confusion among well-intentioned administrators that creates the rifts through which your security can leak. The domain is a powerful centralizing feature, and NT's "exceptions" (like local accounts) keep the domains simpler and therefore more secure. A domain is a sort of controlled security fortress, a compartment. Its features are strongly defensive and can be placed under the complete control of its own administrators.

Auditing

Windows NT security auditing is complete, detailed, and easy to use, bearing the same interface as its other event logs. NT's detailed per-file audit controls are somewhat rare among TCSEC systems, even though they are frequently requested. NT offers a simple filtering scheme for viewing the security log, but no sophisticated analysis. It can, however, save the logs in text files amenable to import by analysis applications, like database programs. Few secure systems offer sophisticated audit analysis, partly because the science of auditing is still young (amazing as it seems).

Networking

NT takes many commonsense networking precautions, like never passing plaintext passwords and requiring a password when identifying other domain controllers. It is also aggressively tracking a host of Internet security standards, many of which are done at the application level (that is, by and between specific applications). While it does not yet encrypt or cryptographically preserve the integrity of all of its NT-to-NT communications, this is not a problem on NT-only networks with no secret "taps."

Third-Party Watch

One of the most exciting aspects of a system like Windows NT is its third-party market for security products. Because NT has a protected kernel that enforces strict separation among its programs, its "protected TCB" is a solid security base on which other products can build. In this section we note a few products for which you should especially watch, and give some salient points that help you judge their security.

Network Encryption

Windows NT does not cryptographically protect its general network data traffic, as do few commercial operating systems. On most computer networks, particularly local area networks like Ethernet, messages can be received by workstations other than those to which they are addressed. All but the addressee ignore the message. Further, on many of these the sender can put any sender address it wants in a message to lead the receiver to believe the message came from another source. Windows NT prevents such skullduggery by preventing all but system programs from placing messages directly on the network. Instead, NT withholds messages from each program not specifically addressed to them and finally formats each message to ensure an accurate sender address.

A malicious element, which we'll call a "tap," can enter these networks one of two ways: an illicit device surreptitiously attached to the network or a legitimate workstation on the network that, unlike NT, allows any of its programs to place messages directly on the network (or example, traditional MS-DOS). Encryption is the only plausible way to thwart taps and is primarily used in one of the following ways (we presented some protecting technologies in "Cryptography" in Chapter 9, The Internet and Intranets):

❖ The first prevents taps from reading the data in messages they intercept by encrypting ("hiding") the data in the message. Sender and receiver act in concert, one or both knowing some "secret" information (usually called a "key") so that entities that don't know these secrets can't decrypt the data, at least not easily.

❖ Encryption can also be used to ensure the *integrity* of a message transmitted. Cryptographically generated information, called a "signature," is attached to a message so that the receiver can detect in-route changes to the message. While taps can perhaps change a message, they can't reattach a legitimate signature.

❖ "Authentication" assures the receiver of the identity of the sender. The sender uses secret information to attach cryptographically generated information (a signature) to a message. The receiver can determine with extremely high probability that the message could have been sent only by the entity that knows the sender secret, presumably only the legitimate sender. While taps can attempt to impersonate senders, they can't attach or adjust a legitimate signature.

❖ Our last technique is called "replay prevention." Suppose one workstation sends a message to another every morning at 7:10 to "unlock the vault." The message is strongly protected by a signature, and perhaps even encrypted, but its network image is always exactly the same. A tap could record the message, then send it to the receiver at some other time. The receiver considers the message legitimate and "unlocks the vault." One of the best countertechniques is for the sender to include a unique sequence number in each request, perhaps the time and date, and the receiver acts only once on a given sequence number.

These techniques are often used together and the algorithms for their use can be quite complicated. There are two generic ways to install encryption. The first way is as a separate hardware "box" (which for some reason is always black) between each workstation and the network. The advantage is that you can secure any workstation, no matter how untrustworthy. The disadvantage is that it's one more box to administrator.

The second way is as software in the workstation itself, which of course requires the workstation's operating system to have a protected TCB, like NT. The advantage is that you can more easily bring administration into the mainstream, but the disadvantage is that the software is only as secure as the underlying operating system. You can, of course, have combinations of hardware and software.

NT's flexible and modular network driver scheme is well positioned for such software, which invariably adds or modifies networking protocols. The problems that third parties have in implementing such software are not so much technical problems as problems of politics and standards, but we hope to see a number of strong products for Windows NT.

Audit Trail Analyzers

Most secure operating systems leave sophisticated audit analysis to third parties, partly because audit analysis is at best an undefined and highly specialized science. Let's consider a few analyses, starting with the simplest and progressing:

Example: A server experiences an inordinately high number of ACL denials over a period of fifteen minutes from a particular workstation. Is there skullduggery afoot?

Example: A particular user has, for years, logged on between 8 AM and 9 AM and out at 5 PM sharp. They suddenly start logging on late a night. Or a user is logged onto three workstations an average of three-quarters of a mile apart. More skull-duggery?

Example: A user with administrative capabilities installs and uses a new program (*.EXE file) that the analyzer does not recognize as "trusted." This presupposes an administrator can tell the analyzer which programs are deemed trusted. The analyzer could, for example, recognize such programs not by their name or location, but by a checksum on the *.EXE file. This lets the user make copies and even rename the program.

Example: You want an audit message that shows which files were printed to each line printer. This is not as easy as it may seem. Word processors, for example, may read a file then print it sometime later. (We assume the word processor doesn't issue its own such audit message. More on this option later.) An analyzer could associate the print job with the file previously read by the word processor, but what if the word processor had read and is "holding" several files? Which was actually printed? Suppose the user wanted to circumvent audit and copied the file, gave it a different name, then printed it, perhaps a few days later. Again, an analyzer should be able to catch specific scenarios like this, but how many such scenarios are there?

As you can begin to appreciate, auditing is not an exact science. The number of particular scenarios an analyzer might need to detect is large.

Personal Identification Devices (PIDs)

PIDs are devices that authenticate through something the user "holds" rather than something they "know" (a password). PIDs range from small tokens, like a key or small card, to small calculatorlike devices that let you participate in challenge-and-response schemes, to the esoteric, like fingerprint and retinal identification. Authentication based on both a PID and a password is excellent (something you hold and something you know). In this case, the password can be much simpler than it needs to be without the PID, simple enough that it is seldom written. NT's modular structure nicely supports such software. Specifically, its logon program interacts with a special subsystem called the GINA.DLL, which can be easily replaced by software that adds smart card authentication to the logon scenario.

Security-Smart Applications

Applications can participate in system security. One of the easiest and most profitable things they can do uniquely is issue meaningful audit events. For example, our text editor in one of the earlier examples knows exactly which file it printed. Of course, you don't want your security log clogged with useless application reports ("chaff"). It's best if the application lets the administrator determine what it audits.

As another example, applications that authenticate their users through their own passwords could rely on NT's authentication instead. Rather than asking for a separate password, likely not through the Trusted Path, an application could accept NT's account identity instead.

Virus Checkers

Trojan Horses, viruses, and other malicious programs are an epidemic on systems like MS-DOS or Macintosh OS without file system access controls. Systems like NT, with a protected TCB and ACLs, are considerably less prone to virus attacks. Presently there are no common NT-specific viruses. However, they will appear. Using a good virus checker never hurts, and we recommend you employ one that specifically addresses Windows NT. Keep it up to date and protect its executable and data files!

Secure Installation

As installed, Windows NT is not protected as tightly as it might be. This appendix lists recommended, specific settings for ACLs on the critical parts of the TCB (the Registry and various system folders), directories that hold application programs, and general directories that should be protected. (We assume that for security you format all drives that hold the directories listed on the following page with the NTFS disk format.) It also specifies a few changes to the Rights policy and a few other miscellaneous changes to make after installation. Many of our recommendations are tighter than in the rest of the text and should suit those who want maximum security from Windows NT.

The Everyone group implicitly includes all accounts, whereas the Users group includes only those you install. Many files, directories, and other objects need an ACL entry for "general users" and the question becomes whether to use Everyone or Users. In this appendix we take the most conservative position and use Users. Therefore, throughout our recommendations for configuring ACLs we use Users instead of Everyone except for a few exceptions, which we note. You may well choose to use Everyone in place of Users in these cases, and while this may be a little less secure, the choice is largely subjective.

Reboot the system after you make these changes.

The Registry

The Windows NT Registry is a centralized database that holds many configuration parameters for the operating system and applications. Many regular user and administrative applications read and set values in the registry outside the user's view. You can manually edit the Registry using the program named REGEDT32.EXE.

The Registry is organized into four hierarchically structured directory (folder) trees, analogous to four logical drives. REGEDT32 lets one navigate the folders (called "keys") in a Registry tree analogous to Explorer, and also edit the values stored in the Registry keys. Consult your system documentation for details on using REGEDT32.

Each Registry key has an ACL analogous to an ACL on a file. It is important to set these so that regular users cannot alter any security or other critical system parameters. Immediately after installation and before any regular users are allowed to log on, use REGEDT32 to modify the ACL on the Registry keys that follow. On each of these keys, give the ACL entry for Everyone "Read" permission.

Do not apply the changes to the subkeys unless noted.

HKEY_LOCAL_MACHINE\
\Software\Microsoft\Rpc ...*and its **subkeys***

HKEY_LOCAL_MACHINE\
\Software\Microsoft\WindowsNT\CurrentVersion

HKEY_LOCAL_MACHINE\Software\Microsoft\WindowsNT\CurrentVersion\
AeDebug
Compatibility
Drivers
Embedding
Fonts
Font Substitutes
GRE_Initialize
MCI
MCI Extensions
Ports ...*and its **subkeys***
ProfileList
WOW ...*and its **subkeys***

HKEY_LOCAL_MACHINE\Software\Windows3.1MigrationStatus
...*if present; and its **subkeys***

HKEY_CLASSES_ROOT ...*and its **subkeys***

In this case we explicitly use the Everyone group (rather than replacing it with Users), since it is difficult to determine how various programs that use the Registry may act. For example, a program may need access to Registry information even in denying a request to an account outside the User group.

File System ACLs

Protect System Files and Directories

Most of the TCB is kept within the WINNT directory. (This is the conventional name—some administrators choose to name it differently, although we discourage this.) You must strengthen the ACLs in several elements of this directory immediately after installation before any regular users are allowed to log on.

Except where noted, apply these changes not only to these directories, but also to all subdirectories and existing files by checking both of these options on the Directory Permissions window. Make these changes in the order shown.

All the files in this section should be owned by the Administrators group. If they are not already, as a full administrator simply take ownership.

C:	...*C: and its files—**not subdirectories****
Administrators:	Full Control
CREATOR OWNER:	Read
Users:	Read
SYSTEM:	Full Control

C:\WINNT	...*WINNT directory **only***
Administrators:	Full Control
CREATOR OWNER:	Full Control
Everyone:	Read
SYSTEM:	Full Control

C:\WINNT\SYSTEM
C:\WINNT\SYSTEM32

Administrators:	Full Control
CREATOR OWNER:	Full Control
Everyone:	Read
SYSTEM:	Full Control

C:\WINNT\REPAIR	
Administrators:	Full Control
SYSTEM:	Full Control

C:\WINNT\SYSTEM32\CONFIG	
Administrators:	Full Control
CREATOR OWNER:	Full Control
Everyone:	List
SYSTEM:	Full Control

C:\WINNT\SYSTEM32\SPOOL	
Administrators:	Full Control
CREATOR OWNER:	Full Control
Users:	List[1]
Power Users[2]:	Change
SYSTEM:	Full Control

---

1. If a user has trouble printing, change this to "Special Access" (**RWXD**) ("Not Specified"). Although it lets users delete other user's jobs, they can't read them.
2. On NT Server, use Server Operators instead.

```
C:\WINNT\SYSTEM32\DHCP
C:\WINNT\SYSTEM32\RAS
C:\WINNT\SYSTEM32\OS2
C:\WINNT\SYSTEM32\WINS
```
Administrators:	Full Control
CREATOR OWNER:	Full Control
Everyone:	Read[1]
SYSTEM:	Full Control

```
C:\BOOT.INI
C:\NTLDR
C:\NTDETECT.COM
```
Administrators:	Full Control
SYSTEM:	Full Control

```
C:\AUTOEXEC.BAT
C:\CONFIG.SYS
```
Administrators:	Full Control
Everyone:	Read
SYSTEM:	Full Control

In most of these cases we retain the use of the Everyone group (rather than replacing it with Users), since it is difficult to determine how various programs access system information. For example, a program may need to access these directories even in denying a request to an account outside the User group.

It is not necessary to use an ACL on an executable file to prevent users from gaining administrative capabilities. All Windows NT programs ensure that their user has particular Rights and/or is a member of a special administrative group before performing sensitive security and operational functions.

General Directories

We've already discussed protecting the system portions of the system file hierarchy. We now turn our attention to other directories. These are initial settings and you may have to adjust selected files and subdirectories so that various applications work correctly. Make these changes for each directory and all its files and subdirectories:

```
C:\TEMP          Owner: Administrators group
```
Administrators:	Full Control
CREATOR OWNER:	Full Control
Users:	Special (RWX)(Not Specified)
SYSTEM:	Full Control

1. If you experience any problems in the corresponding subsystems, you may have to set the ACL entry for Everyone to "Change."

```
C:\BIN
C:\DEV
C:\DOS                         Owner: Administrators group
    Administrators:               Special (All)(RX)
    CREATOR OWNER:                Read
    Users:                        Read
    SYSTEM:                       Full Control
```

The latter three directories are present only if you preloaded DOS. However, if you have converted C: to the NTFS format, DOS can no longer run and you can probably delete these directories. Files in these should be Read-Only and we therefore recommend setting the directory ACL so they are initially Read-Only even for the owner and administrators. This helps to prevent even administrators from installing programs that are not Read-Only. Program files (usually *.EXE files) in BIN, DEV, and DOS that are not to be run by administrators should be set specially to:

```
    Administrators:               No Access
    Account Operators:            No Access
    Backup Operators:             No Access
    Server Operators:             No Access
    Users:                        Read
    SYSTEM:                       Full Control
```

Common Applications Directories

We recommend that only full administrators install new software on the system. By convention, we recommend each application be stored in a subdirectory of C:\WIN32APP, although the following recommendations apply wherever they are stored.

For maximum security, discourage administrators and NT Server Operators from running day-to-day applications from their administrative accounts. To help encourage this, we arrange the following ACL so that by default they do not obtain "Execute" access to executable files created in this directory. (Obviously full administrators can change these default ACLs if they choose.) It is not a security violation for administrators to run such programs if you can ensure that the programs contain no malicious code. If you so ascertain, allow "Read" access to the appropriate groups.

```
C:\WIN32APP                    Owner: Administrators group
    Administrators:               Special (All)(None)
    Account Operators:            Special (All)(None)
    Backup Operators:             Special (All)(None)
    Server Operators:             Special (All)(None)
    Users:                        Read
    SYSTEM:                       Full Control
```
(Some of these groups are not present on NT Workstation.)

Note that the ACL placed by default on all executable (and other) files in this directory tree is therefore:

Administrators:	No Access
Account Operators:	No Access
Backup Operators:	No Access
Server Operators:	No Access
Users:	Read
SYSTEM:	Full Control

This precludes access to these administrative groups, which was our goal.

If you wish to restrict access to applications further, we recommend you create a local or global group for that application. Then, throughout the application's base directories replace the Users (or Everyone) entry of the preceding ACLs with that application-specific group, keeping the same permissions.

There may be cases where applications cannot work properly unless they can modify elements of the trees in which they are installed, and by default they cannot under the foregoing recommendations. There are two cases where you may need to judiciously relax these restrictions:

❖ Directories in which applications create and modify files and/or directories regardless of the user. If possible, isolate such modified files and directories. You can often accomplish this by giving these directories the ACL:

CREATOR OWNER:	Change
SYSTEM:	Full Control

❖ Files modified by the application regardless of the user. You can often accomplish this by giving these files the ACL:

Users:	Change
SYSTEM:	Full Control

Consider such files carefully. Note that anyone can read, modify, and (often) replace these files. The data is unprotected from other users.

If you have difficulty determining which files an application cannot access, enable full object auditing for all the application's files and directories. Examine the audit log to determine where problems lie.

User Home Directories

We assume that the user's home directories are kept inside C:\USERS. Protect this tree as follows:

C:\USERS	Owner: Administrators group
Administrators:	Special (All)(Not Specified)
CREATOR OWNER:	Full Control
Users:	List
SYSTEM:	Full Control

C:\USERS\...	Owner: *the owning user*
...all home directories	
(the user):	Full Control
Administrators:	Read
CREATOR OWNER:	Full Control
SYSTEM:	Full Control

Regarding the two previous items, while one can never preclude members of the Administrators group access to any file, as a point of practice we specify that all files created in the USERS tree be Read-Only by administrators. However, we do not deem it a security violation to grant full administrators more access to these file trees. Granting extended access (like "Full Control") makes it somewhat easier for administrators to manage the file trees when necessary. Users can relax the restrictions on their home directories, but they should, of course, use caution.

C:\USERS\DEFAULT	Owner: Administrators group
Administrators:	Full Control
CREATOR OWNER:	Full Control
Users:	Special (RWX)(Not Specified)
SYSTEM:	Full Control

We regard DEFAULT as a "public" directory for generic use. Hence, access is not tightly controlled. Note however that users may create fully protected files and subdirectories. We recommend against using this directory for regular users unless they have use for a home directory. For example, they may run only "canned" programs that don't use a home directory. Normally, each user is given their own home directory or, in rare cases, a group of users shares a home directory.

Rights Policy

Use the User Manager to manage the Rights policy. Note that a Rights policy applies only to its own computer and you must adjust the rights on each Windows NT computer on the network. We recommend the following changes to the as-installed Rights policy:

Bypass traverse checking   We recommend you disable this Right for all but full administrators and the SYSTEM user.

Debug Programs   Remove Administrators.

Shut Down the system   Remove Everyone and Users, if they exist. We consider it more secure to allow only authorized users to shut down the system (see "Miscellaneous" below).

Access this computer from the network   Change Everyone to Users. Further restrict this Right if prudent.

Log on Locally   Remove Everyone and Guests. Remove Users on NT Server, but leave it on NT Workstation. It is standard NT policy to preclude other than administrators direct (primary) logon to an NT Server, although this policy is more operational than security-minded. Further restrict this Right if prudent.

We remove both the Rights to "Log on Locally" and "Access this computer from the network" from Everyone, and instead extend them only to legitimate, defined groups. It simply seems prudent to disallow completely unlimited access to these Rights.

The disadvantage of giving access to broad groups like Users is that when a new account is added it immediately obtains broad capabilities. Therefore, there may be a considerable security benefit in tightly limiting both of these Rights because they control which users can access which computers on the network. One might even allocate specific user accounts to these Rights. This more specific approach follows the general security dictum "that not specifically allowed is prohibited," which is also the policy of the system ACLs. The disadvantage to detailed Rights policies is that the Rights list must be maintained on each computer, and hence there is no centralized list of who can access what.

More specifically, to tighten your security you can replace Users in both these Rights with a specific list of user accounts. If a list becomes unwieldy, consider specially created groups named, for example, Local Logons and Remote Accessors.

Troubleshooting

Some third party applications and services, particularly administrative tools, may not work with these Registry and system file ACLs. If so, you need to adjust the ACLs accordingly. But how do you know which ones to adjust? One handy technique is to enable object audit failures for the suspected files or Registry keys then run the program that fails. It usually fails soon after it unsuccessfully attempts to modify an object, and this will show in the security log. You can then adjust the object ACLs, but be careful in how you relax them. Avoid giving the general public write access to sensitive objects.

Miscellaneous

Booting the system and shutting it down should be tightly controlled, but some controls are hardware specific.

❖ Disable the computer hardware's ability to boot from alternative sources (CD-ROM, floppy, and so forth). Different hardware employs different means of protection (cabinet key locks, BIOS passwords, and so forth).

❖ Similarly, use all hardware protections available to prevent a user in physical contact with the computer from mechanically shutting off its power.

❖ Allow Windows NT to turn off the computer's power after it shuts down. In the Registry key:

```
HKEY_LOCAL_MACHINE\SOFTWARE\Microsoft\WindowsNT\
        CurrentVersion\WinLogon
```

modify the item PowerDownAfterShutdown to have a value of 1. Those who shut down the system are now given the option of also powering down the computer. Not all computer hardware supports this feature.

❖ If nonadministrators are to be entrusted to shut down the system, consider creating a Shutdown global or local group then grant the Rights "Shut down the system" to that group, as well as system administrators and operators. Populate the Shutdown group as appropriate.

❖ Prevent users other than the user who is logged on from accessing floppies or CD-ROM. In the Registry key:

```
HKEY_LOCAL_MACHINE\SOFTWARE\Microsoft\WindowsNT\
        CurrentVersion\WinLogon
```

add a value named AllocateFloppies with date type RegSize and a value of 1.

❖ Limit redirection of printers and other devices to alternate ports to administrators. In the Registry key:

```
HKEY_LOCAL_MACHINE\SYSTEM\CurrentControlSet\Control\
        SessionManager
```

add a value entry named ProtectionMode with date type RegSize and a value of 1.

Glossary

sĭ–kyoor′ə-tē

*A feeling of confidence; a degree
of trust in your system and
its configuration.*

The following abbreviations are defined inside other glossary entries:

Acronym	See...
ACL	Access Control List
ACE	Access Control List
C2	Trusted Computing Systems Evaluation Criteria
DAC	Discretionary Access Control
DOS	MS-DOS
FAT	Disk Formats
HPFS	Disk Formats
MAC	Mandatory Access Control
NTFS	Disk Formats
RWXDPO	Permissions
SAM	Security Accounts Manager (SAM) Database
SSL	Secure Sockets Layer
TCSEC	Trusted Computing Systems Evaluation Criteria
TCB	Trusted Computing Base
WFW	Windows for Workgroups

Access Control List (ACL) Controls information attached to many NT objects, like NTFS files and directories, that determine in what manner user accounts can access the item (read, modify, delete, and so forth). An ACL consists of a set of **entries**, also called **access control entries** (**ACE**s), each of which pertains to an account or a group. NT uses the special **CREATOR OWNER** entry to assign permissions to the account that creates a new object. See also *Permissions*.

Account and Account Policy A collection of parameters that govern a user's capabilities to use an NT workstation. User's are matched to an account during logon by presenting the account's password. A **domain account** is defined on a domain controller (NT Server) and is allowed and visible throughout that domain and all domains that trust it. A **local account** is defined on a workstation (NT Server or Workstation) and is allowed and visible only on that workstation. The **Account Policy** of a workstation is a collection of parameters that affect all accounts on the workstation and is managed by the User Manager program. See also *Logon and Logoff*.

Administrator   Generically, a user (or more properly, an account) that has capabilities to "administer" the workstation. A **full administrator** has all administrative capabilities while other administrators have fewer. All accounts who are members of the local group named Administrators are full administrators on that workstation. See also *Operators* and *Power Users*.

Auditing and Audit Policy   Also called "security auditing." A group of NT features that records security-relevant **audit events** into a **security log**. The **Audit Policy**, managed through User Manager, determines which of several predefined **categories** of events NT records. **Audit controls** on many objects, like NTFS files and directories, additionally determine which audit events are generated when the objects are accessed. Audit controls and the ACL are kept in the same internal data structure and for this reason some NT documentation speaks of the audit controls as part of the ACL. We don't.

Authenticate   A broad synonym for "logon."

Basic Permissions   See *Permissions*.

Browser   A class of NT windows that presents the domains and workgroups visible on the network, as well as the advertised resources that each makes available to (shares with) other workstations.

Capability   We use this term only generically. It is not a specific NT feature. For example, we might say, "An account has many capabilities: its Rights, group memberships, password controls, logon periods...."

Categories (Audit)   See *Auditing and Audit Policy*.

Client   See *Server*.

Controller   See *Domain Controller*.

CREATOR OWNER   See *Access Control List*.

Desktop   The various icons and windows as well as the task bar that populate your monitor. This style of interface was introduced by Windows 95 and appeared for the first time on Windows NT 4.0.

Discretionary Access Control (DAC)   A term for the kind of access control that ACLs provide. Some NT documents consider audit controls on objects as part of DAC, but this is a misapplication of the term.

Disk Formats NT supports three formats for mass storage devices, like the logical partitions of a hard drive: **FAT**, the traditional DOS format; **HPFS**, a format developed in conjunction with OS/2; and **NTFS**, the new native format for Windows NT. Only NTFS supports ACLs and is used wherever security is a concern. Floppy disks can be only FAT.

Domain Account See *Account and Account Policy.*

Domain Controller A workstation that centrally controls and stores certain data for a domain, including domain accounts and global groups. Only NT Server can be a domain controller. There is only one active controller in each domain, but other NT Servers can serve as backup controllers in case the active controller fails. Domain controllers often function as general data servers, but need not.

Events (Audit) See *Auditing and Audit Policy.*

Event Viewer A standard NT program that lets an administrator view and manage the security log. See also *Auditing and Audit Policy.*

Explorer A standard NT program that lets you manage your logical disks and their files and directories. In particular, it lets you manage their ACLs and audit controls. You can also simply use your desktop. It's a matter of personal preference.

File Default Permissions See *Permissions.*

Firewall A rather imprecise term applied to a class of software systems usually implemented on a stand-alone computer. A firewall stands between a LAN and an intranet. Its main purpose is to protect the computers on the LAN from attack by computers on the intranet by restricting and logging traffic between the two networks. Generally, a firewall removes the LAN as a direct part of the intranet so that remote computers cannot directly send packets to computers on the LAN. (Or, equivalently, the firewall may allow only certain LAN computers direct access to the intranet.) Firewalls often provide proxy servers (see *Proxy Service*) that stand between specific LAN clients and intranet servers. Firewalls may also limit traffic between the LAN and intranet based on their IP address, often called "IP filtering." However, IP addresses can be falsified and this is, therefore, not a strong security protection.

FTP For File Transfer Protocol, a service often provided on intranets (like the Internet) that facilitates the passing of files between two hosts on the network. There are many FTP client programs. Some are graphic and quite easy to use. FTP traditionally requires the client user to type a name and password that must be recognized on the server, although anonymous access is frequently allowed.

Full Administrator See *Administrator.*

Global Group See *Group.*

Gopher An information retrieval service often provided on intranets like the global Internet. Gopher makes geographically diverse libraries of information appear to be organized into a single directory tree so that the libraries appear much like a logical drive (like E:).

Group   A named list of user accounts or other groups. A **global group** is defined only on domain controllers, can include only the accounts on the controller, and is visible and usable throughout the domain and all domains that trust it. A **local group** can be defined on any workstation, can include local and domain accounts and global groups, but is visible and usable only on its own workstation. Groups facilitate the granting of permissions through ACLs and are used to impart administrative capabilities to administrator accounts. Each account must have one group designated its **Primary group** for POSIX compatibility.

Home Directory   A directory associated with a particular account usually intended for the use and control by the account's user(s).

ID   An number that uniquely identifies a user account or group on the entire network. Windows NT uses IDs internally and users seldom see them. Account and group IDs are permanent. They do not change for the life of the account or group and NT never assigns the same ID twice. By contrast, administrators can change the name of an account.

Item   A term we use for "file and/or directory."

Local Account   See *Account and Account Policy.*

Local Group   See *Group.*

Logon and Logoff   The process by which NT identifies a user account under which to provide its services. A user sitting at a workstation must log on before they can use an NT Workstation, called a **primary logon**. Before a workstation provides a service to another workstation on the network, it determines the account with which to associate the service through a **secondary logon** determined from a name and password passed to it by the requesting, client workstation.

Mandatory Access Control (MAC)   Windows NT doesn't have MAC, but it's a term often used in the secure system market so it's worth a little background discussion. MAC is an access control that uses military-style sensitivity labels like the familiar Unclassified, Confidential, Secret, and Top Secret. Access to each file and other "data storage objects" on the system is protected by one of these labels analogous to an ACL. The administrator "clears" each user to one of these labels (usually kept in their "account") and that user may only read files at their "clearance" label or lower. For example, a user cleared to Confidential could read Unclassified and Confidential files, but not those cleared at Secret or Top Secret.

Enforced by the TCB, MAC rules employ the basic principle that users and their programs can't copy data from one place to another in such a way that it leaves the data exposed at a lower level than originally assigned. For example, no user or program could read data from a Secret file and write it to a Confidential file, although they (or it) may well be allowed to read data from a Confidential file and insert it into a Secret file. Similarly, no user or program can change the Secret label on a file to Unclassified, although they (or it) may be allowed to change it to Top Secret. (Actually, "trusted" users and programs can do the operations, but "untrusted" ones cannot.)

What's been long understood but surprises many newcomers is that MAC prevents people only from seeing what they shouldn't see. It does not prevent them from changing what they shouldn't change. In short, it's a strong "read-protect" but is not a "write-protect" security measure. MAC is said to "prevent unauthorized disclosure but does not ensure integrity," which is just a fancy of way saying the same thing. Early security systems added yet another access control that enforces mandatory write control to complement MAC, usually called a "(mandatory) integrity control." However, because the TCSEC does not require them, general security systems of today do not include these integrity controls. Despite being around for a couple of decades, MAC is not widely accepted outside the military.

Malicious Trojan Horse programs can subvert MAC by communicating using aspects of the computer system not intended as a means of data exchange and therefore not protected by MAC. These aspects are called "covert channels." For example, although a malicious program that has read Top Secret data can't write it to an Unclassified file (MAC prevents this), it may be able to communicate the data through a covert channel to a cooperating program at Unclassified that could. As an analogy, you might lock a negotiating team in a room and prevent the unscrupulous among them from using the phones to tip off their partners in crime on the floor below about the status of the negotiations. But the clever lock-in taps their foot in a Morse Code pattern. Not as fast as the phone, but just as effective. Well-designed systems limit covert channels, but it's hard to do so completely without unduly impacting other system requirements. Further, the TCSEC allows channels under 100 bits per second. That's 45,000 bytes per hour. Hardly the kind of hole you'd expect from a "mandatory" access control.

Historically and in practice, programs not specifically designed to work in the MAC environment often work strangely when introduced on a MAC system. Few off-the-shelf applications are yet so designed. While there are usually ways to work around these, they can be bothersome.

MS-DOS The ancestral operating system to Windows NT. Some versions of MS-DOS are called simply **DOS**.

Network Share Directory A directory (including its tree) that one workstation makes available for connection by other workstations. To the connecting client, a remote share directory looks like a logical drive hence the alternative term "network drive."

Notepad A standard NT program to edit text files.

Operators A term applied to several classes of administrators on NT Server: Account Operators, Backup Operators, Print Operators, and Server Operators. Backup Operators are also defined on NT Workstation.

Orange Book   See *Trusted Computing System Evaluation Criteria*.

Owner   An account identity attached to each object that has an ACL. Typically, the account that creates an object becomes its initial owner, although, if allowed by its ACL, other accounts can take ownership of the object replacing the original owner. NT often allows accounts special control of objects they own; in particular, changing its ACL.

Password   A secret phrase or word that lets the person who knows it gain some capabilities that others cannot. NT's most common use of passwords is during logon.

Permissions   Capabilities that an account has toward an object protected by an ACL. **Basic Permissions** permit fundamental access and differ in name between objects. The Basic Permissions for files and directories are (with the common abbreviation in parenthesis): "Read" (**R**), "Write" (**W**), "Delete" (**D**), "Execute" (**X**), "Take Ownership" (**O**), and "Change Permissions" (**P**). We sometimes call these the **RWXDPO** permissions. For convenience, NT programs often offer the user predefined sets of Basic Permissions called **standard permission sets** (or sometimes "access types"). These names also vary according to the kind of object. Sets that are not standard permission sets are sometimes called **special access permissions**. The **file default permissions** are a special set in each ACL entry of a directory that are applied to the corresponding entry in the ACL of newly created files in that directory.

Plaintext   In the science of cryptography, information that is not disguised by encryption. Also called "cleartext."

POSIX   An IEEE committee that maintains a set of operating system standards driven by the UNIX industry. The most prominent standard is P1003.1, which defines the operating system interface for regular (nonsystem) programs. Windows NT supports P1003.1, which means vendors with programs designed to the standard can readily adapt them to run on Windows NT.

Power Users   A specific kind of administrator with few capabilities. Typically, users are made Power Users on their own personal desktop workstation. This lets them add other user accounts and do noncritical functions like change the time and date. An account that is a member of the Power Users local group is a Power User.

Primary Group   See *Group*.

Primary Logon   See *Logon and Logoff*.

Privilege   An alternative, little-used term for Right.

Proxy Service   A program that positions itself between the client and server in a particular client-server scenario, usually on a firewall or gateway. All traffic between the client and server passes through the proxy. Servers are usually unaware of the proxy and clients are sometimes unaware. Proxies are important components of firewalls because they allow clients on a LAN controlled, limited access to services on a wide area network like an intranet. They can also provide certain security features by monitoring, recording, and even blocking certain kinds of transactions. Proxies are usually designed to support specific protocols, like the FTP and WWW protocols.

Registry A large, critical collection of parameters on each NT Workstation that governs the workstation's operations. The Registry is organized into a few logical tree structures, and is managed by administrators and various system programs.

Rights and Rights Policy A Right is a capability assigned on each workstation to accounts and/or groups visible from that workstation. A Right lets an account perform certain critical functions. NT has about two dozen Rights. For example, one Right allows an account to access the workstation from the network, another lets an account change the system time, and yet another lets them shut down the system. The **Rights Policy** is the total assignment of Rights on a particular workstation and is managed by User Manager. The Rights Policy imparts capabilities only on its own workstation.

Screen Saver A program that NT automatically invokes after a period of keyboard and mouse inactivity that paints a low-intensity display on the monitor to keep its phosphors from becoming damaged. Screen savers on NT have security significance because you can require a screen saver to require a logon password to revert to the original screen.

Secondary Logon See *Logon and Logoff*.

Secure Sockets Layer (SSL) A cryptographic protocol commonly used in the WWW that can ensure confidentiality, integrity, and server and client authentication.

Security Accounts Manager (SAM) Database NT's term for the collection of user accounts and group definitions on a computer.

Security Log See *Auditing and Audit Policy*.

Security Window See *Trusted Path*.

Server A generic term for a workstation that provides services to other workstations on the network, which are called **clients**. Strictly speaking, these terms apply only to a specific transaction because two workstations can provide services to each other, in which case each is both a server and a client. The term "server" usually refers to workstations with a primary purpose of acting as a server to many workstation clients. We never use the term "server" in place of "NT Server." Sometimes "server" can refer to a workstation running either NT Workstation or NT Server.

Server Manager A standard NT program to manage various properties of an NT Server, like its domain relationships.

Special Access Permissions See *Permissions*.

Spoof When a program or user attempts to "fool" a user to divulge sensitive information or perform some task that the spoofer can't perform directly. A main purpose of the Trusted Path is to foil spoofing attempts. See also *Untrusted Programs*.

Standard Permission Set   See *Permissions*.

Trojan Horse   A malicious portion of seemingly benign software. An unsuspecting user may run such a program, and because the program itself obtains the capabilities of the user, the Trojan Horse can take actions allowed the user. These actions may be unknown and unintended by the user. Trusted programs are trusted to be free of Trojan Horses. See also *Virus*.

Trust Relationship   A relationship from one domain A to a second B that lets the domain accounts and global groups B be allowed and visible on all workstations in A. In this example we say "A trusts B." The trust relationship is neither reflexive (A can trust B without B trusting A) nor transitive (A trusting B and B trusting C do not by themselves denote that A trusts C). Only administrators manage trust relationships.

Trusted Computing Base (TCB)   The totality of programs and files entrusted to uphold the defined security policies of an operating environment like Windows NT. We can say that any program capable of subverting those rules must be trusted to uphold them or at least not to subvert them. One trusts a program usually because one trusts the source of the program or has examined the program's code in detail. Trust is not an operating system attribute in that you cannot tag particular programs as "trusted," thus giving them special capabilities. Instead, capabilities are granted by mechanisms like Rights and administrators should not grant critical capabilities like Rights to untrusted programs. We also speak of files that hold critical security information as a part of the TCB. Programs that are not trusted, **untrusted programs**, are presumed to contain malicious code and should not, therefore, be given any sensitive capabilities.

Trusted Computing Systems Evaluation Criteria (TCSEC)   A U.S. Department of Defense standard that has become the principal criterion for highly secure computer operating systems. The TCSEC is not a software specification, but rather a criterion intended to guide a team of evaluators in affixing a security grade to a particular computer system. In the order of increasing complexity, these grades are: C1, C2, B1, B2, B3, and A1. The TCSEC is often called the **Orange Book** because its cover is, of course, orange. The National Computer Security Center at the National Security Agency performs evaluations under the TCSEC and also issues companion books that apply to other security areas, like networking. The initial release of Windows NT targets C2 evaluation.

Trusted Path   A feature through which a user sitting at a workstation can demand to be put in touch with a trusted program in a manner that cannot be subverted by malicious, untrusted programs. On Windows NT, you hold down the Ctrl, Alt, and Del keys simultaneously, which immediately produces the **Security window**, which you can trust. Because this window appears only on user demand, malicious programs can't readily spoof a user by producing a bogus copy.

Untrusted Programs   See *Trusted Computing Base*.

User Manager (for Domains) A standard NT program for managing accounts, groups, and the Account, Audit, and Rights Policies. The version for NT Workstation is named User Manager while the version for NT Server is named User Manager for Domains. We refer to them collectively by the shorter term.

Virus Malicious code that often enters the system as a Trojan Horse. Its characteristic is that it "infects" other legitimate programs, usually trusted programs, by changing them or their control data.

Windows for Workgroups (WFW) A Microsoft add-on product for Microsoft Windows. WFW adds mainly networking services for Windows, as well as several convenient utilities. WFW and NT cooperate in certain aspects of WFW security.

Workstation Our term for "computer." A workstation can range from a small desktop PC to a large, dedicated computer often functioning as a workgroup server.

World Wide Web (WWW) An information retrieval service that runs on intranets like the worldwide Internet. WWW clients (called "browsers") fetch "pages" of information (normally for viewing) from WWW servers on the network. A unique aspect is that fetched pages of information can contain named links to other, perhaps distant, pages and these other pages can be easily fetched by "clicking" the link name. WWW is designed to support graphics fully, which makes it an exciting and easy tool to use.

Appendix C

Answers

Accounts and Domains

[1]   No. MANUF users are not allowed into the ACTG domain.

[2]   Yes, because SALES users are allowed into the ACTG domain. Yes, because SALES accounts always have access to the SALES domain's resources, even when the account is being used on a workstation in another domain. The SALES user is just doing a secondary logon to the SALES domain.

[3]   SALES accounts are allowed into the ACTG domain, hence this secondary logon to a workstation in ACTG succeeds.

[4]   NT bases all its decisions on the account you log on to. You may have two accounts: one that gives you certain capabilities that the other does not.

[5]   No. Typically you can use your account on workstations throughout your domain and in other domains that your domain trusts.

[6]   They are the names of the domains whose accounts NT allows to log on at this workstation. All such accounts can also remotely access this workstation (a secondary logon), other security controls allowing.

[7]   **C**'s users are allowed into both **A** and **B** (and of course **C**). NT allows no other domain crossing.

[8]   They are different accounts, but they're both for you. You can access each by logging on to it, but only one at a time. Resources you can access in one may not be accessible from the other. The new SALES\JJones lets you access resources in the SALES domain, which you couldn't access as ACTG\JJones. This is one way your administrator can give you access to the SALES domain without giving access to the other users in ACTG.

[9]   SALES and ACTG only for both cases. SALES accounts are allowed in both SALES and ACTG.

[10] Nothing, really. NT's name lists typically show you only the domains and accounts that can be used in a particular scenario.

[11] The administrator could tell all of them the account's password. The problem is that there's no way to determine which of them did something on the system. And none of them can ever protect anything from the others, at least through the shared account.

[12] No. There are really no disadvantages. Because your account is allowed on your workstation, it's allowed also on the others in your workstation's domain so you can freely access their resources, other controls permitting.

[13] Look at the logon window *Domain* list of a workstation in each domain on your network. Each shows the list of the other domains its domain trusts. If you can't get to the other workstations, use Explorer to expand the network share directories of workstation in other domains. This should get you at least part of the way there.

Your Working Environment

[14] Suppose you walk up to a workstation and see the Security window, or one of the windows its buttons call up. Since you didn't use the Trusted Path to produce the window, you shouldn't believe it. NT erases these windows in a short period of time to keep you from developing bad habits.

[15] Don't believe it. There are only a few cases where NT asks you for a password outside a Trusted Path scenario. This is not one of them. Even if it was, if you don't recognize and expect it, don't give it your password.

[16] You can believe a scenario that instructs you to enter the Trusted Path sequence and when you do, asks for your password.

[17] Without this delay, you could repeatedly change your password until your old favorite is no longer on the list of previous passwords, then choose it again. This negates the whole point of preventing you from using one of your previous passwords.

[18] The browser (or one of its related programs) runs the applet and confines the applet to the designated tree. If one can alter the browser program itself, one could remove these restrictions. The browser is inside the directory tree and unless protected by a strong ACL can be modified!

[19] Type the Trusted Path keys to start a fresh scenario.

[20] Don't believe it. Some program is trying to fool you. Tell your administrator.

[21] You can set the screen saver to ask for your password to restore your screen. This keeps others from using your unattended terminal when you forget to lock it or log off.

[22] It's dangerous to use such programs. Even if you trust the program itself, without the Trusted Path other programs can masquerade as the program and "spoof" you.

[23] It's certainly hard for someone else to guess. It's almost impossible to remember and therefore guaranteed to be written down. Unless you're a memory expert, it's not a good password.

[24] Yes. You may not have the Right to log on primarily to **Y**, but you have the Right to access it remotely.

[25] No. Maybe it writes the passwords it presents you in a little file somewhere that only the program's creator knows. Or maybe it presents you with passwords from a relatively short list, again known by its creator. Or maybe it lists only a few different passwords!

ACLs

[26] These mean the workstation on which the ACL sits, which is just the domain name if it's on a domain controller.

[27] No. **RWXDPO** does not equate to "Full Control." For files they give the same control, but as we see later they are a little different for directories.

[28] For each entry in the ACL, the window remembers the last custom set you defined for that entry and installs that set again when you select *Special Access* (without the "...").

[29]

	ProjX	ProjY	Access
BBrown			Read (**RXP**)
BBrown	✔		Change (**RWXDP**)
BBrown		✔	No Access
BBrown	✔	✔	No Access
JJones			Full Control (**All**)
JJones	✔		Full Control (**All**)
JJones		✔	No Access
JJones	✔	✔	No Access
CClark			No Access
CClark	✔		No Access

DDavis in ProjX has "Change" (**RWXD**) permission. Note in particular that a user given specific permissions, like BBrown, is precluded access if they are a member of a group given "No Access."

[30] Anyone with **R**, **W**, or **X** and the owner JJones can view the ACL. JJones and BBrown can change the ACL. Even when JJones is in ProjY and therefore has no access to the file, as owner they can change the ACL, perhaps giving themselves all permissions. The CClark entry is extraneous if CClark is not a member of these groups. Removing this entry has no affect on who can access the file.

[31] (1) BBrown gets **RX** by being a direct member of ACTG\Accounting and **WXD** by being an indirect member of ProjZ. In total, they get **RWXD**. (2) CClark gets **WXD** by its membership in ProjZ. (3) JJones gets "No Access" even though it's a member of ProjZ. (4) None. Owners gain no permissions unless the ACL grants some. However, owners can change the ACL and give themselves permissions.

[32] We make JJones the owner of the file. Because BBrown does not have "Take Ownership" (**O**) or "Change Permissions" (**P**) permission, JJones alone can adjust the ACL.

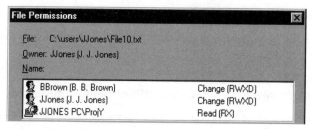

[33] The major ability is to preclude the old owner from accessing the file. Also, the owner of a file can see its permissions regardless of the ACL, but this is a minor point.

[34] JJones fails because it takes only one entry to deny access, even if others would seem to allow it.

[35] That permissions are additive. The JJones entry gives "Read" permission while the Everyone entry gives "Write." Combined we get both "Read" and "Write."

[36] Yes, you can see the name because the name is really protected by the ACL on the parent directory, AA. Yes, because you can always open the ACL on a file you own, providing you can see it from Explorer or in a desktop window.

[37] You can see the file's name, but you can't open the ACL because you don't have **R**, **W**, or **X** permission to the file and are not the owner.

[38] Yes, but note the caution that you can't change it.

[39] **RWXDPO**. Recall that "Full Control" gives you a tiny bit more control than the simple sum of **RWXDPO**. Hence, **RWXDPO** is not strictly equal to "Full Control."

[40] With "Full Access" to a directory you can delete its items regardless of their ACL. With **RWXDPO**, you need "Delete" permission to delete the items.

[41] One advantage of **RWXDPO** to a directory rather than "Full Control" is that you can't accidentally delete its items that you've individually protected from deletion. Hence, **RWXDPO** is a little safer. However, "Full Control" makes it easier to delete these items when you really want to, hence it's a little more convenient.

[42] They get the same ACL as they would if they were newly created.

[43] No.

[44] "Add" does not let you see the contents of a directory but it lets you create new entries, but since "Add" has file default "Not Specified" you get no permissions to files you create. By contrast, "Add and Read" gives you "Read" (**RX**) permission to files you create.

[45] "List" gives BBrown permission only to view the names of the directory's entries but no permission to access its files. "Read" additionally lets it read the files.

[46] You might have tried, for example, an ACL with a single entry for Everyone with "Special Access" (**All**)("Not Specified"). Instead of creating the empty ACL you might expect, NT gives "Full Control" to the owner and SYSTEM. You can probably guess the rationale for owner. We discuss SYSTEM later.

[47] NT replaces CREATOR OWNER with your entry with "Full Control."

[48] Your entry in the new file's ACL is the sum of **RX** and **WXD**: **RWXD**. This illustrates that when the creator is already listed in the ACL, the CREATOR OWNER permissions augment that entry.

[49] When faced with this dilemma, NT chooses the conservative option and gives you "No Access."

[50] All the ones in the tree.

[51] This changes only the files in DirA, so F1 gets a new ACL but F2 does not. It gives the file the same ACL as files newly created.

[52] This changes all the directories and files in the tree.

[53] Once you change an asterisked entry it is no longer asterisked and thereafter propagates normally.

[54] Our choices are:

| CREATOR OWNER | Full Control (All) (All) |
| JJones (J. J. Jones) | Full Control (All) (All) |

ACL on JJones

CREATOR OWNER is redundant because JJones is the only one who can create entries and JJones already gets "Full Control," but it doesn't hurt.

[55] First, we need to give everyone "List" permission to our home directory so they can get through it into Public:

CREATOR OWNER	Full Control (All) (All)
Everyone	List (RX) (Not Specified)
JJones (J. J. Jones)	Full Control (All) (All)

New ACL on JJones

Note our careful use of "List" (as opposed to "Read") because it uses "Not Specified" for file defaults. Now for Public itself:

CREATOR OWNER	Full Control (All) (All)
Everyone	Read (RX) (RX)
JJones (J. J. Jones)	Full Control (All) (All)

ACL on JJones\Public

[56] There's no need to change your home directory. The ACL for DropBox is:

Everyone	Add (WX) (Not Specified)
JJones (J. J. Jones)	Full Control (All) (All)

ACL on JJones\DropBox

[57] People who copy into DropBox lose control of the item. It becomes yours. It's poor practice to include CREATOR OWNER on DropBox.

[58] Don't give these items sensitive names like "Plans to Demote JKJ."

[59]

CREATOR OWNER	Full Control (All) (All)
JJones (J. J. Jones)	Full Control (All) (All)

ACL on JJones\Work

Again, CREATOR OWNER is superfluous, but it does no harm.

[60]

BBrown (B. B. Brown)	Add & Read (RWX) (RX)
CClark (C. C. Clark)	Read (RX) (RX)
CREATOR OWNER	Full Control (All) (All)
JJones (J. J. Jones)	Add & Read (RWX) (RX)

ACL on JJones\LRPlan

This is rather tricky. We chose not to give JJones full access to all files, reasoning that if BBrown creates a file, JJones should not necessarily be able to delete it. However, you might give JJones "Take Ownership" permission in the file defaults, which means JJones can take ownership of BBrown's files and change their ACL.

[61]

BBrown (B. B. Brown)	Full Control (All) (All)
CREATOR OWNER	Full Control (All) (All)
JJones (J. J. Jones)	Special Access (RXP) (RXP)
JJONES PC\ProjX	Add & Read (RWX) (RX)

ACL on JJones\ProjX

The file defaults for JJones are perhaps not exactly what you'd like, but you can of course change the ACLs on new files.

[62]

BBrown (B. B. Brown)	Full Control (All) (All)
CREATOR OWNER	Full Control (All) (All)
JJones (J. J. Jones)	Special Access (RXP) (RXP)
JJONES PC\ProjX	Change (RWXD) (RWXD)

ACL on JJones\ProjX\Public

[63]

BBrown (B. B. Brown)	Full Control (All) (All)	
CREATOR OWNER	Full Control (All) (All)	
JJones (J. J. Jones)	Full Control (All) (All)	
JJONES PC\ProjX	Read (RX) (RX)	

ACL on JJones\ProjX\Manager

We choose to let BBrown fully administer the directory as per our original policy.

[64] You could create a global group JSK and FDT with the two accounts. (Choose the name carefully because you can't rename groups!) This group should be able to change permissions and take ownership of items with which the two people work. Alternately, they could agree to give each of their accounts "Full Control" to all files and directories. The advantage of the group is that you might want to add a third user to the job share group, although the group name is no longer descriptive.

[65] Put all your accounts in all your ACLs with "Full Control" or make a group that holds your accounts giving it "Full Control." The latter is quite useful if you anticipate getting more accounts later.

[66] You can't. They own items they create and as such can change the ACL arbitrarily.

[67] This gives the access to everyone in INTERACTIVE, which may be broader than you intend, since INTERACTIVE includes everyone who can primarily log on to the workstation. Also, if you add other accounts to the ACL they now gain access from remote workstations, which is not the case when you prohibit NETWORK.

[68] Yes. Give INTERACTIVE "Change permission," and NETWORK "Read." Note however that a remote user with, say "Add," gets "Add and Read." In other words, NETWORK does not limit remote users unless it's set to "No Access."

[69] Although global groups can be a members of local groups, local groups cannot. NT doesn't even list local groups in the Add window.

[70] No.

[71] No. It's gone.

[72] No. Once a group is deleted, it's gone for good. A new group of the same name is a totally different group.

[73] "Partners" and "Benefits" seem useful. "A-K" and "L-K" seem useless because it's hard to imagine why access should be based on someone's last name. "Engineers" and "Secretaries" are okay if there's a legitimate use for restricting access based on these criteria. "BS, MS, and PhD" as well as "Men, Women" are probably not useful. It's hard to imagine how they could be used for legitimate access control, although there could be some cases. "Others" although perhaps useful is not descriptive. Maybe the manager meant "Nonemployees."

[74] Since your goal is to control access to printers, a better group may have been Restricted Printers. Then you could select users other than managers which gives you flexibility. One of the problems with the name "Managers" is that if you add non-managers to Managers so they can use a printer, they might gain access to information they aren't supposed to access because people might tag items with "Managers" under the legitimate expectation that only managers have access.

[75] The key test for each of your groups: Are there file directories or other objects (like printers) that members of this group should have that other system users should not or vice versa?

[76] Yes, because logon to the remote workstation requires your account's domain be visible for successful secondary logon. Since your domain is visible, you can use its accounts and groups.

[77] Reprotected.

[78] This is the one relatively rare case where File Manager preserves the ACL.

[79] Yes.

[80] Reprotected.

[81] They reprotect except for the small case where you move a file within a logical drive.

[82]

ACL for a Temporary Directory (Top) and Its Files (Bottom)

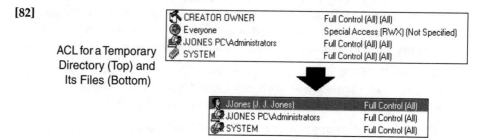

Let Everyone create files in the temporary directory, but prohibit access by the Everyone group by setting Everyone's file default to "Not Specified." CREATOR OWNER is obvious. SYSTEM and Administrators are the usual maintenance entries.

[83] The program could assign temporary files the same ACL as the document on which it's working. Better yet, it could give only the current account access to the temporary file, assuming it doesn't intend other programs to access these files.

[84] Yes.

[85] Not really. Local administrators and SYSTEM don't usually access this tree through the sharing mechanism. However, we have precluded remote administrators from modifying the tree. This may be too strict for some situations.

[86] The most likely case is that their account is not allowed on your workstation. Remember that NT must determine the remote user's account before it can even check whether they pass the share ACL.

[87] Only the share ACL on the logical disk used to access the file. If you connect to the outer share, its ACL governs. If you connect to the inner share, its ACL governs.

[88] No. A user who creates new items can give BBrown arbitrary access. Setting the share ACL Read-Only for BBrown is necessary to keep that account from changing both current items and those later created.

[89] Although NT warns you that it's Read-Only and asks for confirmation, it deletes it. Not much protection! If you are an MS-DOS command line user, the /F option to the "DEL" command also deletes a Read-Only file.

[90] While local groups can hold global groups and regular users can create them, they are limited to the workstation on which they are defined. It's a tough call.

[91] No. The domain trust relationships govern the interdomain use of domain accounts in the same manner as global groups.

[92] None. "No Access" always takes precedence.

[93] It's quite a descriptive one, since they're visible under the same rules as domain accounts.

[94] Technically they're different groups, but they may serve the same purpose. For example, Backup Operators. No, you never see them in the same ACL because each is allowed only in ACLs on its own workstation.

[95] It can only be deleted by someone with "Full Access" to its parent directory. This is the only case where you can delete an object without D permission to the object itself.

[96] Domain Users typically includes all the domain accounts in your workstation's domain, and Users typically includes Domain Users plus local accounts, but administrators can change them. Everyone implicitly includes all accounts allowed on the workstation. No one can be removed from Everyone.

[97] When setting up default ACLs, you almost always give CREATOR OWNER "Full Control."

[98] This is okay. It just means that accounts from the domains you never heard of are allowed into the other workstation's domain, while they're not allowed into yours.

[99] If you move it within the same logical disk, nothing changes, but in all other cases the entire tree is reprotected as it's built in the destination directory according to that directory's default ACLs.

Special Situations

[100] No. Local accounts can appear in only local groups and local groups are visible only on their own workstation. This means a local account can't escape its own workstation by inclusion in a group on another workstation.

[101] Only if you know their password.

[102] No. In usual practice, the Users group on BETA represents only the accounts allowed on BETA, and similarly for JJONES PC.

[103] It's certainly not as safe as when you have to enter the Trusted Path sequence before your password. But it's probably okay for many sites. You can keep your passwords the same across workstations if you deem it unsafe.

[104] Because Windows 95 has no Trusted Path, it's easy for a malicious program to present the unlocking screen and capture your password. You don't want to give it your domain password!

Planning Domains

[105] The GAMMA domain should not trust the department. This means that department accounts are not allowed in the GAMMA domain, and can't be used in ACLs or for secondary logons to GAMMA. It's okay for the department to trust the GAMMA domain, which just means the GAMMA members have access to the department's resources.

[106] Perhaps you want to ensure that neither the defense nor the prosecution has access to each other's domains. Set neither to trust the other. Setting the judicial domain to trust both the others means that common material can be kept in the judicial domain, since accounts from all domains can be included in judicial ACLs.

[107] PUBLIC trusts INTERNAL and SECRET, and INTERNAL trusts SECRET. That's all.

[108] RESCH seems quite sensitive and secretive, so for security you would be reluctant to let it trust any of the other domains. While you may trust members of your research staff, on a practical level they may not need access to the other domains, and have no business in some, like ACTG and SALES. Therefore no other domains should trust RESCH. This may be a good example of an isolated domain. PERS is similar.

[109] Yes. Based on the domain relationships alone, users in SALES can be active in the MANUF domain. For example, they can access network share directories. Someone in sales could carelessly or maliciously copy sensitive sales information onto MANUF workstations where it could be exposed. From a security point of view, the best solution is to isolate a domain like SALES by giving it no trust relationships in either direction. Remember that you can use matching accounts to give selective cross-domain access to the few who need it.

[110] You might feel that passwords in the MANUF domain are not as well protected as in SALES. Perhaps security is not as tight. In this case, you might want to make the PLine accounts' passwords in the SALES domain different than in MANUF. In this way if PLine's password in MANUF is compromised, it can't be used to gain access to the SALES domain. On the other hand, if the passwords are different, NT

may ask for them outside the Trusted Path. We don't like passwords entered outside the Trusted Path so this argues for keeping them the same.

[111] Suppose it's the policy of the subject domains to hold their own accounts and CENTRAL is a major server. You'd probably want to allow all domains' accounts on CENTRAL so they can be used, for example, in ACLs. CENTRAL must trust each subject domain.

[112] This depends on where you keep the accounts. If they're kept on the server, then this is like our master scheme where all clients trust the server. All clients allow the server's accounts and global groups. If you keep them instead in the client domains, the server would trust all the client domains, where all accounts are allowed on the server. This is like our "CENTRAL" example.

[113] No. Multiple servers can share a single domain quite nicely. If they are NT Servers, one can even serve as a backup domain controller for the other. You can also configure NT Server to be a plain server (not domain controller). The criteria for domains is about who needs frequent access to a server. The same domain community may well need frequent access to more than one server.

[114] First, browsing lists are often presented by domain, so the lists are shorter, which is nice when users in each domain primarily reference their own domain's accounts and groups. Second, you may want two separate groups of administrators. In short, all the reasons for having two domains might apply. The fact that each trusts the other just means that users in each domain may need to share with the other domain and that each generally "trusts" users in the other domains.

[115] ACL entries that name domain accounts and groups become deadwood, albeit harmless.

Managing Groups and Accounts

[116] Students Not bad, assuming you mean all students as opposed to only undergraduates. The word "Students" in the description is redundant. Try "Undergrads and grads enrolled at…"

Group A Fine except a group name like Athena is much better.

Tall People First, a description like "People over 190 cm" is better because it's more precise. Second, it's hard to imagine how access control could be based on height, except maybe on a basketball team.

VIPs The membership criteria is vague. How could you know who might be in such a group?

Pat's Friends The name and description is fine. As a local group created by Pat, this seems useful, but as a global group this presupposes everyone knows who is friendly with Pat and who is not.

Mail Room Looks good.

[117] Just because the local account is indirectly a member of a group on ZZZ doesn't mean that ZZZ allows the account. NT authenticates an account before it allows it to establish a presence on the workstation, before it can even attempt operations that check the account's group membership. As an analogy, suppose you are on the guest list for an exclusive ball but you're not allowed in the door of its hotel because you're dressed shabbily. Being on the guest list inside the hotel does you little good if you can't get into the building for other reasons.

[118] You can't remove the Primary group.

[119] For a maximum rate, an attacker quickly guesses up to the reset threshold then waits the reset time before trying again. Hence the maximum overall frequency is approximately the reset time divided by the locking threshold. For example, if the threshold is six guesses and the reset time three minutes, the maximum rate is about two guesses per minute.

[120] Its raw space is 26^5, about twelve million. However, some letters are more likely to begin words than others, for example, "S" is much more likely than "X," so guessing schemes would concentrate on the former. Its effective space is therefore less, but you need to be a mathematician to figure out by how much!

[121] First, you may not know how strongly the application protects its passwords. Second, applications do not require the Trusted Path to enter their passwords so it's easier for malicious programs to pretend to be the application asking for a password.

[122] NT stores the numeric ID in the ACL and fetches up the name only when displayed. Hence, you always see the latest name.

[123] The deleted accounts are gone from the ACLs.

[124] If you let them change the password, one guest can prevent the others from future logons.

[125] No.

[126] It's better to make logon restrictions in the account, especially if the account is a domain account. The Rights Policies are per workstation, and therefore are dispersed and harder to administer. Also, because the Rights are kept in a different window, when you're working on an account you might not notice whether it had the logon Right. However, an account has a limited number of allowed logon workstations and if this is not enough you must use the Rights Policy.

[127] Implement a Shut Me Down group on each workstation with the Right to shut down the system.

[128] No. Rights are not kept in the account and therefore don't get copied. Note that our question carefully used "associate" rather than "add the Rights to the account."

[129] You could create a global group with these two accounts as members then add this group to the local Administrators group of the six workstations.

[130] The simplest way is to keep your original DOM-A accounts and include the global group DOM-A\Domain Admins in all workstations (including domain controllers) in DOM-B. Keep the Administrator account on all workstations in DOM-B with the same password as in DOM-A.

[131] Add both Domain Admins groups to the Administrators local group on each workstation in both domains.

[132] You cannot include the remote domain account in your Administrators group because you don't trust its domain and therefore the account is not allowed in yours. Create a local account of the same name and password that matches to the remote account during secondary logon. Put this new account in your local Administrators group. However, one might question the wisdom of letting an account in a domain you don't trust become a full administrator in yours!

[133] Domain accounts in SALES, because accounts in the SALES domain are allowed in all three.

[134] Place global administrators in the Domain Admins of MAST, then include this group in the Administrators local group on each workstation in the network, including domain controllers. Single domain administrators are placed in the Domain Admins group in their respective domains, which are also placed in the local Administrators group of the workstations in that domain. Hence, each local Administrators group holds MAST\Domain Admins plus the Domain Admins from its own domain.

[135] The reason is a subtle. When MANUF\Administrator used the Server Manager to attach to the ACTG domain, the secondary logon on ACTG could not find the account MANUF\Administrator and therefore matched its own ACTG\Administrator—same name, same password. Working under ACTG\Administrator, that administrator could therefore modify ACTG's accounts. However, when ACTG\Administrator secondarily logged on to MANUF, that account is fully recognized because MANUF trusts ACTG. On MANUF, the account ACTG\Administrator is not a member of the Administrators local group and therefore could not modify the accounts on ACTG.

[136] Only by changing the Rights allocated to the group, and this can change only some of their capabilities. Only full administrators can change the Rights Policy.

[137] Add the remote account to your controller's Server Operators group. Your domain trusts the remote domain so your workstation allows the remote account.

[138] Because the remote Print Operators group is a local group you can't include it in your own domain's groups. You could have a global group created in the other domain named, for example, Domain Print Operators, then include it in your own local Print Operators group. The security disadvantage is that the remote domain administrators can extend this group without your knowledge. An alternative technique is just to add the remote accounts to your local Print Operators group.

[139] Give them domain accounts in SALES because its accounts are the only ones that all three domains allow. Create a global group SALES\Global Acct Ops and add it to the local Account Operators groups on all the domain controllers.

[140] Make a global group named, for example, Domain Power Users and include it in the Power Users local group on each workstation.

[141] Your local Power Users group can't include local groups from any other workstation. You could add specific, remote accounts to your local Power Users groups.

[142] Yes, to a modest degree. While Power Users can create new accounts, careless regular users can give out their passwords, which has the same effect of letting others onto the system. Power Users can also share directories to the network, which can be quite significant if the directories don't have ACLs.

[143] Not usually, since one could never tell which person used the account. Instead, they should create an administrative account for each user with a private password, then put these accounts into the local Account Operators group.

[144] No, because Server Operators can't modify accounts. No, because while Account Operators can modify accounts in general, they can't add accounts to the Account Operators group or modify the Rights Policy.

[145] It's certainly more convenient, but less secure. This is a tough call.

Security Auditing

[146] Because JJones is in both groups, it gets all the controls in both projects plus its own, in total: "Read and Write" successes, and "Read" failures. Note again that, unlike ACLs, even though ProjY is not audited it does not exempt its members from auditing when another entry specifies they shall be.

[147] No.

[148] Like ACLs, when the person creating the file is already in the audit list, NT just adds the CREATOR OWNER events to those already set for that user.

[149] Incorrect passwords are often simple misspellings of correct ones. If you can see a misspelling you can readily guess the real password. NT policy is to not even show administrators users' passwords.

[150] Yes, based on whether the account name is presented or not.

[151] No. This is a benign occurrence.

[152] There are two events: Local Group Created #635, and Local Group Changed #639.

[153] No.

[154] It denotes which events don't appear in the subsequent log. If you miss a "turn off," you might think the absences of an event in the log means that it did not occur, when instead it was never recorded.

[155] Although access to the item has not changed, the person who can manage the ACL has changed and such an event might well be of interest. Taking ownership is rare on most systems and rare events are good ones to audit.

[156] Yes. The record is the same as if you actually changed the ACL.

[157] Again, the #560 event logs the taking of ownership noting a "WRITE_OWNER" access.

[158] The controls pass unchanged to each file and subdirectory, except that CREATOR OWNER is replaced by the account creating the object, or if that account is already in the controls, CREATOR OWNER's **RWXDPO** controls are added to the account.

[159] These names are permanently placed in *.TXT files and, of course, do not thereafter change. These names are usually saved as internal IDs in *.EVT files and Event Viewer presents the names only when you view the logs. While this adapts to name changes, it means that the viewer may not print the names when you transfer a log to another workstation.

[160] When they are both present, the Client ID represents the actual user. The Primary ID represents a service involved in the operation, usually a trusted system service.

[161] First you note that the event occurs only on the workstation that holds the account of the password being changed. The event is #627, Change Password Attempt and NT issues it for both successes and failures. The "target" is the account whose password is changed and the "caller" is the person attempting the change. You can't easily tell from which other workstation the caller made the request, although the Caller Domain helps. Of course, the event doesn't include the new password.

The Internet and Intranets

[162] No. An attacker can simply change the message and attach a new seal using the receiver's public key that will appear genuine to the receiver.

[163] Yes. The receiver can take the entire message packet to a third party and show that the seal for this particular message could only have been computed (within the computational limits of the underlying ciphers) by someone who knew the sender's private key. This is about as close as nonrepudiation gets to fingering the sender.

[164] One technique is to feed the secret phrase and each message to a hash function, then attach the hash result to the message itself. The hash and message are sent as plaintext, and the phrase is not sent at all. The receiver can ensure that the particular message could have been sent only by someone who knew the secret by feeding their copy of the phrase and message through the same hash and ensuring the result is the same as the received hash. Note that it's important that an eavesdropper cannot determine the input to the hash function (in particular, the secret phrase at the beginning) from the hash output, which they can freely see. This is one of the important properties of a hash function and gives rise to the term "one-way" hash. Note that the attacker could change the hash value in transit, but without the secret phrase it's not feasible to attach one that can make the receiver verify the fake message.

[165] No. An attacker could record one transaction and attempt to replay it later. However, the server sends a different challenge the second time so the recorded response based on the first challenge won't check out.

[166] Yes. The client could submit the challenge, password, and user name to a one-way hash function, then pass the result and the plaintext user name back to the server. The critical property is that one cannot deduce the input to the hash function (which includes the password) from its output, which is passed as plaintext.

[167] To note several:

❖ The actual password is not stored on the server, and on the client and controller only briefly. However, NT must protect the hash itself as strongly as the password because an attack can be to use the hash to impersonate its user. However, knowing the hash is less useful than knowing the password because the attacker can present the password (but not its hash) to any legitimate authentication interface.

❖ The user's hash is never present on the network or the server.

❖ The challenge/response scheme eliminates replay attacks.

❖ The server-controller conversation is secured. Although integrity is not ensured, communication between the domain controller and server are quite safe because it's unlikely a penetrator could offer a substitute that would decrypt to the proper plaintext values.

[168] Yes. In this case Mallet sends Bob (the receiver) the false key, which Bob takes to be Alice's (the sender). Mallet can capture Alice's transmission, change the plaintext message, recompute the seal using the false private key, then forward it to Bob. Bob uses the false public key (who he thinks accurately represents Alice) to verify the data, which succeeds.

[169] You can verify the certificate belongs to B. Bell assuming you know the certificate of its CA (or can step through the hierarchical chain to a CA whose certificate

you have independently verified). However, it could have been another B. Bell pretending to be your associate, or someone who convinced their lax CA that they had the identity in the certificate.

Subsystems and Other Security Features

[170] The value left over from the first user's logon, which could be different if a third user were between the two.

[171] Use Policy Editor to edit the Remote Update entry in its Registry, setting up the manual mode parameters. Make sure you set up the new, manual policy file for manual mode naming its own network location. Log out. The next logon should be from the new location. Alternately, you could set this parameter in the automatically loaded file which would eventually trigger a manual load.

[172] No. While you can delete it, the Registry has been changed and will stay that way unless you change it back manually.

[173] Typically, it allows Everyone Read access to files created, which means everyone can read everyone else's spool files. To fix this, set the ACL entry for Everyone to "List" permission. CREATOR OWNER, Administrators, Server Operators, Print Operators, and SYSTEM can retain "Full Control."

[174] No. However, in the normal scheme of things it's not clear that you'd want to let a user from another domain change the share directory ACLs anyway. Such powers are usually reserved to the "owner" of the computer whose account would presumably be in the same domain specified for ACL names on that computer.

The TCB

[175] 1. The infected program remains on the system even after the one that infected it is removed.

2. The infected program might be a standard system program and therefore escape suspicion.

3. Users, especially administrators, may not trust and therefore not run the original. The infected program is a different story.

[176] One of the classic ways to trick an administrator into running a Trojan Horse program is to insert the program in a directory in the administrator's (or even regular user's) search path and give it the name of a common program. The Trojan Horse program mimics the program whose name it takes, and does a lot more!

[177] No. Suppose an administrator runs a seemingly safe program that contains a Trojan Horse. Unknown to the administrator, the Trojan Horse can issue a request to the server, at least in some cases. The trusted server fulfills the request because it has no way of knowing that the administrator did not directly request it.

[178] There's no simple answer. Mostly, you trust a program because you trust the people who wrote it and delivered it to you. If you have access to its source code, you could examine it, but a huge program offers many places for malicious code to hide. Unfortunately you can't safely trust it by just testing it.

[179] "Delete and replace" is where a penetrator can replace an element of the TCB with a fake copy, for example replacing a trusted program with a malicious one that appears to do the same job. Even with "Change" permission to a directory, malicious users can't delete its items without "Delete" access to each, which they don't have in this case, so it's safe. "Full Control" lets them delete the items regardless of the individual protection on the item and therefore is not safe.

Trusted Systems Services, Inc.
Products and Services

1107 South Orchard, Urbana, IL 61801
Phone: (217) 344-0996   FAX: (217) 344-0901
http://www.trustedsystems.com
inform@trustedsystems.com

❖ **NT Security Seminar and Evaluation**

This includes a half-day presentation of Windows NT security combined with a half-day evaluation of your security requirements. Our preseminar questionnaire helps focus our time at your site, and we deliver a summary of our observations and recommendations about a week after our visit.

❖ **User Security Essentials Workshop**

This hands-on, half-day workshop is geared toward general Windows NT users. It covers essential NT security topics and has a Quick Reference handout. This workshop is for full staff training (at least ninety people) and is held at your site using your workstations.

❖ **Key Employee User Security Workshop**

This one-day, hands-on workshop is designed for key employees. It is an in-depth user security course for select groups of day-to-day users. Attendees will receive a copy of *Windows NT Security Guide* , along with a course book.

❖ **Administrator Workshop**

This two-day, hands-on workshop is for administrators of all levels and includes the topics covered in the Key Employee User Security Workshop. You'll learn how to set up your security environment. The discussion focuses on key questions, such as How secure is Windows NT? Attendees will receive a copy of *Windows NT Security Guide*, along with a course book.

❖ **Evaluation and Installation Services**

We offer a variety of Windows NT security services, including site security appraisals (what NT can do for you), installation, and security auditing.

Discovery Workshops

These small (four to six students) hands-on workshops address a variety of flexible topics, from our standard course material to various current third party NT security products. Discussion is geared to those who like to explore with a well-informed guide to assist and direct them. Discovery Workshops are held at our site in Champaign, IL, with one fully loaded workstation per student.